Capital in Banking

Capital in Banking traces the role of capital in US, British, and Swiss banking from the nineteenth to the twenty-first century. The book discusses the impact of perceptions and conventions on capital ratios in the 19th century, the effects of the First and Second World Wars, and the interaction of crises and banking regulation during the 1930s and the 1970s. Moreover, it emphasises the origins of the risk-weighted assets approach for measuring capital adequacy and explains how the 2007/2008 crisis led to a renaissance of unweighted capital ratios. The book shows that undisclosed reserves, shareholders' liability, and hybrid forms of capital must be considered when assessing capital adequacy. As the first long-run historical assessment of the topic, this book represents a reference point for publications in economics, finance, financial regulation, and financial history.

This title is also available as Open Access on Cambridge Core.

Simon Amrein is a lecturer and head of the MSc in Banking and Finance programme at the Lucerne School of Business. He studied finance, economic history, and history at the Lucerne School of Business, the London School of Economics and Political Science, and the European University Institute in Florence.

STUDIES IN MACROECONOMIC HISTORY

Series Editor
Michael D. Bordo, *Rutgers University*

Editors
Owen F. Humpage, *Federal Reserve Bank of Cleveland*
Christopher M. Meissner, *University of California, Davis*
Kris James Mitchener, *Santa Clara University*
David C. Wheelock, *Federal Reserve Bank of St. Louis*

The titles in this series investigate themes of interest to economists and economic historians in the rapidly developing field of macroeconomic history. The four areas covered include the application of monetary and finance theory, international economics, and quantitative methods to historical problems; the historical application of growth and development theory and theories of business fluctuations; the history of domestic and international monetary, financial, and other macroeconomic institutions; and the history of international monetary and financial systems. The series amalgamates the former Cambridge University Press series Studies in Monetary and Financial History and Studies in Quantitative Economic History.

Other Books in the Series:

Stephen Quinn and William Roberds,*How a Ledger Became a Central Bank: A Monetary History of the Bank of Amsterdam* (2023)

Simon Hinrichsen, *When Nations Can't Default: A History of War Reparations and Sovereign Debt* (2023)

Barry Eichengreen and Andreas Kakridis, *The Emergence of the Modern Central Bank and Global Cooperation: 1919–1939* (2023)

Alain Naef, *An Exchange Rate History of the United Kingdom: 1945–1992* (2021)

Barrie A. Wigmore, *The Financial Crisis of 2008: A History of US Financial Markets 2000–2012* (2021)

(*continued after Index*)

Capital in Banking

The Role of Capital in Banking in the 19th and 20th Century: The United Kingdom, the United States, and Switzerland

SIMON AMREIN
Lucerne School of Business

CAMBRIDGE
UNIVERSITY PRESS

CAMBRIDGE
UNIVERSITY PRESS

Shaftesbury Road, Cambridge CB2 8EA, United Kingdom

One Liberty Plaza, 20th Floor, New York, NY 10006, USA

477 Williamstown Road, Port Melbourne, VIC 3207, Australia

314–321, 3rd Floor, Plot 3, Splendor Forum, Jasola District Centre, New Delhi – 110025, India

103 Penang Road, #05–06/07, Visioncrest Commercial, Singapore 238467

Cambridge University Press is part of Cambridge University Press & Assessment, a department of the University of Cambridge.

We share the University's mission to contribute to society through the pursuit of education, learning and research at the highest international levels of excellence.

www.cambridge.org
Information on this title: www.cambridge.org/9781009276894

DOI: 10.1017/9781009276887

Published with the support of the Swiss National Science Foundation.

When citing this work, please include a reference to the DOI 10.1017/9781009276887

First published 2025

A catalogue record for this publication is available from the British Library.

A Cataloging-in-Publication data record for this book is available from the Library of Congress

ISBN 978-1-009-27689-4 Hardback

Contents

Figures

Tables

Acknowledgements

This book would have never been written without the support of numerous people. The book project started as a PhD thesis at the European University Institute (EUI). I owe an outstanding debt of gratitude to my former supervisor, Youssef Cassis, who always encouraged me to pursue my research interests. I would also like to thank Regina Graf, John Turner, and Tobias Straumann for being part of my examining board. I gratefully acknowledge the financial support for my research at the EUI by the Swiss State Secretariat for Education, Research and Innovation (SERI).

Various scholars have contributed to my work through comments on papers at many conferences or in personal conversations. Among them are Carlo Edoardo Altamura, Ioan Balaban, Mark Billings, Michael Bordo, Oskar Broberg, Maria Stella Chiaruttini, Andreas Dietrich, Alexis Drach, Philip Fliers, Armin Jans, Lena Rethel, Hugh Rockoff, Martin Spillmann, Christoph Lengwiler, Alain Naef, Tobias Straumann, John Turner, and Eugene White. Furthermore, I am grateful to two anonymous reviewers for providing valuable feedback on the book. Writing a book covering more than two centuries can only do limited justice to the complexity of the topic. Certain aspects may be neglected or misinterpreted, for which only I am responsible.

I wish to thank the staff at the Bank of England Archive, the London Metropolitan Archives, the British National Archives, the Royal Bank of Scotland Archives, the Swiss Federal Archives, and the Zentrale für Wirtschaftsdokumentation, as well as the library staff at Lucerne's Central Library, for their invaluable assistance.

Lastly, I would like to thank my family. This book would have never been possible without my parents, and would never have been finished without my partner, Patricia. I dedicate the book to our wonderful son, Emil.

Abbreviations

ABC	Analyzing Bank Capital
ABA	American Bankers Association
BankG	Banking Act (Bundesgesetz über die Banken und Sparkassen)
BankV	Banking Ordinance (Vollziehungsverordnung zum Bundesgesetz über die Banken und Sparkassen)
BBA	British Bankers' Association
BCBS	Basel Committee on Banking Supervision
BIS	Bank of International Settlements
bn	billion
BNA	British National Archives
BoE	Bank of England
BoEA	Bank of England Archive
BSD	Bank Supervision Division (of the Bank of England)
C/A ratio	capital/assets ratio
CCC	competition and credit control
CEG	Comptoir d'Escompte de Genève
CH	Switzerland
CHF	Swiss franc
CLCB	Committee of London Clearing Bankers
DM	Deutsche Mark
EEC	European Economic Community
EUI	European University Institute
FBC	Federal Banking Commission
FDIC	Federal Deposit Insurance Corporation
FDICIA	Federal Deposit Insurance Improvement Act
FED	Board of Governors of the Federal Reserve
FFIEC	Federal Financial Institutions Examination Council
FINMA	Swiss Financial Market Supervisory Authority
G10	Group of Ten

GDP	gross domestic product
HSSO	Historical Statistics of Switzerland Online
ILSA	International Lending Supervision Act
IMF	International Monetary Fund
IRB	Internal ratings-based
LDC	Less developed countries
LMA	London Metropolitan Archives
m	million
OCC	Office of the Comptroller of the Currency
OECD	Organisation for Economic Co-operation and Development
p.a.	per annum
pp	percentage points
RBSA	Archive of the Royal Bank of Scotland
RWA	risk-weighted assets
SBA	Swiss Bankers Association
SBC	Swiss Bank Corporation (Schweizerischer Bankverein SBV/ Société de Banque Suisse)
SEC	US Securities and Exchange Commission
SERI	Secretariat for Education, Research and Innovation
SFA	Swiss Federal Archives
SNB	Swiss National Bank
UBS	Union Bank of Switzerland (Schweizerische Bankgesellschaft SBG/Union de Banques Suisses)
USNB	United States National Bank

I

Introduction

Banks play a vital role in economic development by providing credit to businesses and private households. Their lending and investment activities on the asset side are financed by debt or equity capital. Proportionally to the total assets, equity capital has experienced a major change since the nineteenth century. By 1850, for example, the balance sheets of banks in the United States consisted of about 40% equity capital. The figure dropped to 7% in 2000. Similar declines can be observed in countries such as Switzerland and the United Kingdom. Before and during the 2007/2008 financial crisis, some global banks held as little as 2–5% equity capital in their balance sheets.[1]

The decrease of equity capital in proportion to the total assets is a remarkable change in how banks have funded their activities since the emergence of modern banking in the nineteenth century. However, a high level of debt does not come as a surprise. A commercial bank's key function is granting loans and receiving deposits, and customer deposits are considered debt capital. Thus, funding a bank with 'other people's money' is in the very nature of banking. Nonetheless, a certain level of capital is essential for individual banks, and for the financial system as a whole. It serves as an absorber of losses and can affect a bank's default probability. Moreover, a sufficient amount of capital induces trust for creditors. Consequently, adequate capital is – among other factors – important for financial market stability.

Capital adequacy has become a widely discussed issue in the aftermath of the 2007/2008 financial crisis. The suggestions by academics, regulators, and politicians in response to the question of 'how much capital is enough?' have ranged from one-digit percentages to 100%. The variety of opinions is underlined by arguments that promote financial market stability on the one hand, and potential adverse economic effects via reduced credit supply on the

---

[1] See Chapter 6.

other. The latter claim is often based on the argument that equity capital is more expensive than debt capital. Prominent advocates of substantially higher capital requirements include Anat Admati and Martin Hellwig, Eugene Fama, and John Cochrane.[2] Moreover, many economists argue that capital requirements were too low before the 2007/2008 crisis, and that large international banks that defaulted would have survived the crisis with higher capital ratios.[3]

Inherent to the disagreement over capital adequacy are diverging opinions on the role and relevance of capital in banking. From a historical perspective, the assessment of capital/assets ratios is even more complex. Analysing capital/assets ratios without considering a broad set of factors – ranging from the economic, political, and regulatory environment to the risks of bank assets – is misleading. Additionally, the significance of these factors has changed over the past two centuries, resulting in evolving perceptions of what constitutes adequate capital.

Imagine a bank in 1880 primarily focusing on lending to a few railway and industrial companies in an environment without a deposit insurance scheme and a central bank as a 'lender of last resort'. The same bank in today's world, now with a well-diversified loan portfolio, deposits insured, and the ability to discount securities with the central bank in a crisis, might even have the same capital/assets ratio as in 1880. However, this bank's probability of surviving a crisis might differ greatly between 1880 and today. Similarly, a decline of the capital/assets ratio from 10% to 5% over 140 years does not necessarily reflect a more fragile financial system on an aggregated level, nor more risk appetite on the single bank level. It might simply result from different economic, political, and regulatory realities.

This book goes beyond displaying ratios over two centuries by addressing the significant shifts in the environment of banks. Firstly, it traces the role of capital at the beginning of commercial banking in the United States, the United Kingdom, and Switzerland during the late eighteenth and nineteenth centuries. Capital adequacy has been debated since the beginning of banking, and bankers often relied on rules of thumb and conventions when determining their bank's capital. Secondly, banks' contribution to the financing of World War II led to a balance sheet expansion in banking and fundamentally changed how capital adequacy was measured. This was

---

[2] Anat R. Admati and Martin Hellwig, *The Bankers' New Clothes: What's Wrong with Banking and What to Do about It* (Princeton: Princeton University Press, 2014); Marie-Astrid Langer and Michael Rasch, 'Interview with Eugene Fama – Banken brauchen mindestens 25 Prozent Eigenkapital', *Neue Zürcher Zeitung*, 9 November 2013; John H. Cochrane, 'The Grumpy Economist: Equity-Financed Banking', *The Grumpy Economist*, 2016: http://johnhcochrane .blogspot.com/2016/05/equity-financed-banking.html (accessed 22 February 2017).

[3] Charles A. E. Goodhart, 'Lessons for Monetary Policy from the Euro-Area Crisis', *Journal of Macroeconomics*, 39 (2014), 378–82; Andrew G. Haldane and Vasileios Madouros, 'The Dog and the Frisbee', *Speech Presented at the Federal Reserve Bank of Kansas City's Jackson Hole Economic Policy Symposium*, 2012.

the starting point for comparing capital to assets that were adjusted by the risk they posed. Thirdly, the banking crises of the 1930s, 1970s, and 1980s led to the introduction of statutory capital requirements, culminating in the uniform Basel I framework in 1988. Lastly, the 2007/2008 financial crisis and more recent banking instability emphasise that more regulation and higher capital requirements do not necessarily increase banking stability. Following the gradual evolution of the perception of capital over two centuries demonstrates that informal and formal capital requirements were continuously adapted. Regulatory frameworks, particularly the regulation of capital, are path dependent. Reforms that tried to eliminate the weaknesses of the existing banking regulation rather than a fundamental reassessment of regulation aimed at increased banking stability were the norm. With a historical narrative on the role and relevance of capital, this book contributes to the ongoing discussions about financial market stability, banking regulation, and capital requirements. While speaking to present-day debates, the book is rooted in historical context.

1.1   THE SCOPE OF THIS BOOK

This book focuses on the role of bank capital in the United States, the United Kingdom, and Switzerland during the nineteenth and twentieth centuries. The nineteenth century marked a period when many larger commercial banks were established to finance industrial companies, infrastructure, and trade. The main scope is the period leading up to the Basel Accord in 1988 (Basel I). The Basel Accord harmonised the definitions, measurement approaches, and requirements for bank capital on an international level. The book, therefore, follows three loose threads – the perception and role of capital in three countries – until they become one in the late 1980s. An epilogue covers the post-Basel experience from 1988 to the present.

   This book does not constitute an in-depth analysis with a global perspective over two centuries. Instead, the research focuses on particular countries, events, periods, and banks. Emphasis is given to commercial banks, broadly defined as financial intermediaries with the primary functions of receiving capital in the form of deposits, granting loans, and investing money, as well as providing services to facilitate the settlement of financial obligations. In terms of legal forms, the focus is on joint-stock banks, as joint-stock banks require a share capital. However, joint-stock banks vary to a large degree in terms of their assets. Moreover, many large banks have developed from 'pure' borrowing and lending/investing activities in the nineteenth century to global universal banks in the twenty-first century, also providing investment banking, asset management, and private banking services. Pure investment (or merchant) banks, private banks, and other financial service providers are not considered in the book.

Geographically, the book covers the three relevant financial centres.[4] The United Kingdom[5] and the United States represent the major financial centres of the nineteenth and twentieth centuries. Switzerland, with its financial hubs in Geneva in Zurich, became an internationally important financial centre in the 1960s and was home to large commercial banks.[6]

The three countries differ in various dimensions: The United Kingdom and the United States are traditionally market-based financial systems, whereas the Swiss system is a typical example of a bank-based financial system.[7] Moreover, the countries differ regarding the regulation and supervision of banking and have different legal traditions (common law versus civil law). The United States certainly offers the richest bank regulation and supervision history among the three countries. A variety of regulatory and supervisory systems emerged during the period of early American banking (until 1837), the free banking era (1837 to 1863), and the national banking period (1863 to 1913). Additionally, the United States has a long history of measuring capital adequacy during the nineteenth century, as banknotes were often limited to a certain multiple of capital, which at the same time constitutes a capital requirement. However, a formal and legally binding minimum capital ratio on the federal level has existed only since the 1980s.

In the United Kingdom, approaches towards regulating banking were taken between the 1820s and the 1870s. From 1844 to 1857, the Joint Stock Bank Act of 1844 enacted a statutory capital requirement for banks. However, this proved to be a short and relatively unimportant intermezzo of banking regulation. Instead, the United Kingdom opted to regulate not banks but,

---

[4] For an overview of the hierarchy of international financial centres, see Youssef Cassis, 'International Financial Centres', in *The Oxford Handbook of Banking and Financial History*, ed. Youssef Cassis, Richard S. Grossman, and Catherine R. Schenk, Oxford Handbooks (Oxford: Oxford University Press, 2016); Youssef Cassis, *Capitals of Capital: A History of International Financial Centres 1780–2005* (Cambridge: Cambridge University Press, 2006).

[5] The United Kingdom, consisting today of England, Wales, Scotland, and Northern Ireland, was a space of banking markets with different characteristics that developed independently for most of the nineteenth century. Scottish joint-stock banks, for example, had a longer tradition than English joint-stock banks, as they were already allowed to establish before 1826. Moreover, the capital levels of Scottish banks were higher than that of English banks. Thus, the book distinguishes between English and British banks. When considering the nineteenth century, it usually specifically refers to English banks. Once the (English) Big Five banks become the dominant banks in the United Kingdom, the narrative switches to a broader geographical space. On the differences of Scottish and English banking, see Thomas Joplin, *An Essay on the General Principles and Present Practice of Banking in England and Scotland*, 2nd ed. (Newcastle upon Tyne: Printed and published by E. Walker, 1822), p. 30; James William Gilbart, *The Principles and Practice of Banking* (London: George Bell & Sons, 1873).

[6] Youssef Cassis, 'Introduction: The Weight of Finance in European Societies', in *Finance and Financiers in European History, 1880–1960*, ed. Youssef Cassis (Cambridge: Cambridge University Press, 1992), pp. 1–13 (p. 7).

[7] For an overview of bank-based versus market-based financial systems, see Franklin Allen and Douglas Gale, *Comparing Financial Systems* (Cambridge, MA: MIT Press, 2000).

more broadly, companies.[8] It was not until 1979 that the Banking Act introduced statutory banking regulation in the wake of Britain's secondary banking crisis.[9]

Switzerland's first attempts at banking regulation were taken on a regional (cantonal) level from the 1860s onwards. The Federal Banknote Act, introduced in 1883, stipulated minimum capital requirements for note-issuing banks. The Great Depression led to the introduction of the Federal Law on Banks and Savings Banks (Banking Act) in 1934, thereby establishing the first statutory capital requirements in Switzerland on the federal level.

The three countries also vary in their tradition of bank supervisory practice. In the British system, the Bank of England (BoE) supervised banks informally and without a legal mandate until 1979. In Switzerland, the banking legislation of 1934 established the Federal Banking Commission (FBC) as a banking supervisory agency, which later became the Financial Market Authority (FINMA). In the United States, state and federal bank supervisory agencies existed, depending on the period. The three most important federal bank supervisors are the Office of the Comptroller of the Currency (OCC, created 1863), the Board of Governors of the Federal Reserve (FED, 1913), and the Federal Deposit Insurance Corporation (FDIC, 1933).

In summary, these three countries offer three interestingly different cases: a system with a long tradition of supervising bank capital with several bank supervisors already in the nineteenth century (United States), a system based with a strong emphasis on informal supervision and statutory banking legislation only after 1979 (United Kingdom), and a system of statutory legislation with statutory capital requirements after 1934 (Switzerland).

The starting point of the research period varies, depending on the country. The first English joint-stock banks were established in the late 1820s, after the enactment of the Country Bankers Act in 1826. Before 1826, the Bubble Act of 1720 prohibited the formation of joint-stock companies without royal charters. This distinctive regulatory setting led to the emergence of hundreds of small partnership banks (private and country banks) during the second half of the eighteenth century.[10] The new joint-stock model became the dominant legal form of banks in England from the mid-nineteenth century onwards. Joint-stock banks grew in number, size, and geographic scope, reaching a peak of 110 individual banks in England in 1885.[11] A rapid consolidation known as the

---

[8] The shift towards corporate law instead of banking law was marked by the Company Acts in 1879, 1908, 1929, and 1967.

[9] For an overview of these regulatory developments, see Mark Billings and Forrest Capie, 'Transparency and Financial Reporting in Mid-20th Century British Banking', *Accounting Forum*, Financial accounting: Past, present and future, 33.1 (2009), 38–53.

[10] For an overview of the evolution of the UK bank population in the long run, see Ranald Cattanach Michie, *British Banking: Continuity and Change from 1694 to the Present* (Oxford: Oxford University Press, 2016), p. 31.

[11] Banks located in Wales are also included.

Amalgamations Movement followed, with the number of banks dropping to twenty-six by 1918. The concentration process led to the emergence of five large banks, the so-called 'Big Five': Barclays, Lloyds, Westminster, Midland, and National Provincial. Barclays and Lloyds still exist today. Parts of the former Big Five also transferred into HSBC and the NatWest Group.[12]

In Switzerland, economic development rather than a regulatory change triggered the establishment of joint-stock banks. Towards the end of the eighteenth century, the savings banks were the first to emerge alongside the existing private banks. It was only in the 1850s that the first large joint-stock banks were established after the model of the French Crédit Mobilier to finance infrastructure, trade, and industry. Besides providing loans for larger projects and financing firms as the 'steam engines of credit',[13] joint-stock banks were also active in the underwriting business.[14] This group of banks became known as the 'big banks'. By 1918, Switzerland counted eight large joint-stock banks.[15] Severe losses in the Great Depression reduced the number of big banks to five. The 1990s was another period of rapid market consolidation in Swiss banking, leaving only UBS and Credit Suisse. In 2023, UBS took over Credit Suisse.

The banking market's structure in the United States fundamentally differed from the United Kingdom and Switzerland. The US system was marked by a decentral organisation, different regulatory levels (state versus federal) and a large number of small banks. Throughout the free banking period (1837 to 1863), regulation and supervision were left to the individual states, and banks could obtain a charter and enter the market freely if they could raise a certain amount of capital. By 1860, about 1,600 state banks existed, and almost every bank issued banknotes.[16] From 1863, banks could charter as national banks,

---

[12] Barclays was incorporated in 1896 as Barclay and Company, Limited and was previously a private bank. Lloyds was incorporated in 1865 as Lloyds and Company. Westminster was established in 1834 as London and Westminster Bank. It merged in 1909 with the London and County Bank and 1918 with Parr's Bank. National Provincial was established in 1833 as National Provincial Bank of England and merged in 1968 with Westminster to become NatWest. NatWest was integrated into the Royal Bank of Scotland in 2000 and renamed as the NatWest Group in 2020. Midland was established 1836 and was acquired in 1992 by HSBC.

[13] Handels- und Gewerbe-Zeitung, 'Die grossen Unternehmungen der Westschweiz', *Handels- und Gewerbe-Zeitung* (Zurich, 26 April 1856), pp. 189–90 (p. 190).

[14] See, for example, Albert Linder, *Die schweizerischen Grossbanken*, Beiträge zur schweizerischen Wirtschaftskunde (Bern: Stämpfli & Cie, 1927); and Adolf Jöhr, *Die schweizerischen Grossbanken und Privatbankiers* (Zurich: Polygraphischer Verlag, 1940), pp. 13ff.

[15] Schweizerischer Bankverein SBV, Basel; Schweizerische Kreditanstalt SKA, Zurich; Schweizerische Volksbank SVB, Bern; Bank Leu, Zurich: Eidgenössische Bank, Zurich; Schweizerische Bankgesellschaft SBG, Winterthur; Basler Handelsbank, Basel; Comptoir d'Escompte de Genève CEG, Genf.

[16] Howard Bodenhorn, 'State Banks – Number, Assets, and Liabilities: 1834–1896, Table Cj149-157', in *Historical Statistics of the United States, Earliest Times to the Present*, ed. Susan B. Carter, Scott Sigmund Gartner, Michael R. Haines, et al. (New York: Cambridge University Press, 2006): http://dx.doi.org/10.1017/ISBN-9780511132971.

creating a dual-banking system. The number of banks reached about 10,000 by the late 1890s and peaked at around 20,000 in the early 1920s.[17]

The roots of the large commercial banks in the United States reach back to the eighteenth and nineteenth centuries. The first commercial banks were founded in the 1780s. The Bank of North America was created in 1781, the Bank of Massachusetts and Alexander Hamilton's Bank of New York in 1784. The Bank of New York is the oldest among the old New York City–based banks. Other important banks from New York City include the City Bank of New York (1812, now BNY Mellon) and Chase National Bank (1877, now JP Morgan). Especially the latter merged with some of the largest New York banks during the twentieth century, among them the Manhattan Company (established 1799), the Chemical Bank (1823), Hanover Bank (1873), and Manufacturers Trust (1905).[18] JP Morgan Chase and Citigroup are still among the four largest banks in the United States. The other two 'Big Four' banks currently are Bank of America and Wells Fargo.[19]

This book uses bank-level data from major banks in the United States, the United Kingdom, and Switzerland, as well as data on nationally aggregated levels provided by bank supervising agencies, national statistical offices, and central banks. Banks' balance sheet data was obtained from printed sources such as historical and academic publications, newspapers, magazines, and banks' annual reports.

The existing literature in fields which most typically deal with banks' capital structure, such as corporate finance, does usually not address the historical evolution of capital ratios.[20] Other strands of literature, such as that on

---

[17] *Historical Statistics of the United States. Colonial Times to 1970*, ed. United States Bureau of the Census, 1975, Series X580.

[18] The Bank of New York merged in 2007 with the Mellon Financial Corporation to become BNY Mellon. City Bank merged in 1955 with the First National Bank. It was formally renamed Citibank in the 1970s and became Citigroup in 1998. Chase National Bank merged with the Manhattan Company in 1955, with the Chemical Bank (founded in 1823) in 1996, and with JP Morgan in 2000 to become JP Morgan Chase. The Hanover Bank merged with the Manufacturers Trust Company in 1961 and Chemical Bank in 1991.

[19] Federal Deposit Insurance Corporation, 'BankFind Suite: Find Institution Financial & Regulatory Data': https://banks.data.fdic.gov/bankfind-suite/financialreporting (accessed 11 April 2022).

[20] Two exceptions with long-run empirical analyses are Allen N. Berger, Richard J. Herring, and Giorgio P. Szegö, 'The Role of Capital in Financial Institutions', *Journal of Banking & Finance*, 19.3 (1995), 393–430; and Anthony Saunders and Berry Wilson, 'The Impact of Consolidation and Safety-Net Support on Canadian, US and UK Banks: 1893–1992', *Journal of Banking & Finance*, 23.2 (1999), 537–71. Key theories on capital structures include the seminal paper by Modigliani and Miller (Franco Modigliani and Merton H. Miller, 'The Cost of Capital, Corporation Finance and the Theory of Investment', *The American Economic Review*, 1958, 261–97), the trade-off theory (Franco Modigliani and Merton H. Miller, 'Corporate Income Taxes and the Cost of Capital: A Correction', *The American Economic Review*, 1963, 433–43; Merton H. Miller, 'Debt and Taxes', *The Journal of Finance*, 1977, 261–75; Alan Kraus and Robert H. Litzenberger, 'A State-Preference Model of Optimal Financial Leverage', *The Journal*

banking crises, financialisation, or discussions of regulation and financial market stability, frequently refer to the relative decline of capital over time but often fail to elaborate on the historical context in which these changes occurred.[21] Within the discipline of financial history, a few contributions provide a more thorough analysis of bank capital. Grossman provides data for twelve countries from 1834 to 1939.[22] Moreover, the author discusses capital and capital regulation in his book on the history of banking in the industrialised world.[23] Jordà, Richter, Schularick, and Taylor provide the broadest dataset on capital/assets ratios, covering seventeen advanced economies from 1870 to 2015.[24] Billings and Capie published the most detailed analysis of bank capital, focusing on British banks from 1920 to 1970.[25] For Switzerland, Amrein discusses the evolution of capital ratios from 1874 to 2014.[26] A broader set of financial history publications cover the topic of capital in banking indirectly. Such publications are often concerned with banking and financial stability, banking regulation, or the role of banks within the economy. Turner, for example, discusses crises and stability in British banking, and also covers the role of capital. Similarly, Bordo, Redish,

of Finance, 28.4 (1973), 911–22), the pecking order theory (Stewart C. Myers and Nicholas S. Majluf, 'Corporate Financing and Investment Decisions When Firms Have Information That Investors Do Not Have', *Journal of Financial Economics*, 13.2 (1984), 187–221), the signalling theory (Stephen A. Ross, 'The Determination of Financial Structure: The Incentive-Signalling Approach', *The Bell Journal of Economics*, 8.1 (1977), 23–40 (p. 23)), and the market timing theory (Deborah J. Lucas and Robert L. McDonald, 'Equity Issues and Stock Price Dynamics', *The Journal of Finance*, 45.4 (1990), 1019–43; Robert A. Korajczyk, Deborah J. Lucas, and Robert L. McDonald, 'Equity Issues with Time-Varying Asymmetric Information', *The Journal of Financial and Quantitative Analysis*, 27.3 (1992), 397–417).

[21] See, for example, Admati and Hellwig, *The Bankers' New Clothes*.

[22] Richard S. Grossman, 'Other People's Money: The Evolution of Bank Capital in the Industrialized World', in *The New Comparative Economic History: Essays in Honor of Jeffrey G. Williamson*, ed. Jeffrey G. Williamson, T. J. Hatton, Kevin H. O'Rourke, and Alan M. Taylor (Cambridge, MA: MIT Press, 2007). See also Richard S. Grossman, *Unsettled Account: The Evolution of Banking in the Industrialized World since 1800*, Princeton Economic History of the Western World (Princeton NJ: Princeton University Press, 2010), pp. 145ff. The analysed countries are Australia, Belgium, Canada, Denmark, Finland, Germany, Italy, Japan, Norway, Sweden, the United Kingdom, and the United States.

[23] Grossman, *Unsettled Account*.

[24] Òscar Jordà, Björn Richter, Moritz H. P. Schularick, and Alan M. Taylor, 'Bank Capital before and after Financial Crises', in *Leveraged the New Economics of Debt and Financial Fragility*, ed. Moritz Schularick (Chicago: The University of Chicago Press, 2022), pp. 116–33.

[25] Mark Billings and Forrest Capie, 'Capital in British Banking, 1920–1970', *Business History*, 49.2 (2007), 139–62. See also Forrest Capie and Mark Billings, 'Profitability in English Banking in the Twentieth Century', *European Review of Economic History*, 5.3 (2001), 367–401, for a discussion of profitability in English banking.

[26] Simon Amrein, 'Eigenmittel der Schweizer Banken im historischen Kontext', in *Krisenfeste Schweizer Banken? Die Regulierung von Eigenmitteln, Liquidität und 'Too big to fail'*, ed. Armin Jans, Christoph Lengwiler, and Marco Passardi (Zurich: NZZ Libro, 2018), pp. 87–116.

and Rockoff compare the financial stability of Canada and the United States, discussing capital too.[27]

However, bank capital and its relevance in a historical context seldom take centre stage. Moreover, most publications refer to the same time series covering capital/assets ratios on a nationally aggregated level. These time series are often obtained from different sources and then assembled. Additionally, key aggregates, such as capital, total assets, or even banks as entities, are often defined differently from one country to another.

1.2 THE ROLE AND RELEVANCE OF CAPITAL IN BANKING

Capital in banking is a source of trust. Since the emergence of commercial banks in the nineteenth century, two roles are usually attributed to bank capital. The first is the loss absorbency function. This function relates directly to paid-up share capital and reserves, which should cover a bank's unexpected losses.[28] The second function of capital is the guarantee function. A high level of equity capital in a bank induces trust for creditors. Without trust, creditors (i.e. depositors) withdraw their funds. In the most extreme case, a bank run leads to immediate illiquidity. A high level of capital can increase the trust of stakeholders in a bank. However, various other elements can also provide trust for creditors, or even replace capital entirely in its role as a facilitator of trust.

The elemental form for providing trust in banking are guarantees. A guarantee for a bank confirms that liabilities are secured by a substantial degree in case of losses. Historically, three entities often provided such guarantees and thus induced trust in banking: the state through regulation (i.e. capital requirements, safety nets, explicit or implicit guarantees by governments), the shareholders (i.e. by the extent of their liability), and the bank itself (i.e. by choosing the degree of risk of its business model and its capital policy). One may even argue that paid-up capital is entirely unnecessary in the presence of trust-inducing guarantees and reserves for unexpected losses. In fact, history provides many cases of banks without share capital. Thus, a simple numerical leverage ratio cannot answer the ubiquitous question of how much capital is adequate in banking. It depends on the factors facilitating the trust and loss absorbency functions of capital. Moreover, there is not one optimal set of distribution of the guarantee function among the government, shareholders, and a bank's management that makes a banking market less prone to bankruptcy. This book aims to outline the various environments in which banks operated throughout the last two centuries – and the relevance of capital over time.

---

[27] Michael D. Bordo, Angela Redish, and Hugh Rockoff, 'Why Didn't Canada Have a Banking Crisis in 2008 (or in 1930, or 1907, or . . .)?', *The Economic History Review*, 68.1 (2015), 218–43 (pp. 238–9).
[28] Unexpected, because provisions are made for expected losses.

Bank balance sheets are unlike the balance sheets of any other company. A specificity of commercial banks is that a substantial part of their funding is usually collected from depositors. Firms in the non-financial sector often depend to a more significant degree on funding from banks and investors. Even among banks themselves, balance sheet structures vary substantially, depending on their business model. For example, the type of credit and its duration varies from bank to bank. Whereas the joint-stock banks in the United Kingdom and the United States focused more on short-term investing, their counterparts in Switzerland engaged in long-term investments at an early stage. Thus, understanding the structure of a balance sheet is crucial for recognising the risks involved in banking and the role of capital. Moreover, measuring capital requires a consistent definition of capital and balance sheet items such as deposits or total assets. Such definitions are even more important in a historical context. Current accounting and regulatory views on capital shape our relatively uniform understanding of capital. In the past, however, the definition of capital varied.

1.2.1 Defining Capital

Figure 1.1 shows a simplified commercial bank balance sheet. The asset side summarises a company's investments, whereas the liability side shows how it finances its operations. In this simple accounting view, equity capital consists of three elements: shareholders' capital, reserves, and retained earnings. Companies can raise shareholders' capital by issuing shares. Equity capital refers to the book value of equity capital. The nominal (book) value and the market value of equity capital can deviate substantially, depending on investors' expectations.

The (disclosed) reserves stem from two sources: Banks can attribute a part of the annual profit to the reserves. Moreover, banks often issue shares at a price above the nominal value of the share. The share premium (agio) is allocated to the reserves. Reserves can also be released – for example, to absorb losses.

Assets	Liabilities
Cash	Due to banks
Money market, bills of exchange, drafts	Due to customers, cheques
Due from banks	Bonds
Due from customers	Bills of exchange
Mortgages	General provisions
Financial investments	Other debt
Tangible assets	
Other assets	*Equity capital*
	• Share capital
	• Reserves
	• Retained earnings
Total assets	**Total liabilities**

FIGURE 1.1 Simplified balance sheet of a bank

Finally, the retained earnings consist of the profit remaining after reserves are allocated and dividends are distributed to shareholders.

Two types of capital were common historically but not visible in a bank's public balance sheet: undisclosed (hidden) reserves and unlimited or extended shareholder liabilities. Hidden reserves constitute an issue when measuring capital based on public balance sheet data, as the actual capital might exceed the disclosed amount of capital. A second form of capital is shareholder liabilities. The potential loss of a shareholder is (nowadays) limited to the initial investment. However, shareholders are subject to potential losses above their investment in a system of extended or even unlimited liability. All three countries – the United Kingdom, the United States, and Switzerland – provide examples of extended or unlimited shareholder liabilities in the past.

Historically, the understanding of what capital is varied across time and geography. A crucial step towards a uniform understanding of capital in banking was the Basel Accord of 1988. In 1988, the Basel Committee on Banking Supervision (BCBS) at the Bank of International Settlement (BIS) published a framework for measuring capital adequacy. The framework – known as Basel I – became a global standard, and its guidelines were translated into many national banking regulations.

The most evident example of varying national traditions in capital definitions is mezzanine capital, such as subordinated debt or preferred equity. Such hybrid forms of capital represent claims on the asset side that are senior to common share capital. Historically, subordinated debt became a crucial funding source in the second half of the twentieth century. In the United Kingdom, subordinated debt was used almost interchangeably with share capital and reserves until the 1980s. The BoE did not even differentiate the different capital forms in its official statistics and classified subordinated debt (called 'loan stock') as a part of equity capital. Swiss banks could use subordinated debt for regulatory purposes as part of the required capital after 1981. In the United States, some federal bank supervisory agencies have also allowed banks to use subordinated debt for capital requirements since the 1960s.

Another example of varying capital definitions were general provisions (or general loan-/loss reserves). A bank creates provisions if it expects a loss. In contrast to general reserves, general provisions are created for a specific, anticipated future loss. It is the expectation of using the provision which characterises it as debt rather than equity capital.

The BCBS responded to the heterogeneity in capital definitions by defining two capital tiers. Tier 1 consisted of share capital and disclosed reserves. Other forms of capital, such as hidden reserves, revaluation reserves, general provisions, and hybrid forms of capital, were assigned to the supplementary Tier 2 capital.[29] Since 1988, the definitions of capital have been further

---

[29] Basel Committee on Banking Supervision, *International Convergence of Capital Measurement and Capital Standards (Basel I)*, 1988, pp. 5–6.

broadened, incorporating new types of capital instruments. The main categories used under the latest Basel framework (Basel III) are Common Equity Tier 1, Additional Tier 1, and Tier 2 Capital.[30]

1.2.2   Assets, Liabilities, and the Risk of Insolvency and Illiquidity

Banks allocate their funds to various investments on the asset side, the safest being simple cash holdings. Cash is stable in value in the absence of inflation and is also liquid. If the share of cash increases, a bank's overall risk does not increase. This level of safety, however, comes with a price, as cash does not yield any interest. Other assets in a bank's balance sheet may be government or corporate bonds, stocks from companies, or lending to other banks. Their characteristics differ widely: some are easy to sell even in crises (hence very liquid); others are not. Some assets are subject to substantial price fluctuations; others are relatively stable. In other words, they pose different risks, which are rewarded with a risk-adjusted return if markets are efficient.

On the liability side, commercial banks finance themselves via deposits from customers, loans from other banks or central banks, or bonds. These balance sheet items on the liabilities side are considered debt capital. The difference between total assets and debt capital is considered equity capital.

A particular type of bank is a note-issuing bank. Its currency in circulation is a liability. In systems with a note-issuing monopoly, the central bank is the only bank with such liability. However, in systems with several or numerous note-issuing banks in the past, banknotes often constituted a substantial share of these banks' liabilities, in some cases proportionally more relevant than deposits.

The different maturities of assets and liabilities pose various risks that can lead to illiquidity or insolvency. Illiquidity describes what happens when depositors or other short-term creditors call in their funds immediately and the bank cannot sell off assets in due time to cover these withdrawals. Managing such a maturity mismatch of assets and liabilities results from a bank's basic economic function as a financial intermediary, accepting deposits and providing loans. Even the mere threat of possible illiquidity might trigger bank customers to demand their deposits in cash. Thus, customers are incentivised to be first in line in such a case.[31] Therefore, even stable banks can face bank runs triggered by a ripple of fear caused by neighbouring banks falling into trouble.

A bank is insolvent if the total assets are equal to or smaller than the liabilities. Losses – for example, on loans – diminish a bank's equity capital.

---

[30] Common Equity Tier 1 consists of common shares, share premia, retained earnings, and disclosed reserves. Additional Tier 1 consists, for example, of contingent convertible bonds (CoCo bonds). Tier 2 Capital consists, for example, of subordinated debt. For detailed definitions, see Basel Committee on Banking Supervision, *Basel III: A Global Regulatory Framework for More Resilient Banks and Banking Systems*, 2010.

[31] Douglas W. Diamond and Philip H. Dybvig, 'Bank Runs, Deposit Insurance, and Liquidity', *Journal of Political Economy*, 91.3 (1983), 401–19.

However, disentangling insolvency and illiquidity in a crisis is often difficult. Illiquidity occurs when creditors question solvency. Furthermore, once creditors initiate a bank run, it further weakens a bank's capital base if it is forced to sell assets below market prices, thus realising losses. A distinction between liquidity and solvency is often made through the use of different time horizons: a bank is liquid if it can settle debts by a fixed due date and solvent if it can settle debts in due course.[32] Therefore, solvency and liquidity are crucial for a bank's stability.

1.2.3 Measuring Capital Adequacy: A Brief Historical Overview

Assessing the size of capital in absolute terms provides little information as it neglects the size or risk of a bank. Therefore, comparisons with balance sheet items are necessary. Historically, bank capital was often compared with five aggregates: banknotes, deposits, total liabilities, total assets, and risk-weighted assets. Dividing the capital by these aggregates leads to five capital ratios, which provide the basis for discussing capital adequacy.[33] The capital ratios increase if the equity capital grows and total assets, risk-weighted assets, deposits, or liabilities are held constant. The book uses the capital/assets ratio as the primary ratio to assess capital adequacy, as it is unaffected by changing balance sheet structures and asset risk over time.

One of the first capital ratios used in banking was the one comparing banknotes with capital for note-issuing banks. The roots of such ratios can be traced back to old note-issuing banks in Europe, such as the BoE, and were frequently used among note-issuing banks in the United States from the late eighteenth century. Among commercial banks in the United Kingdom and Switzerland that did not issue banknotes, the capital/deposits ratio was the standard measure. Early references to the capital/deposits ratio can be found in James William Gilbart's *A Practical Treatise on Banking* (1827). In the United States, capital/deposits ratios became more popular towards the end of the nineteenth century once deposits replaced banknotes as the primary liability of banks.

Broader ratios comparing capital with total liabilities or total assets have become more popular with the increasing heterogeneity of bank balance sheets. By the 1930s, it was evident that the extent of capital should reflect a bank's risk on the asset side, but actual methodologies to implement it were missing. An example of a first crude approach with two different asset classes and varying capital requirements is provided by the Swiss banking legislation of 1934.

---

[32] Jack Revell, *Solvency and Regulation of Banks: Theoretical and Practical Implications*, Bangor Occasional Papers in Economics (Bangor: University of Wales Press, 1975), pp. 12–17.

[33] The terms 'solvency' and 'capital adequacy' were and still are often used. In the 1950s and 1960s, 'solvency' was more commonly used in the United Kingdom, whereas 'capital adequacy' was the usual term in the United States. Revell, *Solvency and Regulation of Banks*, p. 12.

However, the accelerator towards more sophisticated capital requirements was the Second World War: rising government debt levels guided bank supervising agencies in the United States into the future of capital adequacy. War-related financing initiated a rapid expansion of deposits and total assets among banks in many countries. Federal bank supervisors in the United States realised that banks had started to fail to meet the informal capital requirements. Careful not to weaken the crucial role of banks in government financing, bank supervisors resorted to a new capital adequacy ratio. The capital/risk-assets ratio deducted cash and government securities from total assets, as bank supervisors argued that such investments posed no risk. This was the initial step towards a risk-adjusted view when measuring capital. More sophisticated risk-weighting methodologies followed this first crude approach. The Board of Governors of the Federal Reserve in the United States developed what was probably the most advanced and earliest methodology in the pre-Basel I-era: its 'ABC formula' of the 1950s. By the 1980s, various other countries also used risk-based capital requirements; among them were major countries such as France (from 1979), Switzerland, the United Kingdom (1980), and Germany (1985).[34] The Basel Accord of 1988 (Basel I) harmonised the varying approaches towards risk-adjusted capital measurements internationally.

The Basel II requirements of 2004 refined the risk-weighted approach and addressed the various deficiencies of Basel I.[35] One of the most severe changes was probably that proprietary risk-weighting models were also allowed. This gave large banks leeway in assessing the risks and, depending on those, the size of their capital buffers. In the area of credit risk, for example, banks could also use the so-called 'internal rating-based approach'.[36] Finally, the Basel III requirement in 2010 also introduced a non-risk-weighted measure: the leverage ratio.[37]

1.3   BOOK OUTLINE

Chapter 2 describes the evolution of capital/assets ratios in Germany, the United States, the United Kingdom, and Switzerland from the nineteenth century to the present. The capital/assets ratio is chosen to outline the increased leverage in the banking systems over time. A closer analysis of capital ratios in the United States, the United Kingdom, and Switzerland shows that these ratios must be

---

[34] In 1985, seven out of the nine European countries that were members of the Basel committee had already adopted risk-weighted approaches. Daniel K. Tarullo, *Banking on Basel: The Future of International Financial Regulation* (Washington, DC: Peterson Institute for International Economics, 2008), p. 41.

[35] Basel Committee on Banking Supervision, *Basel II: International Convergence of Capital Measurement and Capital Standards: A Revised Framework*, 2004.

[36] Basel Committee on Banking Supervision, *Basel II*, pp. 48–112.

[37] Basel Committee on Banking Supervision, *Basel III Leverage Ratio Framework and Disclosure Requirements*, 2014.

assessed carefully, and comparisons across countries are difficult in specific periods. Firstly, the capital/assets ratios used by the academic literature usually consider paid-up capital and disclosed reserves only. However, the total liability of shareholders can go beyond the paid-up capital. For certain periods or types of banks, there was even an unlimited liability of shareholders, which influenced the level of capital/assets ratios. Secondly, accounting standards allowed the extensive build-up of hidden reserves in the United Kingdom and Switzerland. The chapter shows that the capital strength of banks, considering hidden reserves and shareholder liabilities, is often underestimated by published figures. Thirdly, the underlying definitions used to construct time series data have varied, sometimes even with regards to the financial institutions that were considered as banks and thus were included in such statistics – or not. The academic literature comparing capital/assets ratios on an international level often neglects such issues. Thus, a historical narrative discussing the long-run evolution of capital in banking is crucial. Additionally, the chapter analyses structural changes in the assets of British, Swiss, and US banks using the Basel I framework of 1988 for a historical simulation.

The remaining chapters are arranged chronologically. Chapter 3 deals with the emergence of commercial banking in the United Kingdom, the United States, and Switzerland for the period leading up to the First World War. The First World War marks a fundamental change in the financial system, ending the first wave of globalisation and the classical gold standard. The chapter emphasises the role of the early banking literature in shaping the ideas of what adequate capital meant in numbers. Moreover, the chapter looks at individual banks in all three countries and how they determined the size of their capital. In Switzerland, simple rules of thumb such as the 1:3 capital/deposits ratio were surprisingly persistent, while the English banks – holding much shorter maturities on their asset side – abandoned such strict guidelines from very early on. In the United States, capital ratios were considered from the very beginning of banking. The chapter argues that the decentral or central organisation of the banknote issuance was an important determinant for the relevance of capital in the respective countries.

Chapter 4 focuses on the period of the two World Wars. Both wars led to substantial declines in capital/assets ratios in the United Kingdom, the United States, and Switzerland. The chapter shows that three drivers had a severe impact on the capitalisation of banks. Banks held high shares of the total government debt, which led to an expansion of balance sheets. At the same time, high inflation ratios devalued the paid-up capital of banks. Moreover, formal and informal constraints restricted banks from issuing capital in wartime.

The Second World War, in particular, had long-lasting effects on the evolution of banks and their capital. The United Kingdom had already entered a period of cheap money during the 1930s, and the control of capital issuances after 1939 reinforced the financial repression of the banks. The BoE conducted the country's monetary policy with the aim of securing demand for government debt. In this role, the BoE was an informal supervisor controlling the banks through liquidity ratios. As the research shows, British banks wanted to increase their capital during and after the Second World War but were prevented from doing so by the BoE.

The Swiss banks operated in a regulated but much more liberal framework. The 1930s led to the emergence of a formal supervisor and banking legislation, but (compared to their British counterparts) banks had substantially more leeway in making their own decisions. There was no widespread recapitalisation after the Second World War, as was the case after 1918. On the one hand, the big banks were still restructuring themselves due to the Great Depression – a process that had come to a halt due to the war. On the other hand, there was also a genuine feeling that the business models of banks would no longer require that much capital.

The belief in informal guidelines was much more pronounced in the United States than in the other two countries. By the mid-1930s, the United States already had three federal bank supervisory agencies – the OCC, the FED, and the FDIC – which all had developed opinions on how capital adequacy was assessed. At the core was a capital/deposits ratio of 10%. However, the rapidly growing government debt in banks' balance sheets overturned this convention, leading to the first risk-adjusted measurements for capital and triggering the development of new measurement approaches that became the forerunner of the Basel I guidelines.

Chapter 5 analyses the relationship of crises and regulation after the Second World War in the case of the United States and the United Kingdom, and after 1934 in Switzerland. The post–World War Two period is marked by high growth, the globalisation of banking, and a trend towards a harmonised framework for banking regulation. The Basel Accord in 1988 resulted from a gradual evolution towards risk-weighted assets models. However, the path towards Basel I was different in all three countries. When minimum capital ratios were introduced in Switzerland in 1935, most banks were indifferent, either because their capital surpassed the minimum requirements or because, having just found themselves in the middle of a crisis, they lacked bargaining power. This indifference changed towards the end of the 1950s. With the balance sheets of Swiss banks rapidly expanding, the regulation of capital through capital ratios suddenly became a bottleneck for growth. The regulatory framework was developed collaboratively, and the capital requirements were relaxed. Swiss banking could not have grown to such an extent without these changes.

The United Kingdom lacked the experience of a solvency crisis during the 1930s, resulting in the capital in banking becoming an almost irrelevant topic. It took until the secondary banking crisis in 1973/1974 for banks' regulation and supervision to finally be reconsidered.

The United States did experience a deep banking crisis in the 1930s but introduced statutory capital requirements only in the 1980s, following increased domestic banking instability and the threat of potentially high losses from the Latin American debt crisis. In contrast to Switzerland, the various US banking supervisors first had to go through a process of internal harmonisation of banking supervision and regulation from the 1970s.

As the chapter shows, there were also commonalities among the three countries in the pre-Basel period. All countries developed risk-based capital adequacy frameworks. Banks in all three countries grew rapidly, and in some cases, capital ratios limited the growth of banks. Moreover, banks actively participated in shaping their regulatory environment, albeit to different degrees within the three countries.

Chapter 6 provides an epilogue covering the development from Basel I to Basel III and reflections on the evolution of capital regulation in the long run. Both capital requirements between the 1990s and 2020 and the leveraging of the banking sector have been covered by many authors in the wake of the 2007/2008 financial crisis. Particular emphasis is given to the divergence of risk-weighted and risk-unweighted capital ratios among large, global banks – most of which have their roots in the nineteenth century. The chapter finishes with a call for a reassessment of banking regulation. In a historical perspective, regulatory frameworks are highly path dependent and are seldom fundamentally reconsidered with the aim to increase financial stability. Moreover, once we accept a certain degree of instability in modern banking, the focus should be on who covers losses and how significant such losses can potentially be without the involvement of the public.

2

Capital Ratios in the Long Run

Commercial banks have steadily increased the amount of debt capital compared to their equity capital since their emergence in the nineteenth century. The capital/assets ratio allows the tracing of this evolution in the long run and for various countries. This chapter considers the capital/assets ratios of four countries – the United States, the United Kingdom, Switzerland, and Germany – from 1840 to 2020. Banks in all four countries show a remarkable downward trend in the capital/assets ratio, except for a few periods of recovery.

Presenting a time series covering 180 years requires diligent work, but is ultimately not very complex. However, little emphasis has been given to issues related to the collection and aggregation of data so far. The time series showing capital/assets ratios for the four countries under consideration, for example, consist of thirteen different aggregated time series. Many of these time series do not fully represent the respective banking market. Certain banking groups, for example, are missing for specific periods. Moreover, the underlying definition of a bank, capital, and accounting standards varies between countries.

Other aspects that have received limited attention in a very long-run perspective are structural changes in banks' balance sheets. A key issue is that the underlying risk of assets in banking might have changed over time. The risk of default, for example, is fundamentally different if a bank holds 80% government debt on its balance sheet compared to a bank investing 80% of its assets in low-rated corporate bonds. Were capital ratios still decreasing if such risks of assets were considered? A simple Basel I methodology is applied in a historical context to adjust for the degree of risk. As such calculations require detailed balance sheet data, only British, Swiss, and US banks are analysed. This exercise highlights that decreasing capital ratios are not simply the result of structural changes on the assets side but can be observed even after accounting for such structural differences.

Finally, two other aspects can substantially alter capital ratios: a bank's 'actual' capital position may differ from the published figures because of hidden (undisclosed) reserves or due to unpaid shareholder capital.

2.1   CAPITAL RATIOS SINCE 1840

Figure 2.1 shows the evolution of bank capital as a percentage of the total assets from 1840 to 2020 for Germany, the United Kingdom, the United States, and Switzerland. From the early 1880s, data is only available for Switzerland and the United States. The capital/assets ratios in both countries remained above the 30% threshold until 1871 (Switzerland) and 1873 (United States). In the

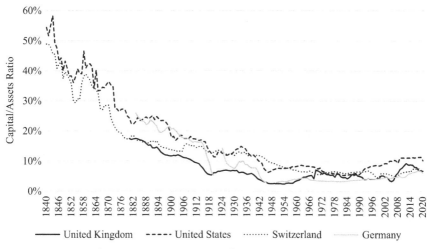

FIGURE 2.1   Capital/assets ratios, 1840–2020[1]

---

[1] Data and composition of time series: Germany: 1883–1920, Aktien-Kreditbanken and Hypothekenbanken (Deutsche Bundesbank, *Deutsches Geld- und Bankwesen in Zahlen, 1876–1975* (Frankfurt am Main: Knapp, 1976)); 1924–45 and 1950–2020, all banks (Deutsche Bundesbank, 'Deutsche Bundesbank – Statistics (Table BBK01.OU0322; BBK01.OU0308)', 2022, www.bundesbank.de/de/statistiken (accessed 3 February 2024)). United Kingdom: 1880–1966, all banks (David K. Sheppard, *The Growth and Role of UK Financial Institutions, 1880–1962* (London: Methuen, 1971); 1967–78: Big Four banks (data obtained from individual annual reports); 1979–83, clearing banks (Jack Revell, *Costs and Margins in Banking: Statistical Supplement 1978–1982*, ed. Organisation for Economic Co-Operation and Development (OECD) (Paris: OECD, 1985)); 1984–2008, all banks (OECD, *Income Statement and Balance Sheet Statistics* (Paris: Organisation for Economic Co-operation and Development, 13 April 2010) www.oecd-ilibrary.org/content/data/data-00270-en (accessed 8 December 2015)), 2009–20, 'ECB Statistical Data Warehouse (Series T00/L60)' https://sdw.ecb.europa.eu/home.do (accessed 28 February 2022). Switzerland: 1835–1905, note-issuing banks (Adolf Jöhr, *Die Schweizerischen Notenbanken: 1826–1913* (Zurich: Orell Füssli, 1915)); 1906–2020, all banks (Swiss National Bank, 'Historical Time Series', 2009). United States: 1835–1970, all banks (United States. Bureau of the Census, *Historical Statistics of the United States. Colonial Times to 1970*); 1971–9, commercial banks (Federal Deposit Insurance Corporation, 'Historical Bank Data', 2017, www2.fdic.gov/hsob/index.asp (accessed 21 February 2017)); 1980–2009, all banks (OECD, *Income Statement and Balance Sheet Statistics*); 2010–20: Federal Deposit Insurance Corporation, *Historical Bank Data*.

subsequent decade, both countries' capital/assets ratios experienced a further decline, falling to the 20% level.

From the 1880s until the end of the First World War, the capital/assets ratios of all four countries fell rapidly. By 1918, the ratio stood at 9.3% in Germany, 13.1% in Switzerland, 5.5% in the United Kingdom, and 13.3% in the United States. During the war, the ratios fell by 7.1 percentage points (pp) in Germany, 1.9pp in Switzerland, 3.7pp in the United States, and 2.8pp in the United Kingdom.

During the inter-war period (1918–39), the capital/assets ratios in all four countries recovered somewhat. The ratios grew after the First World War and accelerated their growth during the years of the Great Depression. Towards 1939, the ratios started to decline again. They then deteriorated even more rapidly during the Second World War. In Germany, the ratios dropped by 4.8pp during the Second World War, in the United Kingdom by 2.5pp, in Switzerland by 1.6pp, and in the United States by 5.3pp. The ratios of the four countries converged during the second half of the twentieth century. Capital/assets ratios grew again for US banks from the 1990s, and in Switzerland, the United Kingdom, and Germany after the last financial crisis.

Compared to the other countries, US banks' capital/assets ratio seems to have been the highest over most of the period covered. On the other hand, the capital/assets ratios in the United Kingdom were comparably low for a long time. However, in the second half of the twentieth century, there was less variation among the capital/assets ratios of the four countries.[2]

2.2 THE PROBLEMS OF CONSTRUCTING LONG-RUN TIME SERIES

Presenting capital ratios over 180 years seems to be a simple exercise and has been done in many publications. However, most publications do not discuss the cascade of issues related to showing long-run data. One of the critical problems is that reliable time series covering capital/assets ratios for more than one century seldom exist. For some years, there might be no data, or the data might be based only on a small number of banks. Moreover, long-run time series often consist of several individual datasets. Many of these sources are secondary sources, and obtaining the original source is not always possible. In addition, only a few sources discuss the methodology used in collecting and aggregating the data. However, identical definitions of capital and assets across time and space would be a condition for producing consistent data. A case in point is illustrated in Figure 2.1. It might give the impression of presenting four different time series covering four countries; in fact, thirteen individual time series have been aggregated to provide a long-run view of capital ratios.

---

[2] For an overview of capital/assets ratios of a broader set of countries, see Grossman, *Other People's Money*; Grossman, *Unsettled Account*; Òscar Jordà, Björn Richter, Moritz Schularick, and Alan M. Taylor, *Bank Capital Redux: Solvency, Liquidity, and Crisis* (Cambridge, MA: National Bureau of Economic Research, March 2017), www.nber.org/papers/w23287.

A second issue is that datasets sometimes cover different groups of banks. Finding datasets without a selection bias is difficult or even impossible for some periods. The German dataset before 1920 only incorporates certain bank types: joint-stock banks (*Aktien-Kreditbanken*) with a balance sheet total above one million DM and mortgage banks (*Hypothekenbanken*).[3] Other banking groups, most notably the savings banks (*Sparkassen*), are neglected.

Similar problems exist in the case of Switzerland. The time series from 1840 to 1906 consists of note-issuing banks only, which were usually regionally active banks with a primary focus on mortgage lending and receiving savings from customers (apart from note-issuing). Two important bank types are missing: small savings banks and large joint-stock banks.[4] The issue is even more apparent when considering that savings banks in Switzerland (and Germany, too) were often organised as 'clubs' or cooperatives, starting their business with little or no capital.[5] The data availability for Switzerland allows some insights into how representative the time series from 1840 to 1906 is. Only 7% (measured in the number of banks) or 37% (measured in total assets) of the bank population is covered from 1840 to 1906.[6]

Similar problems appear with the time series of banks in the United Kingdom. Until 1968, the time series covers joint-stock banks only. The banking model of private banks is not represented in the time series, even though private banks (based on partnerships) were the standard banking model until the 1830s. The number of private banks gradually fell towards the beginning of the twentieth century. Regarding joint-stock banks, however, the dataset represents the banking market, even though the data from 1968 to 1983 consists of only the 'Big Four' banks. The market at the time was highly concentrated.[7] Moreover, data on the whole market produced by the Bank of England (BoE) did not provide details on bank capital.

Another even more fundamental problem for bank statistics in British banking during the 1960s and 1970s emerges when considering the definition of a bank. The BoE asked only the so-called statistical banks in the United Kingdom to contribute their data to its statistical publications. The BoE defined statistical

---

[3] The joint-stock banks consist of the big banks in Berlin (*Berliner Grossbanken*) and Provincial Banks (*Provinzbanken*). See Deutsche Bundesbank, *Deutsches Geld- und Bankwesen in Zahlen*, p. 53. The data was first published in *Der Deutsche Oekonomist* and aggregated by the German Bundesbank.

[4] The exception was the Eidgenössische Bank. It was part of the group of big banks and issued banknotes.

[5] Johannes Ludwig Spyri, *Die Ersparnisskassen der Schweiz (1852–1862)*, Schweizerische Statistik (Zurich: Druck von Gebrüder Gull, 1864).

[6] See Adolf Jöhr, *Die Schweizerischen Notenbanken* and Franz Ritzmann, *Die Schweizer Banken: Geschichte, Theorie, Statistik*, Bankwirtschaftliche Forschungen (Bern: Haupt, 1973) for estimates on the number and total assets of all banks in Switzerland. Unfortunately, Ritzmann does not provide information about the capital of banks.

[7] Barclays, Midland, Westminster, Lloyds. The data was collected from the annual reports of the respective banks by the author.

banks as banks that were on the Schedule 8 or Schedule 127 lists.[8] Therefore, a substantial part of the market that emerged during that time – the secondary banks – was not represented in official statistics. The definition of a bank is a general problem: in order to measure, statistical offices or central banks need to define what is measured. Entities outside that definition are not covered.

Finally, the time series for the United States supposedly consists of 'all banks' for most of the years covered. However, 'all banks' is inaccurate, even though the US Bureau of the Census used the term in its statistical publications. The primary source of the data until the end of the nineteenth century was the Comptroller of the Currency, which discloses an incomplete coverage of banks as non-national banks were underrepresented.[9] The data after 1971 consists of FDIC-insured banks only. Moreover, investment banks regulated by the US Securities and Exchange Commission (SEC) were excluded.[10]

The shortcomings of long-run time series on capital/assets ratios are numerous. The data may serve as an analytical departure point but require further differentiation. Awareness of the problems of long-run data is therefore crucial when it comes to interpreting it, along with an understanding that long-run time series are more an approximation than an exact measurement.

2.3   STRUCTURAL CHANGES IN BALANCE SHEETS

Figure 2.1 shows decreasing capital/assets ratios in the long run, but did the leverage among banks increase once the risks on the asset side were considered? The Basel Capital Accord of 1988 provides a straightforward methodology to address this question. It allows for measuring structural changes in the balance sheets over long periods.

In 1988, the member countries of the Basel Committee on Banking Supervision at the Bank for International Settlements agreed on a common framework for the regulation of the capital adequacy of international banks. Basel I put forward a methodology that aimed to measure the credit risks of assets.[11] Each asset group carried a particular risk weight. Cash and government securities, for example, were given a zero risk weight. If a bank held USD 50 million in cash, it did not contribute to the overall total of risk-weighted assets (RWA) since its weight was 0%. Investments in company shares carried more risk and were weighted with 100%. This risk-weighting process led to total assets substantially lower than the non-risk-weighted asset total. The capital requirements were set relative to these RWA total at

---

[8] George Blunden, 'The Supervision of the UK Banking System', ed. Bank of England, *Quarterly Bulletin*, Q2 (1975).
[9] For a detailed discussion of the original sources, see United States Bureau of the Census, *Historical Statistics of the United States. Colonial Times to 1970*, p. 1011.
[10] This problem is addressed in Chapter 6.
[11] Basel Committee on Banking Supervision, *Basel I*.

a minimum of 8%, of which half had to be so-called core capital (equity capital and disclosed reserves).[12]

A Basel I simulation requires relatively granular data – for example, on banks' investment portfolios. The available data allows applying the Basel framework for British banks from 1880 to 1966, US banks from 1896 to 1980 and from 1984 to 2020, and Swiss banks from 1924 to 2020.[13] Table 2.1 shows the

TABLE 2.1 *Categorisation of balance sheet assets according to Basel I risk-weights*[1]

Asset	Risk Weight	United Kingdom	Switzerland	United States
Cash and government investments	0%	Cash, treasury deposit receipts, treasury bills, government investments	Liquid assets, government investments[2]	Currency and coin, cash items in process of collection, government obligations, obligations of States and other political subdivisions
Short-term investments	20%	Money at call, discounts	Money market papers, claims against banks	Bankers' balances
Mortgages	50%		Mortgage claims	Real estate loans
Other investments, discounts, loans	100%	Non-government investments, loans and other accounts, premises and other assets	Claims against customers, securities & precious metals, financial investments, participations, tangible assets, other assets	Other loans, other investments

[1] Own classification according to the Basel I framework: Basel Committee on Banking Supervision, *Basel I*, pp. 21–2.
[2] Government investments are bonds or debt register claims (*Schuldbuchforderungen*) from the federal government, cantonal governments, municipalities, and the Swiss Federal Railways, or loans to the respective entities.

[12] The other 4% could consist of undisclosed reserves, revaluation reserves, general provisions, hybrid debt capital, and subordinated debt. Basel Committee on Banking Supervision, *Basel I*, pp. 3–8.
[13] For a Basel I simulation for British banks, see also Billings and Capie, *Capital in British Banking*.

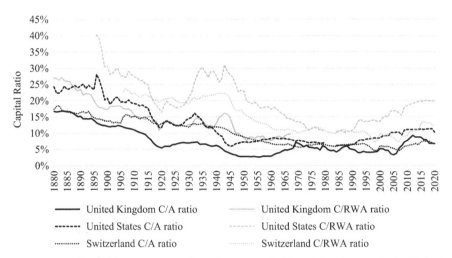

FIGURE 2.2 Capital in percentage of total assets and risk-weighted assets in the United Kingdom, the United States, and Switzerland, 1880–2020[15]

weights for calculating the RWA as defined by Basel I and the classification of the main balance sheet items in the respective countries.[14] The methodology used in this thesis differs slightly from the Basel I approach because of limited data availability: off-balance-sheet items could not be considered. Regarding capital, the calculations in Figure 2.2 only incorporate shareholder capital and disclosed reserves (defined as Tier I in Basel I). Other forms of capital according to Basel I (hidden reserves, subordinated debt, defined as Tier II) are excluded.

Figure 2.2 shows two ratios for each country: a risk-weighted and a risk-unweighted capital assets ratio. The dotted lines represent the capital as a percentage of the RWA. The capital/RWA ratio often developed parallel to the capital/assets ratio. There were periods, however, where the two ratios deviated. Most apparent are the periods of the 1930s in the United States, the Second World War in all three countries, and the period from 2008 to 2020 in the United States and Switzerland (no data on the United Kingdom is available for 2008–20). The reasons for these deviations can be found in the

---

[14] Classified according to Basel Committee on Banking Supervision, *Basel I*, pp. 21–2. The terminology of the balance sheet items relates to that in the source materials. See footnote 15 for data sources.

[15] Author's calculations. Data sources: Switzerland: Swiss National Bank, *Historical Time Series*; United Kingdom: Sheppard, *The Growth and Role of UK Financial Institutions*; United States: Howard Bodenhorn, 'Commercial Banks – Number and Assets: 1834–1980, Table Cj251-264', in *Historical Statistics of the United States, Earliest Times to the Present*, ed. Susan B. Carter, Scott Sigmund Gartner, Michael R. Haines, et al. (New York: Cambridge University Press, 2006), p. 2, http://dx.doi.org/10.1017/ISBN-9780511132971; Federal Deposit Insurance Corporation, *Historical Bank Data*.

banks' increased involvement in government debt or liquid assets. Both categories are weighted with zero per cent, leading to an increase in the capital/RWA ratio.

In the United Kingdom, for example, banks' capital/assets ratio fell by 2.3 percentage points to 5.2% between 1939 and 1945. At the same time, the capital/RWA ratio grew by 1.4 pp. The change resulted from holdings in British treasury deposits. In 1945, treasury deposits accounted for 30.7% of all assets. Meanwhile, government bonds increased from 21.4% to 23.4% of the total assets.

The time series on Switzerland show similar patterns. The capital/assets ratio fell by 1.5 pp between 1939 and 1945, whereas the capital/RWA ratio slightly increased. As in the United Kingdom, these changes were directly related to government investments. By 1939, 4.6% of the balance sheet total of Swiss banks were loans to the government, government bonds, or government debt register claims (*Schuldbuchforderungen*) held by the banks. In 1945, government investments as a percentage of the balance sheet total reached 11.5%.[16]

The asset composition of US banks has changed fundamentally from the early 1930s. By 1930, the share of government bonds in the banks' balance sheet was 10.9%. Six years later, one-third of the assets consisted of government bonds. The capital/assets ratio fell during that period (−2.6pp), while the capital/RWA ratio grew (+6.1pp). A similar effect can be observed from 2008 to 2014, when the share of liquid assets and government securities increased.

2.4 HIDDEN RESERVES

The time series presented so far were based on public figures published in annual reports. Undisclosed (hidden) reserves are not included as part of a bank's published capital even though such reserves serve as buffers against losses – one of the primary functions of capital. Adjusting the capital for hidden reserves leads to higher capital/assets ratios.

Companies create hidden reserves through two processes if not legally prohibited or limited. Firstly, a reserve is not listed under reserves but as a liability in the balance sheet.[17] Therefore, the liability is overvalued (book value exceeds the actual market price). Secondly, an asset in the published financial statement is undervalued (book value is below the actual market value) or not listed at all in the balance sheet. By keeping an asset undervalued or a liability overvalued, a bank avoids realising a profit, which would become

---

[16] Data on government investments: Swiss National Bank, 'Das Schweizerische Bankwesen 1946' (Zurich: Orell Füssli, 1947), p. 128.

[17] A typical example is the use of provisions. Depending on the definition of provisions, it is debatable whether it represents debt or equity capital.

part of the capital if not paid out to the shareholders. However, if a loss occurs, the bank can revalue an asset or liability and release hidden reserves to cover losses or smooth profits. Hidden reserves are, therefore, a form of capital and a safety cushion in crises when, for example, more loan defaults occur. Consequently, the function of hidden reserves is somewhat similar to that of disclosed reserves, with the notable exception that the public is not aware of their true extent.

Historically, there seemed to be three motives for maintaining hidden reserves. Firstly, many banks aimed for stable profits and stable dividends in order to signal stability. Secondly, banks pay dividends on nominal capital. Especially in the nineteenth century and the first half of the twentieth century, a high dividend was also a matter of reputation. Maintaining high (disclosed or undisclosed) reserves while having a comparatively small nominal capital allows for substantial and stable dividend payments on the nominal capital. Thirdly, building up hidden reserves instead of realising profits might avoid taxes on profits.[18]

Academic literature on hidden reserves in the financial sector is sparse.[19] Billings and Capie offer the only long-run data on hidden reserves based on internal accounts from archives covering British banks from 1920 to 1970.[20] For Switzerland and the United States, there are no encompassing assessments of hidden reserves.[21] Swiss banking regulation provides an alternative method for estimating hidden reserves. From the 1960s onwards, banks could use their hidden reserves as a part of the capital they were required to hold. In order to get hidden reserves approved as part of the required capital, auditors of banks had to submit a form confirming the extent of hidden reserves to the Federal Banking Commission (FBC).

For the United States, the estimations of asset values by the FDIC's bank examiners are an indication of hidden reserves. The FDIC published data from 1939 to 1951 summarising these adjustments. As part of their supervisory task, bank examiners estimated the value of assets. The examiners noted differences if the value of their assessment deviated from the value stated in

---

[18] For a review of the regulation of hidden reserves in the 1970s, covering the EEC countries, Japan, Switzerland, and the United States, see Wolf-Dieter Becker, Reinhold Falk, Ottokar W. Breycha, and Godehard Puckler, *Stille Reserven in den Jahresabschlüssen von Kreditinstituten: Eine Studie über die Handhabung in den Ländern der Europäischen Gemeinschaft sowie in der Schweiz, in den USA und in Japan*, ed. Peat, Marwick, Mitchell and Co., Schriften des Verbandes öffentlicher Banken (Göttingen: O. Schwartz, 1979).

[19] For an overview on the regulation of hidden reserves at the end of the 1970s in eleven European countries, see Becker et al., *Stille Reserven*.

[20] Billings and Capie, *Capital in British Banking*.

[21] Malik Mazbouri provides a brief overview of the role of hidden reserves in Switzerland. See Malik Mazbouri, 'A Retrospective Illusion? Reflections on the "Longevity" of Swiss Big Banks 1850–2000', in *Immortal Banks: Strategies, Structures and Performances of Major Banks*, ed. Michel Lescure (Geneva: Librairie Droz, 2016), pp. 231–51.

the bank's balance sheet. Additionally, examiners listed assets that were not in the books of banks. Their value, however, was negligible. Between 1939 and 1951, the ratio of 'assets not on the books' to total assets was 0.02% on average. Assets that were valued by examiners lower than the published value in the banks' balance sheet were about four times larger than the 'assets not on the books'.[22] If negative and positive value adjustments are netted against each other, the FDIC-insured banks hid losses instead of holding hidden reserves in their balance sheets.

2.4.1 Hidden Reserves in British Banking

Billings and Capie provide data on the extent of hidden reserves for six banks (Barclays Bank, Lloyds Bank, Martins Bank, Midland Bank, National Provincial Bank, Westminster Bank) from 1920 to 1968. Hidden reserves were allowed until 1970.[23] On average, the capital, including hidden reserves, was about 61% higher than the published capital.[24] The capital/assets ratio including hidden reserves was 2.5pp higher than the ratio without (minimum: 1.2pp; maximum: 3.4pp).

Figure 2.3 shows the capital/assets ratio of the Big Five banks with and without considering hidden reserves as a part of the banks' capital. The hidden reserves among the six banks grew until the late 1920s. They fell in 1927–30 and 1932–3 before recovering again. During the Second World War, the ratio of hidden reserves decreased and entered another period of growth until the 1960s. These figures are fairly representative of the banking market in the United Kingdom for most of the time covered by the data in Figure 2.3, as from 1920 onwards, the (originally English) Big Five banks had market shares in the UK banking market of between 80% and 90%.[25]

The public was aware of the extensive use of hidden reserves in banking. The *Journal of the Institute of Bankers*, for example, pointed out that 'It is, of course, common knowledge that all the large banks in England have written down their premises accounts to a fraction of their actual worth.'[26] Similarly, *The Economist* pointed out the existence of substantial hidden reserves in the 1920s:

---

[22] FDIC, 'Annual Report of the Federal Deposit Insurance Corporation 1945', 1946, p. 122; FDIC, 'Annual Report of the Federal Deposit Insurance Corporation 1951', 1951, pp. 154–5.

[23] Billings and Capie, *Capital in British Banking*, p. 141.

[24] Billings and Capie, *Capital in British Banking*, pp. 150–1.

[25] Depending on whether the calculations are based on deposits, total assets or number of branches. Author's calculations based on data from 'Banking Supplement, Various, 1861–1946', *The Economist*, 1946.

[26] Institute of Bankers, *Journal of the Institute of Bankers*, XXXIII (London: Blades, East & Blades, 1912), p. 2.

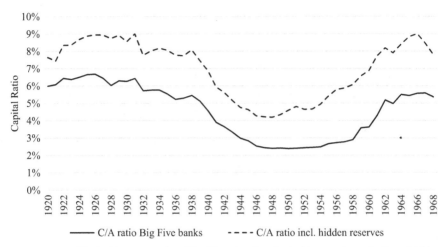

FIGURE 2.3 Capital/assets ratio, Big Five banks, including and excluding hidden reserves[27]

The banks, it must be remembered, have admittedly very large reserves, in addition to those figuring in the balance-sheets. During the past decade an enormous amount has been written off the book value of investments. The latter, mostly British Government securities, have greatly appreciated in value during the past two years, but, as far as we are aware, no bank has written up its investments. Here, therefore, is a very substantial 'hidden' reserve, to which may be added the fact that premises, from which large amounts have been steadily written off year by year, must be now worth a great deal more than the figures at which they appear in the balance-sheets.[28]

The statement above is representative of many others made in *The Economist*'s Banking Supplement, mentioning the presence of undisclosed reserves in English banking as well as the potential use of such reserves to ensure stable dividend payments.

2.4.2 Hidden Reserves in Swiss Banking

In 1934, Switzerland introduced its first national bank regulations. The Banking Act required banks to hold an 'adequate' amount of capital, specified in the Banking Ordinance as a 5% or 10% capital/liabilities ratio.[29] The Banking

---

[27] Capital and assets from 1920 to 1945: 'Banking Supplement, Various, 1861–1946'; capital and assets from 1946–67 and 'actual' (internal) capital from Billings and Capie, *Capital in British Banking*, based on their 'capital measure 1', consisting of published capital plus hidden reserves. Data represents mean value of Big Five banks. Data is missing for the following banks and years: Lloyds (1920–1; 1928–31;1942–6; 1967–8); Westminster (1920–1); National Provincial (1935–6; 1940–5; 1953–64; 1968).

[28] 'Banking Supplement 1923', *The Economist* (London, 19 May 1923), pp. 1059–60.

[29] *Bundesgesetz über die Banken und Sparkassen vom 8. November 1934*, 1934. Article 4.

Ordinance was not revised until 1961. One significant change in capital regulation in 1961 was that hidden reserves were allowed as part of a bank's statutory capital.[30] Allowing hidden reserves as part of the required capital became more restricted again between 1990 and 1995.[31]

According to Switzerland's capital regulations, disclosing hidden reserves was not mandatory. However, if banks wanted to use hidden reserves as part of their required capital, their auditors would have to report them to the bank supervisor: the FBC. Consequently, data on hidden reserves used as a statutory capital component was reported to the FBC and is accessible in its archives. Moreover, the Swiss National Bank (SNB) published annual statistics on hidden reserves for certain years.[32]

Despite these sources, the exact amount of hidden reserves is unknown as the use of hidden reserves for regulatory requirements was limited. From 1961 to 1967, the legally required capital could consist of a maximum of 15% hidden reserves. From 1968 to 1971, the regulator raised the limit to 25%, and in 1972 it removed the limit altogether. Thus, the legally required capital could, theoretically, consist entirely of hidden reserves in 1972. However, if banks had sufficient paid-up capital and disclosed reserves, they might not have reported undisclosed reserves to the supervisor. Data on undisclosed reserves in official statistics and from the archive of the FBC are, therefore, lower-bound estimates only and do not allow for an exact estimate of hidden reserves in Swiss banking.

Figure 2.4 shows the estimates of hidden reserves of all banks in Switzerland as a percentage of the total assets (axis on the left, black bars) and the share that hidden reserves contributed to the required capital (right axis, grey line). On average, banks reported 5.4% (maximum allowed: 15%) of their required capital as hidden reserves from 1961 to 1967. From 1968 to 1971, the average was 11.3% (maximum allowed 25%) and 14% from 1972 to 1994 (no limits).

Compared to the total assets, hidden reserves reached, on average, 0.3% (1961–7), 0.6% (1968–71), and 0.9% (1972–94). The reported hidden reserves grew immediately after the regulatory changes in 1968 and 1972, indicating that the newly reported hidden reserves existed already before these changes. While these figures represent lower bound estimates, the figures of one banking group among the Swiss banks provide more accurate insights.

---

[30] Eidgenössische Bankenkommission, *Circular*, 1961; Eidgenössische Bankenkommission, *Circular*, 1968. Hidden reserves could be only used as regulatory capital if they were taxed.

[31] From 1990 onwards, the build-up of hidden reserves and the reduction of hidden reserves to increase profits had to be disclosed in the annual reports. Eidgenössische Bankenkommission, *Circular*, 1990.

[32] The Swiss National Bank published data on hidden reserves in its annual banking statistics from 1961 to 1994, aggregated for all banks, and on the level of individual bank groups from 1970 to 1994.

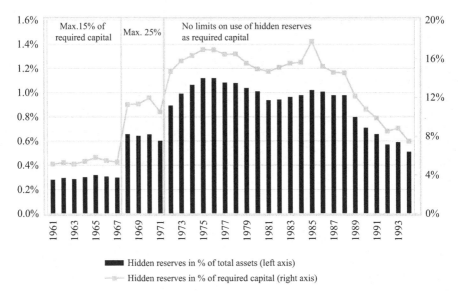

FIGURE 2.4 Hidden reserves reported to the Federal Banking Commission in percent of total assets (left axis) and hidden reserves in percent of required capital (right axis), all Swiss banks, 1961–94[33]

The big banks frequently struggled to meet capital requirements in the 1950s, '60s and '70s.[34] If the big banks had problems meeting capital requirements, they likely reported all their hidden reserves to the supervisor. By 1960, the big banks lacked 16% of the required capital, thus failing to meet capital requirements to a large extent. The big banks narrowly managed to fulfil the capital requirements for some subsequent years but fell below the requirements again in the first half of the 1970s.

Hidden reserves held by the big banks from 1972 to 1994 were on average 1.2% of total assets. The reported hidden reserves reached their high point in 1975 and 1976, reaching 2% of total assets, and fell again rapidly in the 1990s. The reason for this can most likely be found in regulatory changes and the real estate crisis that hit Switzerland in the early 1990s. The revision of the Banking Ordinance in 1995 finally prohibited hidden reserves on a consolidated level. Furthermore, the real estate crisis at the beginning of the 1990s led to losses among the Swiss banks of CHF 42.3 bn, of which CHF 30.1 bn was attributed to

[33] Data: Swiss National Bank, 'Das Schweizerische Bankwesen/Die Banken in der Schweiz (annual issues 1906–2015)', various, 1906–2015 (2015). From 1970 to 1994, the statistics of the Swiss National Bank also contained information on the capital structure of individual bank groups. Archival material: Eidgenössische Bankenkommission, *Anrechnung stiller Reserven als eigene Mittel* (Bern, 1966), Swiss Federal Archives, E6520A#1983/50#49*.

[34] Amrein, *Eigenmittel der Schweizer Banken im historischen Kontext*.

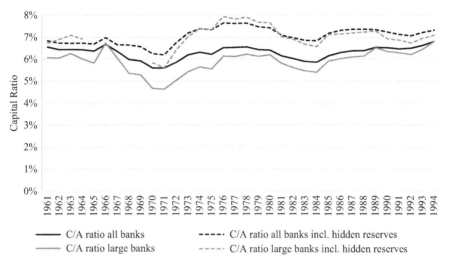

FIGURE 2.5   Capital/assets ratio including and excluding hidden reserves, all banks and big banks, 1961–94[37]

the big banks.[35] The banks likely covered substantial amounts of these losses with hidden reserves, as the total volume of capital (including reserves) was even increasing at the time, and published profits were stable.[36]

Figure 2.5 shows the capital/assets ratios for 'all banks' and the big banks with and without the hidden reserves estimates. It indicates that the actual capital/assets ratios were substantially higher than the capital/assets ratios derived from published accounts. With regards to the whole banking market, the capital/assets ratio, including hidden reserves, was at least 0.8pp higher than the published capital/assets ratio (1961–94). For the big banks, the difference between the actual and the published capital/assets ratio was even more substantial.

2.5   EXTENDED SHAREHOLDER LIABILITIES

In the absence of extended forms of liabilities, an investor is liable only for the paid-up nominal value of a share. The maximum potential loss is the price paid for the stock. With extended shareholder liabilities, the potential losses for

[35] Eidgenössische Bankenkommission, *Jahresbericht 1997 der Eidgenössischen Bankenkommission* (Bern, April 1998), p. 16.

[37] The data was collected from various annual issues of Schweizerische Nationalbank SNB, 'Das Schweizerische Bankwesen/Die Banken in Der Schweiz', 1906–2015, and archival material from the Federal Banking Commission: Eidgenössische Bankenkommission, *Anrechnung stiller Reserven, SFA, E6520A#1983/50#49**.

[36] See Swiss National Bank, *Historical Time Series*.

investors can be much higher, either limited to a certain amount or even unlimited. Under which circumstances can or must shareholders pay in more equity capital? It depends on the regulatory framework. First, a bank might be able to call up more capital based on a decision by the bank's management or the general assembly if needed. There are several reasons to call up additional capital: for example, to expand business activities or to recapitalise after losses and write off a part of the capital. Secondly, capital can be called up if a bank is in liquidation. In that case, calling up capital is contingent on an event (bankruptcy). Given the bank's limited or unlimited claim on its shareholders' wealth, it can be argued that such non-contingent or contingent claims are a form of capital. Consequently, capital/assets ratios can be adjusted by shareholder liabilities, providing a more comprehensive view of a bank's 'capital strength' bank.

Estimating the extent of the shareholder liability is straightforward if it is limited to a specific maximum (e.g. double liability, limited to an amount). If it is unlimited, the liability depends on the individual wealth of each shareholder, making the valuation of the liability almost impossible. In England, all banks could limit shareholder liability from 1857 onwards, but most banks only changed to limited liability after the collapse of the City of Glasgow Bank in 1878. In Switzerland, unlimited liability would still be allowed today for cooperative banks.[38] In practice, however, extended forms of liability lost their importance during the nineteenth century.[39] The United States, finally, provides numerous examples of extended liabilities in banking on the state level. Moreover, the federally chartered national banks were under double liability provisions from 1864 to 1937.

2.5.1 Shareholder Liability in British Banking

By the mid-nineteenth century, banks in England could operate under three different acts. While the acts of 1826 and 1833 did not allow banks to register with limited liability, it was compulsory under the Banking Act of 1844.[40] Most banks at the time, however, operated under the Banking Acts of 1826 and 1833.[41] It was not until 1857 that all English banks could register with limited liability, but only a few banks took the opportunity and changed their

---

[38] Art. 869 & 870, *Bundesgesetz betreffend die Ergänzung des Schweizerischen Zivilgesetzbuches (Fünfter Teil: Obligationenrecht), (Stand am 1. April 2017)*, 1911.

[39] There was only one banking group, the Raiffeisen banks, which made extensive use of unlimited liability until 1989 and limited liability until 2014. For comments on the end of limited liability, see Raiffeisen Schweiz Genossenschaft, 'Geschäftsbericht der Raiffeisen Gruppe 2013', 2014, p. 54.

[40] The Banking Co-Partnerships Act, 1826, 7 Geo. IV, c. 46. Bank of England Act, 1833, Will IV, c. 98. Bank Charter Act 1844 (Act 7 & 8 Vict., c. 32)

[41] Arthur Meredith Allen and others, *Commercial Banking Legislation And Control* (London: Macmillan, 1938), p. 230.

legal status.[42] The collapse of the City of Glasgow Bank in 1878 was a turning point. By 1874, about 20% of English deposits were held by banks with limited liability.[43] In 1880, only around every fourth bank still operated with unlimited liability. In 1885, almost all joint-stock banks were on limited liability.[44]

Most banks that changed to limited liability after the City of Glasgow failure created a 'reserve liability' based on the Companies Act of 1879. This reserve liability could be called up in case of bankruptcy.[45] Thus, unlimited liability was replaced by a certain amount of uncalled capital and reserve capital. The former could be called up anytime, the latter only in the event of a bank failure. On the one hand, the reserve liability protected shareholders from unwanted and uncontrollable calls for capital from bank directors. Shareholders knew how much of the total amount they were liable for. On the other hand, a reserve was established for the depositors, signalling bank safety.[46] However, the transition from unlimited to limited liability banking raises the question of whether banks substantially increased their paid-up capital and reserves once they switched from one to the other regime. Turner has shown that banks with limited liability had substantially higher capital ratios than unlimited liability banks.[47] A look at journalistic articles at the time also shows that an increase of paid-up capital was also expected.

Grossman and Imai also show that uncalled capital and reserve liability restrained the banks' risk-taking. English banks with higher amounts of uncalled capital and reserve liability tended to take less risk. Their loan portfolios grew more slowly, and their assets were less risky.[48]

---

[42] The Limited Liability Act of 1855 (18 & 19 Vict., c. 133) was extended to banks in 1857 (Joint Stock Companies Act of 1857, 20 & 21 Vict., c. 49)

[43] Graeme G. Acheson and John D. Turner, 'The Death Blow to Unlimited Liability in Victorian Britain: The City of Glasgow Failure', *Explorations in Economic History*, 45.3 (2008), 235–53 (p. 237).

[44] Less than 4% of English joint-stock banks had unlimited liability in 1885. Measured in deposits, these banks held less than 1% of all deposits in England and Wales. Author's calculations, data: 'The Economist Banking Supplement, Various, 1861–1946'.

[45] Companies Act of 1879, 42 & 43 Vict., c. 76, Section V. According to the Companies Act, banks could increase the nominal capital per share in case the capital was already fully paid up to create a reserve liability. Alternatively, a portion of the uncalled capital could be defined as having reserve liability.

[46] On the perceptions of unlimited and limited liability in the nineteenth century, see John D. Turner, 'The Last Acre and Sixpence': Views on Bank Liability Regimes in Nineteenth Century Britain', *Financial History Review*, 16.2 (2009), 111–27.

[47] John D. Turner, *Banking in Crisis: The Rise and Fall of British Banking Stability, 1800 to the Present*, Cambridge Studies in Economic History (Cambridge: Cambridge University Press, 2014), p. 126.

[48] Richard S. Grossman and Masami Imai, 'Contingent Capital and Bank Risk-Taking among British Banks before the First World War', *Economic History Review*, 66.1 (2013), 132–55. Both Esty and Grossman find similar results for the reduced risk-taking effect of double liability in the United States. See Benjamin C. Esty, 'The Impact of Contingent Liability on Commercial

Assessing the value of the unlimited liability depends on the individual wealth of a bank's shareholders. Based on an analysis of the City of Glasgow's shareholder composition, Acheson and Turner showed that the bank's shareholders were 'from the wealthier sections of society'.[49] Looking at the shareholders of four different banks in a separate study, Turner came to a similar result.[50] The same can be concluded when looking at the socio-occupational backgrounds of shareholders.[51] Turner also argued that wealthier individuals had a great incentive to act as the directors of banks in order to conduct a vetting role. In the period of unlimited liability, the vetting of shareholders allowed their directors to avoid a dilution of the aggregate shareholder wealth, which would have increased their own liability.[52]

In the period of unlimited liability, quantifying the actual value of the joint and several liabilities would require an analysis of each individual shareholder. For the period after the 1870s, however, the amount of the limited liability can be measured for most of the banks, assuming the limited liability could be paid up entirely by the shareholders in the case of a failure. Including this contingent capital, the total capital resources would consist of (1) the subscribed capital, divided into paid-up and unpaid (uncalled and reserve) capital, (2) the banks' reserves, (3) retained profits, and (4) hidden reserves.

Table 2.2 shows the unpaid capital, hidden reserves and the 'total capital strength' (summarising all capital components) of British joint-stock banks.[53] Most major banks extinguished their unpaid capital between 1956 and 1958 in a capital reorganisation led by the BoE.[54] The small amounts of unpaid capital in later years result from the difference in the authorised share capital and the called-up share capital (allotted and fully paid).[55]

The calculations highlight that the extended limited liability was an integral part of the capital resources in the banking system. In the 1890s, for example,

---

Bank Risk Taking', *Journal of Financial Economics*, 1998, 189; Richard S. Grossman, 'Double Liability and Bank Risk Taking', *Journal of Money, Credit and Banking*, 33.2 (2001), 143.

[49] Acheson and Turner, *The Death Blow to Unlimited Liability*, p. 243.

[50] Turner, *Banking in Crisis*, p. 113.

[51] See Turner, *Banking in Crisis*, p. 117, table 5.5. based on Graeme G. Acheson and John D. Turner, 'The Impact of Limited Liability on Ownership and Control: Irish Banking, 1877–1914', *The Economic History Review*, 59.2 (2006), 320–46; Acheson and Turner, *The Death Blow to Unlimited Liability*; John D. Turner, 'Wider Share Ownership? Investors in English and Welsh Bank Shares in the Nineteenth Century', *The Economic History Review*, 62.S1 (2009), 167–92; Graeme G. Acheson and John D. Turner, 'Investor Behaviour in a Nascent Capital Market: Scottish Bank Shareholders in the Nineteenth Century', *The Economic History Review*, 64.1 (2011), 188.

[52] Turner, *Banking in Crisis*, pp. 111–13.

[53] The total capital strength ratio is a theoretical view measuring the overall liability, capital, as well as disclosed and undisclosed reserves in percent of total assets. It disregards the fact that the total assets would increase if unpaid capital would be paid up or undisclosed reserves disclosed.

[54] Turner, *Banking in Crisis*, pp. 131–2.

[55] See annual reports of the Big Four.

TABLE 2.2 *Total capital resources in percent of total assets, British banks, averages per decade, 1881–2000*[1]

Decade	C/A Ratio	Unpaid Capital/ Total Assets	Hidden Reserves/ Total Assets	Total Capital Strength Ratio
1881–1890	16.6%	36.0%	n.a.	52.6%
1891–1900	13.0%	28.5%	n.a.	41.5%
1901–1910	11.2%	23.4%	n.a.	34.6%
1911–1920	7.3%	15.8%	n.a.	23.1%
1921–1930	6.7%	8.8%	*2.2%	15.5%
1931–1940	5.9%	7.6%	*2.4%	+15.9%
1941–1950	3.0%	2.7%	*1.9%	+7.6%
1951–1960	2.7%	*2.1%	*2.8%	+7.6%
1961–1970	4.6%	*0.7%	*3.2%	+8.6%
1971–1980	*5.9%	*0.4%	0.0%	+6.3%
1981–1990	4.6%	*0.2%	0.0%	+4.8%
1991–2000	5.1%	n.a.	0.0%	5.1%

[1] Author's calculations. Data: Unpaid capital, 1951–90: Individual balance sheets of Big Five/Big Four, collected by author; 1881–50: 'The Economist Banking Supplement, Various, 1861–1946'. Hidden reserves: Billings and Capie, *Capital in British Banking*. Other data: Sheppard, *The Growth and Role of UK Financial Institutions*. Notes: * denotes the Big Five/Big Four banks. This data was used due to a lack of alternative data covering the whole market. + marks estimated figures, as these figures mix data from the whole market with aggregated data for the Big Five/Big Four banks. Note that all forms of capital are measured against the same amount of total assets. This is a theoretical view with a constant standard of comparison. In practice, however, a higher capital in the balance sheet would increase the total assets. For a similar analysis comparing the total capital resources to deposits, see also Turner, *Banking in Crisis*, p. 128, figure 5.1.

the unpaid capital amounted to 28.5% of the total assets. Compared to the deposits, 55% of the banks' deposits were covered by capital resources of various forms in the 1890s. The importance of unpaid capital decreased over time. In the 1930s, the unpaid capital as a percentage of the total assets was down to 2.7%.

2.5.2 Shareholder Liability in Swiss Banking

So far, academic literature has not yet estimated the extent of shareholder liabilities in Swiss banking. Swiss corporate law was and still is part of the Swiss Code of Obligations, introduced in 1883. Besides regulating basic principles, such as accounting standards, disclosure requirements, and audits, it also dealt with the liability of shareholders. According to the Code of Obligations, only 20% of the capital of a joint-stock company had to be paid-up.[56] Consequently, there was no unlimited liability for the shareholders of joint-stock banks after 1883, but the size of the liability in the form of unpaid capital varied up to a limit of four-fifths of a bank's total capital. A different rule applied to banks with the legal form of a cooperative. Many savings banks were founded as cooperatives. If not stated otherwise in the articles of association of a bank, the cooperation members were jointly liable with their personal wealth in the case of bankruptcy.[57]

Besides the general regulatory framework provided by the Code of Obligations, the Federal Banknote Act, also introduced in 1883, was the first law on a national level to regulate a particular banking activity.[58] The Act obliged note-issuing banks to hold a paid-up capital of at least CHF 500,000. If the paid-up capital was above CHF 500,000, note-issuing banks çould – theoretically – still operate with unpaid capital. The paid-up capital of CHF 500,000, however, would have to represent 20% of the total capital (according to the Code of Obligations).

When Switzerland's first National Banking Act was introduced in 1934, it allowed the use of unpaid capital for regulatory purposes, therefore building on the corporate law anchored in the Code of Obligations. The Banking Act stipulated a so-called required capital: the statutory minimum threshold of capital. Both joint-stock banks and cooperative banks could use up to 50% of their unpaid capital as being counted as their required capital from a legal point of view. The regulatory practice of allowing unpaid capital to be part of the statutory capital was maintained until 2012.[59]

Based on the regulatory framework, extensive use of unpaid capital and unlimited liability was possible. Table 2.3 provides estimates for the extent of unpaid capital as well as the 'total capital strength' (including both unpaid capital and hidden reserves) of the Swiss banking system from 1841 to 2000. The data availability for the nineteenth century is low. The numbers shown in Table 2.3 up to 1906 are taken from Adolf Jöhr's compilation and cover only note-issuing banks.[60] Small banks are underrepresented in this period. After 1906, the data in

---

[56] Art. 618 & 633, *Bundesgesetz über das Obligationenrecht vom 14. Juni 1881*, 1883. This rule is still in place today: see Art. 632, *Bundesgesetz betreffend die Ergänzung des Schweizerischen Zivilgesetzbuches (Fünfter Teil: Obligationenrecht), (Stand am 1. April 2017).*

[57] Art. 688 & 689, *Bundesgesetz über das Obligationenrecht vom 14. Juni 1881.*

[58] *Bundesgesetz über die Ausgabe und die Einlösung von Banknoten vom 8. März 1881*, 1883. On Switzerland's monetary history, see Ernst Baltensperger and Peter Kugler, *Swiss Monetary History since the Early 19th Century*, Studies in Macroeconomic History (Cambridge: Cambridge University Press, 2017).

[59] Eidgenössische Finanzmarktaufsicht FINMA, Jahresbericht 2009 (2010), p. 45. The most prominent bank using unpaid capital for regulatory purposes was the Raiffeisen group. Between the 1970s and 1990s, on average more than 60% of the bank's required capital consisted of unpaid capital. The Raiffeisen banks could simply change the amount of their members' liability in the articles of association, and thereby substantially increase their regulatory capital. See Amrein, *Eigenmittel der Schweizer Banken im historischen Kontext*, p. 108.

[60] Jöhr, *Die Schweizerischen Notenbanken*. Adolf Jöhr was General Secretary of the Swiss National Bank, 1907–15; Member of the Board of Governors of the Swiss National Bank,

TABLE 2.3 *Total capital resources in percent of total assets, Swiss banks, averages per decade, 1841–2000*[1]

Decade	Capital/ Assets Ratio	Unpaid Capital/ Total Assets (Estimate)	Hidden Reserves/ Total Assets (Minimum Estimate)	Total Capital Strength Ratio (Minimum Estimate)
[+]1841–1850	44.0%	0.8%	n.a.	44.8%
[+]1851–1860	34.5%	4.0%	n.a.	38.5%
[+]1861–1870	32.1%	6.9%	n.a.	39.0%
[+]1871–1880	20.9%	2.5%	n.a.	23.3%
[+]1881–1890	17.0%	1.8%	n.a.	18.7%
[+]1891–1900	15.3%	0.9%	n.a.	16.2%
[+]1901–1910	13.2%	0.4%	n.a.	13.7%
1911–1920	13.5%	0.4%	n.a.	13.8%
1921–1930	12.5%	0.1%	n.a.	12.6%
1931–1940	12.3%	n.a.	n.a.	n.a.
1941–1950	10.3%	n.a.	n.a.	n.a.
1951–1960	7.6%	n.a.	n.a.	n.a.
1961–1970	6.3%	0.1%	0.4%	6.7%
1971–1980	6.3%	0.4%	1.0%	7.6%
1981–1990	6.2%	0.4%	0.9%	7.5%
1991–2000	5.9%	*0.4%	*0.6%	6.8%

[1] Data: 1841–1900: Adolf Jöhr, *Die Schweizerischen Notenbanken*; Capital/Assets Ratios 1901–2010: Swiss National Bank, *Die Banken in der Schweiz (annual issues 1906–2015)*. Various Issues 1906–2010. Notes: The period from 1841 to 1900 covers note-issuing banks only. * The data is available from 1991–4 only. [+] Note-issuing banks only, no other data available. Please note that all forms of capital are measured against the same amount of total assets. This is a theoretical view with a constant standard of comparison. In practice, however, a higher capital in the balance sheet would increase the total assets.

Table 2.3 become increasingly representative of the banking market as the SNB started to collect and aggregate data. In the first decade of the SNB banking statistics, however, the SNB also struggled to obtain a complete set of data. The reason for this can be found in the lack of publication requirements. According to the Code of Obligations, banks were not obliged to produce an annual public

1915–18; General Manager of Credit Suisse, 1918–39; and Member of the Bank Council of the Swiss National Bank, 1939–51. See Katja Hürlimann, 'Jöhr, Adolf ', *Historisches Lexikon der Schweiz – Dictionnaire historique de la Suisse – Dizionario storico della Svizzera* (Bern): www .hls-dhs-dss.ch/textes/d/D46271.php (accessed 30 April 2019).

statement. Moreover, providing data to the SNB was not mandatory. Many of the smaller savings banks did not publish a balance sheet or income statement for the public.[61] Publication requirements in banking were only introduced with the Banking Act in 1934.

The data in Table 2.3 underline that unpaid capital was common and substantial in the nineteenth century. Measured as a percentage of total assets, unpaid capital reached its highest point at 6.9% in the 1860s. The numbers were substantially lower during the twentieth century for the whole banking market. In the 1970s, for example, unpaid capital added, on average, 0.4pp to the capital/assets ratio of 6.3%. Including hidden reserves, this would lead to an adjusted capital/assets ratio of 7.6%, which was still 20% higher than the published capital/assets ratio.

2.5.3   Shareholder Liability in US Banking

The United States offer a broad experience of experimenting with liability provisions, ranging from limited (single) liability to unlimited liability. Early commercial banks in the United States often operated without extended liability for shareholders. However, during the period leading up to the US Civil War, there was a clear trend towards double liability among banks chartered by states.[62] Double liability typically meant that shareholders were, in addition to their initial investment in the stock, liable for the par (nominal) value of the stock in case of bankruptcy.

The trend toward double liability was further accelerated on the federal level by the introduction of the National Banking Act of 1864.[63] Newly chartered national banks all operated under double liability.[64] Many states followed and implemented liability provisions for state banks. By 1910, for example, eleven states had no additional liability requirements or no incorporation laws for banks. Out of the thirty-two states that required additional liability, however, thirty states imposed double liability.[65] In 1930, only a few states were left with single or voluntary liability, which left the introduction of liability to the banks.[66]

Double liability became increasingly unpopular in the 1930s. Macey and Miller identify three reasons for the demise of double liability. The high number

---

[61] Swiss National Bank, 'Das Schweizerische Bankwesen 1909–1913' (Bern: Buchdruckerei Stämpfli & Cie, 1915), p. 5.

[62] Davis R. Dewey, *State Banking Before the Civil War*, Congressional Documents (Government Printing Office, 1910), pp. 117–20; Ralph W. Marquis and Frank P. Smith, 'Double Liability for Bank Stock', *The American Economic Review*, 27.3 (1937), 490–502.

[63] *National Banking Act*, 1864, Sec. 12.

[64] For an overview, see Grossman, *Double Liability and Bank Risk Taking*; Richard S. Grossman, 'Fear and Greed: The Evolution of Double Liability in American Banking, 1865—1930', *Explorations in Economic History*, 44.1 (2007), 59–80.

[65] Marquis and Smith, *Double Liability for Bank Stock*, p. 498.

[66] Grossman, *Fear and Greed*, pp. 62–64.

TABLE 2.4 *Total capital resources in percent of total assets, United States national banks, averages per decade, 1863–1937*[1]

Decade	Capital/Assets Ratio	Unpaid Capital/Total Assets	Total Capital Strength Ratio
1863–1870	35.1%	29.8%	65.0%
1871–1880	35.0%	25.9%	60.8%
1881–1890	30.0%	21.3%	51.3%
1891–1900	27.0%	17.8%	44.8%
1901–1910	19.3%	10.9%	30.1%
1911–1920	15.4%	7.8%	23.2%
1921–1930	12.9%	5.9%	18.8%
1931–1937	12.4%	6.5%	18.9%

[1] Data: 1863–1931: Office of the Comptroller of the Currency, 'Annual Report of the Comptroller of the Currency 1931', 1932, pp. 1021–2, Tab. 95. 1932–9: Office of the Comptroller of the Currency, 'Annual Report of the Comptroller of the Currency 1939', 1940, p. 301, Tab. 59. Note that all forms of capital are measured against the same amount of total assets. This is a theoretical view with a constant standard of comparison. In practice, however, a higher capital in the balance sheet would increase the total assets.

of bankruptcies between 1929 and 1932 showed that double liability did not contribute to banking stability. Moreover, the bank failures also led to bankruptcies among individual shareholders. Finally, the introduction of federal deposit insurance in 1933 made double liability redundant.[67]

The Banking Acts of 1933 and 1935 led to the end of double liability in the national banking system. The Act of 1933 allowed banks to issue shares without double liability.[68] The Act of 1935 repealed double liability on existing shares of all national banks from July 1937.[69] At the state level, every state had dropped double liability provisions by 1941.[70]

Measuring the extent of double liability for state banks is challenging due to the variety of liability provisions and frequent regulatory changes. However, national banks' liability provisions were stable from 1864 to 1937. Official statistics by the Office of the Comptroller of the Currency, responsible for administering the federal banking system and chartering national banks, provide insights into the capital structure of national banks.

Table 2.4 shows the capital/assets ratio, the unpaid capital relative to total assets, and the 'total capital strength' ratio of national banks from

[67] Johnathan R. Macey and Geoffrey P. Miller, 'Double Liability of Bank Shareholders: History and Implications', *Wake Forest Law Review*, 27.33 (1992), pp. 37–8.

[68] United States Congress, *Banking Act of 1933*, H.R. 5661, 1933, Sec. 22.

[69] United States Congress, *Banking Act of 1935*, H.R. 7617, 1935, Sec. 304.

[70] Grossman, *Unsettled Account*, p. 240. For a discussion of reasons to stipulate double liability provision on state level, see Grossman, *Fear and Greed*.

1863 to 1937. The double liability led to a substantial amount of unpaid capital during the nineteenth century. Over time, the importance of double liability diminished to some extent as banks accumulated reserves. At the turn of the century, for example, such published reserves already made up nearly 40% of the national banks' published capital.

3

The Nineteenth Century

How Ideas Shape Capital Structures

Modern statutory capital requirements heavily influence banks' capital levels. In most countries, the regulation of bank capital specifies minimum capital requirements for establishing and running a bank. According to the World Bank's Bank Regulation and Supervision Survey in 2016, only 5 out of 158 countries did not stipulate a minimum capital requirement.[1] When joint-stock banks were established in the late eighteenth and nineteenth centuries, capital regulation in two of the three countries analysed in the following – England and Switzerland – was light at best.[2] Only the United States regulated capital on the state and federal levels.

One of the main reasons for regulating bank capital was the right of individual banks to issue notes, which was monopolised in the United States as late as the 1930s. The concern for an over-issue of banknotes often led to a limitation of note issuing as a multiple of a bank's capital. Limiting the note issue to a multiple of bank capital is a capital requirement too.

In contrast to the United States, England and Switzerland did not have many note-issuing banks, only one (England) or a few (Switzerland). Therefore, the liabilities side of a commercial bank's balance sheet looked very different to that of note-issuing banks in the United States. In the case of England and Switzerland, not banknotes but customers' deposits were the most important balance sheet item on the liability side. Thus, contemporaries compared capital with deposits to measure if a bank's capital was sufficient.

Comparing capital with the most dominant liability item in the balance sheet is strongly linked to the perception of capital in the late eighteenth and

---

[1] Refers to a minimum required risk-based regulatory capital ratio in 2016. The World Bank, *Bank Regulation and Supervision Survey*, November 2019.

[2] The chapter focuses mostly on one of the constituent countries of the United Kingdom only (England) due to the differences of the banking markets in the respective countries in the nineteenth century.

nineteenth centuries. The key roles of capital discussed in early banking literature were twofold: Firstly, authors viewed capital as an element to strengthen depositors' or noteholders' confidence in the banks and the whole banking system. Secondly, capital served as an absorber for losses.

The advantages and disadvantages of high or low capital ratios were well understood when large commercial banks emerged in England, Switzerland, and the United States. To choose an adequate capital ratio, bank managers considered the conflicting interests of shareholders (in having a high dividend) and those of depositors or noteholders (in having a high capital ratio).

Pursuing capital adequacy has led to the application of various informal and formal rules for capital ratios. Bank managers in England and Switzerland aimed for capital/deposits ratios of about 1:3 when establishing the first joint-stock banks. By the end of the nineteenth century, capital/deposits ratios of 10% were considered sufficient for English banks. In Switzerland, the 1:3 rule of thumb was more persistent. In the United States, banks were usually subject to notes-to-capital limitations. An often-used notes-to-capital ratio was 3:1. Once banknotes' share in balance sheets decreased and deposits' relevance increased, supervisors started to use a capital/deposits ratio of 10% as an informal guideline. The US supervisory agencies used the 10% capital/deposits ratio as a yardstick to measure capital adequacy until the 1930s.

What was the basis for such guidelines aiming to quantify adequate bank capital? The nineteenth-century literature on banking published in English and German provides insights into the discussion of capital in banking. The banking literature in the United States, the United Kingdom, and German-speaking countries had shared roots in the form of publications on monetary theory. This common starting point highlighted the relevance of money supply for the economy and emphasised the importance of liquidity in banking. Thus, the goal of monetary control was an important rationale for the regulation of banking. The consequence was a focus on investment doctrines in banks or, more specifically, the maturity of banks' assets. Within the monetary theory, liquidity concerns dominated, and the discussion of capital adequacy was often only a side product. Beyond the shared roots, publications on banking developed somewhat independently, reflecting country-specific issues such as a country's monetary and fiscal organisation or economic and banking crises. Finally, a second discipline also emerged in the nineteenth century: one dedicated to the specific banking practice, providing advice for the banker on how to manage a bank.

Given the banking literature, the economic environment, and banking regulation, what was banking practitioners' perception of the role and adequacy of capital in the nineteenth century? How were capital policies developed in practice? The environment in which banking practitioners operated varied from one country to another. One can find everything from the speculative behaviour of bankers and their shareholders to remarkable (public) self-reflections of bankers on what an optimal level of capital could be. Moreover, the three banking markets varied regarding banking concentration, development, regulation, and frequency of banking crises.

Beyond the analysis of nineteenth century banking literature, this chapter focuses on large banks and their capital policies in England, Switzerland, and the United States. In the case of England, the focus is on the so-called 'big banks', which were established from the 1820s. For Switzerland, the group of big banks emerging from the 1850s are analysed. In the United States, capital among the first commercial banks of the 1780s and later the large New York City–based banks is discussed.

3.1 EARLY BANKING LITERATURE: SHARED ROOTS, DIFFERENT TRAJECTORIES

The late eighteenth and nineteenth centuries produced a wealth of literature on the theory and practice of banking. James Steuart, for example, published his famous *Inquiry into the Principles of Political Economy* in 1767. Among other subjects, he also elaborated on banking and summarised contemporary banking knowledge.[3] Likewise, Adam Smith provided various paragraphs on banking in *The Wealth of Nations* (1776).[4] Publications by numerous authors on banking followed on both sides of the Atlantic. The nature of such publications throughout the nineteenth century was usually of two kinds. Many authors engaged in theoretical discussions on topics such as note-issuing, investment doctrines, and liquidity in the banking market, and, more generally, the macroeconomic effects of banking. The second stream of literature was practical in orientation. It dealt with the management of banks and elaborated on specific questions arising from banking practice.

The two streams of literature cannot be separated entirely, as theoretical debates on monetary and banking theory had practical implications. The most prominent example is probably Smith's real bills doctrine, which argued that banks should engage in short-term lending against real bills (bills of exchange) only. Such bills of exchange originated from the sale of goods and were discounted by banks. Following the arguments of Smith and later proponents of the doctrine, the asset side of a bank would consist of short-term and, thus, 'self-liquidating' bills.[5] The real bills doctrine became the dominating banking doctrine in the nineteenth century, impacting banking practice and theory in the United States and Europe.[6] The real bills doctrine contrasted the arguments of

---

[3] James Steuart, *An Inquiry Into The Principles Of Political Economy, Volume 2* (London: A. Millar and T. Cadell, 1767), see book IV, part II.

[4] Adam Smith, *An Inquiry into the Nature and Causes of the Wealth of Nations* (London, 1776).

[5] Smith, *An Inquiry into the Nature and Causes of the Wealth of Nations*, book II, chapter II.

[6] For an overview on investment doctrines, see Juha Tarkka, 'Investment Doctrines for Banks, from Real Bills to Post-Crisis Reforms', in *Preparing for the Next Financial Crisis: Policies, Tools and Models*, ed. Esa Jokivuolle and Radu Tunaru (Cambridge: Cambridge University Press, 2017), pp. 63–88 (pp. 66–7): https://doi.org/10.1017/9781316884560.006.

Steuart, who suggested lending against land as collateral (mortgages).[7]
Guidelines on how banks should invest their assets – as proposed by Steuart,
Smith, and others – had obvious practical implications for the individual bank
and its lending policy. Beyond the practical relevance, however, these debates
also had a theoretical dimension, elaborating on the effects of money supply on
the price level.

The publications in different regions and languages showed many
interactions too. The literature on banking theory published in the United
States and the United Kingdom share its roots, the authors Steuart and Smith
being two examples of influential figures contributing to that origin. At the same
time, the publications in the United Kingdom and the United States also
followed their individual paths throughout the nineteenth century, reflecting
on the challenges of the two banking markets.[8] A similar observation can be
made when comparing publications in English and German. Authors writing in
German often drew from the contemporary classic English banking textbooks
while also dealing with country-specific issues.

Along with growing professionalism in banking during the nineteenth
century came publications specifically written for banking practitioners.
Moreover, bankers established organisations that dedicated themselves to
practical issues and education. The organisations and their publications
contributed to the accumulation of knowledge on the management of banks.
In London, the Institute of Bankers was founded in 1879. The Institute's *Journal
of the Institute of Bankers* served as a standard source of information for
bankers, covering theoretical issues and answering practical questions. These
questions were also regularly published as *Questions on Banking Practice* from
1885 onwards. Both publications complemented an existing one, *The Bankers'
Magazine*, founded in 1843, which had quickly become the most relevant
publication for bankers in the United Kingdom. In the United States, banking
practitioners formed the American Bankers Association (ABA) in 1875. The
ABA first published the *Journal of the American Bankers Association* in 1908.
Moreover, *The Bankers' Magazine* (not to be confused with the British version
under the same title) was published from 1847 onwards.

Banking practitioners and people connected to banking engaged in
theoretical debates and published on practical matters. Among the key figures
in the United Kingdom were Thomas Joplin, James William Gilbart, Walter

---

[7] Discussions on the use of land to back money supply started already in the eighteenth century with
John Law, *Money and Trade Considered* (Edinburgh, 1705).

[8] Many British authors also analysed the US market and vice versa. Examples are James William
Gilbart, writing on US-American banking (James William Gilbart, *The History of Banking in
America* (London: Longman, Rees, Orme, Brown, Green, and Longman, 1837); Henry Charles
Carey, criticising English joint-stock banking (Henry Charles Carey, *Principles of Social Science,
Volume 2* (Philadelphia: J. B. Lippincott & Co., 1860), p. 405); and Albert Gallatin, analysing
British Banking (Albert Gallatin, *Considerations on the Currency and Banking* (Philadelphia:
Carey and Lea, 1831).

Bagehot, George Rae, and later Walter Leaf. Thomas Joplin, one of the early banking theorists, took part in the foundation of various banks, including the Provincial Bank of Ireland in 1825, the National Provincial Bank of England in 1833, and the London and County Banking Co. in 1839. James William Gilbart was the general manager of the Westminster Bank from 1833 to 1860. Walter Bagehot was the secretary of Stuckey's Banking Company and later editor of *The Economist*. George Rae worked as general manager and later chairman (1873–98) of the North and South Wales Bank in Liverpool. Walter Leaf was chairman of the Westminster Bank from 1918 to 1927 and president of the Institute of Bankers. Many of their works became 'classics' in British banking literature.

Joplin's *An Essay on the General Principles and Present Practice of Banking in England and Scotland* (1822) was a pamphlet against the note-issuance monopoly of the Bank of England (BoE) and an analysis of the banking system from a theoretical point of view.[9] Gilbart authored the two standard textbooks of the time: *A Practical Treatise on Banking* (1827) and *The History and Principles of Banking* (1834).[10] Bagehot's famous *Lombard Street: A Description of the Money Market* (1873) also featured a chapter on joint-stock banking.[11] Rae, meanwhile, published *The Country Banker* in 1885.[12] Leaf authored the classic textbook *Banking* in 1927. It was re-published in several editions up to 1943.[13]

Among key figures contributing to the US banking literature of the nineteenth century were Erick Bollmann, John McVickar, Eleazar Lord, Albert Gallatin, George Tucker, Charles Carey, William M. Gouge, and Charles F. Dunbar.[14] These authors were less involved in banking activities than their British counterparts. Henry Charles Carey was an American publisher and self-trained economist and sociologist.[15] He wrote on banking

---

[9] Joplin, *Essay on Principles of Banking*.

[10] James William Gilbart, *A Practical Treatise on Banking* (London: Effingham Wilson, 1827). James William Gilbart, *The History and Principles of Banking* (London: Longman, Rees, Orme, Brown, Green, and Longman, 1834).

[11] Walter Bagehot, *Lombard Street: A Description of the Money Market* (London: Henry S. King & Co., 1873).

[12] George Rae, *The Country Banker, His Clients, Cares, and Work: From an Experience of Forty Years* (London: John Murray, 1885).

[13] Walter Leaf, *Banking* (London: Williams & Norgate Ltd., 1927). For a good overview of the British banking literature, see Forrest Capie and Geoffrey Edward Wood, *Banking Theory, 1870–1930*, History of Banking and Finance (New York: Routledge, 1999).

[14] For an overview of influential figures on banking theory, see Harry E. Miller, *Banking Theories in the United States before 1860* (Cambridge, MA: Harvard University Press/A. M. Kelley, 1927); Fritz Redlich, *Eric Bollmann and Studies in Banking*, Essays in American Economic History (New York: G. E. Stechert & Co., 1944).

[15] American National Biography, 'Carey, Henry Charles (1793–1879), Economist, Publisher, and Social Scientist': https://doi.org/10.1093/anb/9780198606697.article.1400098 (accessed 4 May 2022).

in his *Essays on Banking* in 1816 and *Principals of Social Science* in 1860.[16] William M. Gouge was an economist who published *A Short History of Paper Money and Banking in the United States* in 1833.[17] Eleazar Lord, financier and economic theorist, published *Principles of Currency and Banking* in 1829.[18] Albert Gallatin, who was secretary of the US Treasury from 1801 to 1814, wrote his *Considerations on the Currency and Banking* in 1831. John McVickar, George Tucker, and Charles F. Dunbar were university professors.[19] Among these publications, George Tucker provided the most practical treatment of the banking subject.

Banking literature from German-speaking countries emerged later than that in the United Kingdom and the United States. One of the earliest classic publications on banking was Otto Hübner's *Die Banken* (1854). It was followed by Adolph Wagner's *Beiträge zur Lehre von Banken* three years later. Both Hübner and Wagner were economists from Germany. Other classic publications were written by Max Wirth (*Handbuch des Bankwesens*, 1870), Adolf Weber (*Depositenbanken und Spekulationsbanken*, 1902; *Geld, Banken, Börse*, 1939), and Georg Obst (*Banken und Bankpolitik*, 1909).[20] Academics rather than practitioners dominated the German banking literature. Most comparable to the publications of British banking practitioners is Felix Somary's *Bankpolitik*, published as late as

---

[16] Mathew Carey, *Essays on Banking (Reprint)*, ed. Herman E Krooss (Clifton: Kelley, 1972); Carey, *Principles of Social Science, Volume 2*.
[17] William M Gouge, *A Short History of Paper Money and Banking in the United States* (Philadelphia: Ustick, 1833).
[18] American National Biography, 'Lord, Eleazar (1788–1871), Financier, Railway President, and Theologian': https://doi.org/10.1093/anb/9780198606697.article.1001015 (accessed 4 May 2022). Eleazar Lord, *Principles of Currency and Banking* (New York: G. & C. & H. Carvill, 1829).
[19] John McVickar and George Tucker were Professors of Moral Philosophy (Columbia College, University of Virginia). Charles F. Dunbar was a professor at Harvard University. William A. McVickar, *The Life of the Reverend John McVickar* (New York: Hurd and Houghton; Riverside Press, 1872). George Tucker, *The Theory of Money and Banks Investigated* (Boston, C. C. Little and J. Brown, 1839). Charles F. Dunbar, *Theory and History of Banking* (New York: G. P. Putnam's Sons, 1891). Parts of the book had already been published as *Chapters on Banking* in 1885.
[20] Max Wirth, *Grundzüge der National-Ökonomie: Handbuch des Bankwesens* (Köln: DuMont-Schauberg, 1870). Adolf Weber, 'Depositenbanken und Spekulationsbanken: Ein Vergleich deutschen und englischen Bankwesens' (Rheinische Friedrich-Wilhelms-Universität, 1902). Georg Obst, *Banken und Bankpolitik* (Leipzig: Verlag von Carl Ernst Poeschel, 1909). Adolf Weber, *Geld, Banken, Börsen* (Leipzig: Quelle & Meyer, 1939). A general work of reference was also *Die Deutsche Bankwirtschaft*, an encompassing compendium of five volumes published between 1935 and 1938 that covered everything from bank products and accounting principles to capital markets and organisational questions. Walzer Kunze, Hans Schippel, and Otto Schoele, *Die deutsche Bankwirtschaft: Ein Schulungs- und Nachschlagewerk für das deutsche Geld- und Kreditwesen* (Berlin: Verlag der Betriebswirt, 1935).

1915.[21] Somary was an Austrian–Swiss banker, economist, and political analyst.[22]

Within the aforementioned publications in German, not a single book missed referring to Gilbart's banking textbooks. The publication of German magazines covering banking practice evolved only about half a century after its British and US-American equivalents. The *Bank-Archiv*, for example, was published first in 1901, *Die Bank* and *Zahlungsverkehr und Bankbetrieb* from 1908, and the *Bankwissenschaft* from 1927.

3.1.1 The Link Between Liquidity and Solvency Guidelines

Liquidity rather than capital adequacy was the dominating topic in nineteenth century banking literature. The idea that banks should focus on short-term lending was widespread in the nineteenth century. Many contemporaries thought that the real bills doctrine would allow banks to adjust the asset side flexibly, reducing the risks involved in banking.

In the United Kingdom, the crises of 1847, 1857, and 1866 fostered the view that liquidity was vital in avoiding financial turbulence.[23] Rae, for example, argued that the 'financial reserve' should be one-third of the liabilities to the public in order 'to guard against all probable demands'.[24] Similarly, Bagehot highlighted the crucial role of reserves, and that the 'greatest strain on the banking reserve is a "panic"'.[25] Financial reserves meant liquid assets such as cash, money at call and short notice, consols, and reserves at the BoE, and are not to be mistaken with reserves built up by retained profits as a form of capital. Similar discussions on liquidity evolved in the United States. Here, too, the ratio of liquid assets (in the US often defined as cash items, specie, and legal-tender notes) to liabilities was constantly discussed, and later authors related to Bagehot's treatment of the topic.[26]

The two German authors, Hübner and Wagner, also emphasised the relevance of liquidity. Hübner's book was the first to formulate what came to be known as the famous 'Goldene Bankregel' in the German-speaking space. The 'golden bank rule' concerned banks' liquidity and stipulated matching maturities of assets and liabilities.[27] Three years later, Wagner

[21] Felix Somary, *Bankpolitik* (Tübingen: J. C. B. Mohr, 1915).

[22] See Tobias Straumann's introduction in Felix Somary, *Erinnerungen aus meinem Leben*, NZZ Libro (Zurich: Verlag Neue Zürcher Zeitung, 2013), pp. 9–22.

[23] Capie and Wood, *Banking Theory, 1870–1930*, p. 8.

[24] Rae, *The Country Banker*, p. 206.

[25] Bagehot, *Lombard Street*, p. 129.

[26] See, for example, Charles F. Dunbar, *Chapters on Banking* (Cambridge, 1885), p. 22.

[27] 'The credit which a bank can give, without running the risk of being unable to meet its obligations, must correspond not only in amount but also in quality to the credit which it enjoys. ... One cannot give the long-term credit if one has received only the short-term one without running the great risk of not being able to give the latter back.' Otto Hübner, *Die Banken* (Leipzig: Verlag von Heinrich Hübner, 1854), p. 28.

published a critique of the 'golden bank rule', introducing a second famous banking principle: the 'Bodensatztheorie'. Wagner argued that certain deposits could be used for long-term loans, as not all depositors withdraw their capital simultaneously.[28] The theory was further extended by the 'Realisationstheorie' (in English: shiftability theory) of Karl Knies in 1879.[29] Knies emphasised the relevance of being able to liquidate assets to ameliorate short-term liquidity problems if needed.[30] The increasingly differentiated view on liquidity in the German literature developed simultaneously with that in the United States and the United Kingdom, where the shiftability doctrine in banking became increasingly dominant too.[31] According to the shiftability theory, banks could sell assets (including assets with longer maturities) on the market at short notice, thus shifting their assets to other banks or the central bank in case demand for liquidity increased. The shiftability theory, therefore, relaxed the guidelines of the real bills doctrine and changed the understanding of liquidity.

Despite the similarity in rules for liquidity across the banking literature in German and English, the context of the discussions in banking theory was very different due to the varying monetary environments. It becomes most evident when comparing banking theory in English, focusing on England and the United States.

In England, the BoE had a partial note-issue monopoly from 1708 and received a full monopoly in 1844. In the United States, the First Bank of the United States (1791–1811), the Second Bank of the United States (1816–36), state-chartered banks (until 1865), and national banks were allowed to issue notes, resulting in a high number of note-issuing banks. The Federal Reserve received its note-issue monopoly only in 1935. Given the decentral organisation of the note issue, one of the central concerns in the US banking literature was the over-issue of banknotes.[32] Many discussions surrounded the topics of asset liquidity and asset diversification (i.e. how to invest as a bank) and the question of whether note issuing should be limited to a particular proportion of a bank's capital. The limitation of note issuance, however, directly links the two topics of liquidity and solvency. While the central concern of a note-issue limitation is liquidity, it is a solvency rule too. Banknotes are a liability in a bank's balance sheet. If a bank can issue notes equivalent to three times its capital, it implies a capital requirement of one-third (compared to notes). Thus, liquidity considerations had consequences for capital adequacy guidelines. However, even though bank capital was not the

---

[28] Adolph Wagner, *Beiträge zur Lehre von den Banken* (Leipzig: Voss, 1857), p. 167.

[29] The classic contribution to the shiftability theory from the United States is provided by Harold G. Moulton: see 'Commercial Banking and Capital Formation: III', *Journal of Political Economy*, 26 (1918), 484–508.

[30] Karl Knies, *Geld und Credit* (Berlin: Weidmann, 1879).

[31] Jan Körnert, 'Liquiditäts- oder Solvabilitätsnormen für Banken? Zu den Anfängen eines Paradigmenwechsels und zur Einführung von Solvabilitätsnormen zwischen 1850 und 1934', *VSWG: Vierteljahrschrift für Sozial- und Wirtschaftsgeschichte*, 99.2 (2012), 171–88.

[32] Dewey, *State Banking Before the Civil War*, pp. 53–63.

central theme, many authors of banking textbooks had developed a clear understanding of what adequate capital would be.

3.1.2 How Much Capital Is Adequate?

The nineteenth-century banking literature used various terms for what is nowadays defined as equity capital. Gilbart, for example, distinguished between invested capital and banking capital.[33] The former refers to the capital provided by shareholders (equity capital), the latter to capital raised by the bank through deposits, the issuance of notes, and the drawing of bills (debt capital). In the United States, capital was referred to as 'capital stock'.

Apart from discussing equity capital, many authors argued that the use of debt capital is what defines a bank. Most famous is probably Bagehot's statement in *Lombard Street* (1873), emphasising that 'a banker's business – his proper business – does not begin while he is using his own money: it commences when he begins to use the capital of others.'[34] The idea was not new: in 1827, Gilbart had described the profession of a banker as 'a dealer in capital', meaning debt and equity capital.[35] The US literature also used this idea. Dunbar, for example, highlighted that an 'establishment becomes in reality a bank' only if it starts to 'use its credit' to discount commercial papers.[36]

Authors across the banking literature in English and German had a clear and common understanding on what the role of capital was. The use of capital was to provide trust and cover losses. In the United States, Gallatin outlined in 1831 that bank capital needs 'to be sufficient to cover all the bad debts, and all the losses'. At the same time, Gallatin emphasised that the 'ultimate solvency of a bank always depends on the solidity of the paper it discounts'.[37] Other authors, such as Lord and McVickar, had already emphasised the trust component in the late 1820s. McVickar wrote that capital provides assurance to creditors[38]. Lord argued that capital was 'a necessary basis of public confidence, and a guarantee against the consequences of imprudence, unfaithfulness and casualty'.[39] Similarly, Bagehot stressed the role of capital as a source of public trust in a bank and a guarantee for its operations.[40] German economists, such as Hübner and Wagner, shared these views.[41]

---

[33] Gilbart, *The Principles and Practice of Banking.*
[34] Bagehot, *Lombard Street*, p. 113.
[35] Gilbart, *A Practical Treatise on Banking*, pp. 1–2.
[36] Dunbar, *Chapters on Banking*, p. 16.
[37] Gallatin, *Considerations on the Currency and Banking*, p. 41.
[38] As cited in Miller, *Banking Theories in the United States before 1860*, p. 147.
[39] Lord, *Principles of Currency and Banking*, p. 104.
[40] Bagehot, *Lombard Street*, p. 113.
[41] Hübner, *Die Banken*, p. 29. Adolph Wagner, *System der Zettelbankpolitik: Mit besonderer Rücksicht auf das geltende Recht und auf deutsche Verhältnisse – ein Handbuch des Zettelbankwesens* (Freiburg i. Br.: F. Wagner, 1873), p. 425.

In the United Kingdom, only one author ventured to suggest a specific minimum capital/liability ratio for banks. In 1827, Gilbart wrote in *A Practical Treatise on Banking*:

Although the proportion which the capital of a bank should bear to its liabilities may vary with different banks, perhaps we should not go far astray in saying it should never be less than one-third of its liabilities. I would exclude, however, from this comparison all liabilities except those arising from notes and deposits.[42]

Gilbart derived the requirement probably from two roots. He analysed and referenced the Scottish banking market.[43] At the time – the late 1820s – joint-stock banks had just started to emerge in England, while Scotland already had a much more established joint-stock banking market. The second possible source is the BoE, which followed the rule of one-third for its metallic reserve (specie) ratio in proportion to notes (paper money).[44] The rule addressed the liquidity of the bank and its ability to redeem notes for specie. However, such a liquidity guideline has practical implications for capital adequacy too at the time when a bank is established. It raises the question of what equity capital should consist of when paid-in (specie or other assets) at the beginning and what it is invested in when a bank starts to operate.

The probably most advanced discussion of 'sufficient' capital in the first half of the nineteenth century was published by Joplin in 1822. Joplin refrained from suggesting a specific figure but made 'sufficient' dependent on the efficient use of resources.[45] The author seemed to have a well-founded idea of how much capital was adequate. In the context of Scottish banking, he noted that the capital of both the Bank of Scotland and the Royal Bank of Scotland were 'unnecessarily large'. Compared to the trade in Edinburgh and considering the stability of the banks, Joplin argued that they would be equally sound if they reduced their capital by 50%, with beneficial effects for the profit per stock.[46] With this argument, Joplin had already considered various factors determining a bank's capital in 1822: the risks involved in the business, the effect of leveraging on returns for shareholders, and the efficient allocation of capital.

For the emerging English joint-stock banks, deposits were a crucial funding source. Towards the end of the nineteenth century, deposits provided 80–90%

---

[42] Gilbart, *A Practical Treatise on Banking*, p. 309. Gilbart added that he would exclude everything but notes and deposits from the liabilities.

[43] Gilbart, *A Practical Treatise on Banking*, p. 312.

[44] See, for example, Tucker, *The Theory of Money and Banks Investigated*, p. 210, for a discussion of the 'one-third rule' and referring back to the Bank of Venice and Bank of Amsterdam.

[45] Joplin, *Essay on Principles of Banking*, p. 30. 'All that a Bank can gain by capital is credit. And when its capital is sufficiently large to put that upon the most solid basis, it is as large as there is any occasion for; more than that only incumbers it, and would be as well in the hands of the original Stock-holder, many of whom would probably turn it to better account.'

[46] Joplin, *Essay on Principles of Banking*, p. 30. Related to that, Bagehot also observed that Scottish banks paid comparatively lower dividends than English banks. Bagehot, *Lombard Street*, p. 121.

to the total liabilities of the large joint-stock banks.[47] Consequently, deposits were used to assess capital adequacy. In 1877, *The Bankers' Magazine* first attempted to measure the size of banks' capital in the United Kingdom.[48] It noted that a comparison of capital with deposits would have been desirable, but data on deposits was not available for the United Kingdom at the time.[49] Thus, the magazine was not able to publish capital ratios. Instead, it compared the total amount of capital in the United Kingdom and the United States. As of 1876, the capital of British joint-stock banks was estimated at £87.5m, divided into paid-up capital of £64.3m and reserves of £23.2m.[50] The capital of US banks reached £143.8m.[51] *The Bankers' Magazine* considered the figures for the United Kingdom's banks to be comparatively high.[52] The magazine stressed the importance of capital for public confidence and viewed capital formation in banking as a measure of the progress of banking. Regarding the appropriate level of capital in banking, *The Bankers' Magazine* referred to Gilbart's 'one-third guideline', underlining the validity of his views published fifty years earlier.[53]

Thereafter, *The Banker's Magazine* published annual reviews of bank capital in the United Kingdom. From 1902, the magazine also began comparing capital and reserves to deposits and all liabilities.[54] With regard to the optimal capital/liability ratio, *The Banker's Magazine* changed its position. In 1903, the magazine stated – for the first time – that no specific ratio should be followed.[55]

However, the move towards a more differentiated view on the adequate size of bank capital seemed to have happened even earlier. In 1885, Rae referred to the capital/liability ratio as a measure of a bank's 'ultimate stability'. In contrast to Gilbart's view on capital adequacy about sixty years earlier, Rae considered

---

[47] In the case of the Westminster Bank, for example, the share of deposits to total assets was about 50% in the 1830s. It ranged between 80% and 90% from 1850 to 1900. Similar figures can be observed towards the end of the twentieth century for Lloyds, Midland, and National Provincial.

[48] *The Bankers' Magazine*, 1877, 361–9.

[49] *The Bankers' Magazine*, 1877, p. 362.

[50] This includes the BoE and joint-stock banks from England, Scotland, and the Isle of Man. The total capital of joint-stock banks from England (excl. BoE) was £46.8m.

[51] This includes national banks, state banks, savings banks, and private banks. The original sources for the number cited in *The Bankers' Magazine* was the report of the Currency of the Comptroller.

[52] *The Bankers' Magazine*, 1877, pp. 363–4.

[53] *The Bankers' Magazine*, 1877, p. 365.

[54] *The Bankers' Magazine*, 1903, p. 826. 'Experience appears to point out to some banks that it is advisable for them to hold a larger amount of capital in proportion to their liabilities than other banks do. This might naturally be expected, from the different circumstances of the various businesses. Some banks may require in certain stages of their career to possess much larger sums as capital than others may do. They may be called on to make considerable advances, and may feel it necessary to hold a considerable capital while they are collecting the deposits which eventually gather round their business and help them.'

[55] *The Bankers' Magazine*, 1903, p. 828.

the soundness of bank assets as a determining factor for adequate capital. The author emphasised that 'there is no accepted rule in the matter, and it would be difficult to frame one'.[56]

The German banking literature also offers evidence of an increasingly nuanced view on capital adequacy. In 1873, Wagner wrote extensively about the role of bank capital, viewing it as a form of guarantee for depositors. The guarantee would not necessarily have to take the form of paid-up capital. It could also be an unlimited or limited liability. When making this point, Wagner referred to the British joint-stock banks as an example, noting that 'a highly magnificent banking operation does not necessarily require a substantial amount of own capital'.[57] Without providing a specific minimum capital ratio, Wagner concluded that adequate capital would have to be a compromise between the amount, risk, and coverage of assets.[58] Wagner also noted that younger banks tended to have higher capital ratios, whereas older banks tended to have lower ratios.[59] Bagehot made the same observation in the context of English joint-stock banking in the very same year.[60]

Somary provided a further example of advancing views on capital adequacy in 1915, arguing that the amount of capital should depend on the duration of liabilities. Banks holding substantial amounts of short-term liabilities would require less capital. Comparing German and Swiss banks to their English counterparts, Somary noted that English banks did not engage in long-term lending, leading to lower capital ratios as compared to Germany and Switzerland.[61] Reflecting on Gilbart's 'one-third-requirement' stipulated around ninety years earlier, Somary stated that such ratios were 'unimaginable in present times'.[62]

The experience of the United States concerning guidelines on capital ratios in the nineteenth century was very different to that in England, Germany, or Switzerland because capital was often regulated on the state or federal levels. Before the National Banking Act of 1864, banks were chartered by states; thus, rules varied according to the state. Many bank charters stipulated a minimum *liabilities-(or debt)-to-capital ratio* or, more narrowly, a *notes-to-capital ratio*. The purpose of such ratios – popular in practice and in banking theory – was to avoid the over-issue of banknotes in a system where many note-issuing banks existed. Tucker, for example, stated that 'an over-issue of paper is one of the greatest mischiefs of banks', adding that banks are 'most strongly tempted by the desire of increasing their profits'. Limits on note issues in states often ranged

[56] Rae, *The Country Banker*, p. 260.
[57] Wagner, *System der Zettelbankpolitik*, p. 428.
[58] Wagner, *System der Zettelbankpolitik*, p. 431.
[59] Wagner, *System der Zettelbankpolitik*, p. 425.
[60] Bagehot, *Lombard Street*, p. 121.
[61] Somary, *Bankpolitik*, pp. 5–9.
[62] Somary, *Bankpolitik*, p. 10.

between one and three times the capital.[63] Tucker argued that the idea of such a ratio was derived from the BoE's old notes-to-specie ratio of 3:1.[64] Tucker provides a path-dependency argument, reasoning that the provision ('the great rule of one third') was transferred from England to the United States and then copied from one bank charter to another.

This argument is supported by a related discussion on the nature of capital at the time. Key debates centred around the form of capital that shareholders could pay in (specie or other forms, such as securities) and how that capital should be invested on the asset side (e.g. bills or government bonds). Many writers, such as McVickar, Lord, Gallatin, and Gouge, argued that capital banks should only invest their capital in very safe assets such as government bonds.[65]

The National Banking Act of 1864 also set minimum capital requirements for national banks in absolute numbers. The Act made the amount of required capital dependent on the town population where the bank was located. The requirements were set at $50,000 for towns with a population of less than 6,000, $100,000 for towns with a population between 6,000 and 50,000, and $200,000 for larger towns. One-third of the capital of national banks had to be invested in US government bonds. The minimum capital requirements for state banks varied substantially, depending on state regulation. On average, these state-level requirements were lower than the capital requirements for national banks – in many cases, as low as $5,000. Some states also had no banking legislation at all. The varieties of capital requirements led to regulatory competition between states and between the state and federal levels.[66] As a result, the Gold Standard Act of 1900 decreased the minimum capital requirement for national banks from $50,000 to $25,000.

The root of linking capital requirements to a town's population probably lies in several peculiarities of the US banking market. Branch banking was ruled out on the national level and almost non-existent on the state level. A geographic limit on the expansion of banks allowed tying capital requirements of banks to their location. A town's size was likely considered a proxy for the extent of business conducted. The business activity, in turn, impacted the bills of exchange discounted at banks. Moreover, the total assets and liabilities grew or fell based on the discounted or matured bills of exchange.

---

[63] Gouge, *A Short History of Paper Money and Banking in the United States*, p. 51; Tucker, *The Theory of Money and Banks Investigated*, pp. 204–5; Miller, *Banking Theories in the United States before 1860*, p. 149. For an overview on note issue limitations, see Dewey, *State Banking Before the Civil War*, pp. 53–63.

[64] Tucker traces this 'great rule of one-third' back the Bank of Venice and the Bank of Amsterdam. Tucker, *The Theory of Money and Banks Investigated*, pp. 205, 210.

[65] Miller, *Banking Theories in the United States before 1860*, p. 174.

[66] For an overview of capital requirements in the years 1895 and 1909, see Eugene N. White, *The Regulation and Reform of the American Banking System, 1900–1929* (Princeton: Princeton University Press, 1983), pp. 18–21.

As in other countries, discussions on capital requirements in the United States became more differentiated over time. By 1891, Dunbar, for example, had a well-developed view of the topic. He highlighted that there could be no rule for the minimum capital amount, as it should depend on 'the extent of business'. The moment when 'the business passes the line of safety', requiring additional capital, however, should be determined independently by each bank.[67]

Authors of nineteenth-century banking literature not only had an understanding of the relevance and role of capital but also of the relationship between capital and risk. Later contributions emphasised that assets with longer durations that could not be sold quickly would require higher capital ratios, as did assets with high potential losses. What did the literature reveal about the effect of a high capital/assets ratio on return on equity? Were trade-offs between these two ratios discussed?

Although the terms 'leverage', 'return on equity', and 'capital/assets ratio' were not used in the nineteenth century, contemporaries understood their meaning and their relationships. Instead of 'return on equity', bank managers would discuss the extent of dividends. In 1873, Bagehot commented on the leverage effect with the concise notion that 'the main source of the profitableness of established banking is the smallness of the requisite capital'.[68]

The discussion on the adequate relationship between 'profitableness' and 'capital' in nineteenth-century England usually materialised as a conflict of interest between shareholders and depositors. In 1834, Gilbart referred to the diverging interests of depositors and shareholders as the 'evil' of having 'too small a capital' and 'too large a capital' at the same time.[69] On the one hand, Gilbart emphasised the high potential losses of large banks in absolute terms. He also believed it would be alarming if banks paid dividends as high as 15% or 20%. On the other hand, he argued that capital might be used inefficiently in the case of abundance.[70] Joplin made similar considerations. The idea of capital being a guarantee for depositors was featured in almost all publications discussing capital. Moreover, contemporaries perceived adequate capital as a compromise between the capital's role as a guarantee and the profitability of capital for the shareholders.

In the United States, deposits as a source of funding were (compared to England) less important during the first half of the nineteenth century. Measured against the balance sheet total, the share of deposits grew constantly. By 1834, deposits and banknotes each contributed about a quarter to the balance sheet total (the remaining half was contributed by capital). At the turn of the century, deposits made up about 80% (comparable to ratios of English joint-stock banks) of the balance sheet total, and banknotes became almost irrelevant (2%). A change in the banking literature discourse also reflected this structural

---

[67] Dunbar, _Theory and History of Banking_, p. 20.
[68] Bagehot, _Lombard Street_, p. 114.
[69] Gilbart, _The Principles and Practice of Banking_, p. 309.
[70] Gilbart, _The Principles and Practice of Banking_, p. 309.

change. Contemporaries became less concerned about the safety of banknote holders and more worried about the safety of depositors. Liquidity risks resulting from sudden withdrawals of deposits gradually received more attention.[71]

3.2 ENGLAND: BALANCING THE INTERESTS OF SHAREHOLDERS AND DEPOSITORS

The English banking market is unique as banking practitioners of the nineteenth century published frequently on the matter of banking. Did the decisions of bank managers regarding capital policy reflect the theoretical discourse? The London & Westminster Bank and the London and County Bank serve as examples of large and influential English joint-stock banks. The London & Westminster Bank was the first joint-stock bank established in London in 1834. Professional banking circles greeted the bank with hostility. Neither private banks, nor country banks, nor the BoE welcomed the establishment of a new competitor in London.[72] Two years later, in 1836, the London and County Bank was established as the Surrey, Kent and Sussex Banking Company in London (Southwark).[73]

By the turn of the century, the two banks ranked third and sixth in size among the English joint-stock banks.[74] They merged in 1909 to form the London County & Westminster Bank. This amalgamation was the first among joint-stock banks of 'the first magnitude', creating the second largest joint-stock bank in England at the time.[75] Another merger took place with Parr's Bank in 1918. By 1919, the then London County Westminster & Parr's Bank was the third-largest bank in England, ranked in size after Lloyds and the London Joint City & Midland Bank.[76] In 1968, Westminster merged with the National Provincial Bank, becoming the National Westminster Bank.[77] The Royal Bank of Scotland took over National Westminster (NatWest) in 2000. The bank was renamed as the NatWest Group in 2020.

Two people who contributed substantially to the British banking literature were also crucial figures in establishing the London and County Bank and the London & Westminster Bank. Thomas Joplin, who had published essays on

---

[71] For a contemporary treatment of the topic of liquidity risk and deposits, see, for example Dunbar, *Chapters on Banking*, pp. 28–9.

[72] Theodor Emanuel Gregory, *The Westminster Bank Through a Century*, Volume 1 (London: Oxford University Press, H. Milford, 1936), pp. 63ff.

[73] Gregory, *Westminster Bank, Vol. 1*, pp. 322ff.

[74] Measured by total assets. Author's calculations, based on the Banking Supplement of *The Economist*.

[75] *The Bankers' Magazine*, 'The Important London Amalgamation', 1909, 346–50 (p. 346).

[76] The year 1918 marked the end of a series of large amalgamations in English banking. London Joint City and Midland Bank itself was the result of a merger of the London City and Midland Bank with the London Joint Stock Bank.

[77] For a history of the London and Westminster Bank, the London and County Bank, as well as Parr's Bank, which amalgamated with London County & Westminster in 1918, see Gregory, *Westminster Bank, Vol. 1*; Theodor Emanuel Gregory, *The Westminster Bank Through*

banking in 1822 and was a strong proponent of joint-stock banking, was involved in establishing the London and County Bank.[78] James William Gilbart became the first general manager of the London and Westminster Bank in 1833. He stayed in this position for twenty-seven years, shaping the bank's evolution during its first decades.[79]

There are several reasons for choosing these two banks for a closer analysis of capital ideas. As discussed, the two banks became influential joint-stock banks and were among the first large banks with roots in the early period of English joint-stock banking. Thus, their capital position can be traced from the early period of English joint-stock banking. Moreover, balance sheets and income statements are available from the beginning of their establishment. Banks did not have to publish assets and liabilities if they were established under the Country Banker's Act of 1826 (as was the case for these two banks).[80] Nevertheless, the respective data is available, as well as being partly compiled and discussed by Theodor E. Gregory's two-volume history of the Westminster Bank.[81] Finally, the limited data available for the English banking market also leaves no other option than to turn to individual banks. Aggregated data for the whole English banking market was only published after 1880.[82]

3.2.1 Capital Structures at the Beginning of English Joint-Stock Banking: The Example of the Westminster Bank

Figure 3.1 shows the capital structure of the London and Westminster Bank in 1844, ten years after the establishment of the bank. It serves as an example of capital structures in English joint-stock banking. Westminster had an authorised capital of £5m, split up into 50,000 shares of £100 each. By then, shareholders had subscribed £4m of the authorised capital. Of the subscribed capital of £4m, £800,000 was paid-up. The rest was capital liability. The total shareholder liability, however, was far greater than the capital liability because the bank operated under unlimited liability until 1880. Moreover, it must be noted that the London and Westminster Bank shares were not fully subscribed until 1847 – thirteen years after the bank's foundation.[83]

a Century, Volume 2 (London: Oxford University Press, H. Milford, 1936); Ralph Hale Mottram, *The Westminster Bank, 1836–1936* (London: Westminster Bank, 1936).

[78] Gregory, *Westminster Bank, Vol. 1*, p. 322ff.

[79] RBS Heritage Hub, 'James William Gilbart': www.natwestgroup.com/heritage/people/james-william-gilbart.html (accessed 3 February 2024).

[80] *Country Bankers Act*, 1826, c. 46.

[81] Gregory, *Westminster Bank, Vol. 1*; Gregory, *Westminster Bank, Vol. 2*.

[82] See 'The Economist Banking Supplement, Various, 1861–1946'. Another, early data source is John Dun, *British Banking Statistics: With Remarks on the Bullion Reserve and Non-Legal-Tender Note Circulation of the United Kingdom* (London: E. Stanford, 1876).

[83] *The Bankers' Magazine*, 'Reports of Joint-Stock Banks. London and Westminster Bank', 1848, 264–5 (p. 264).

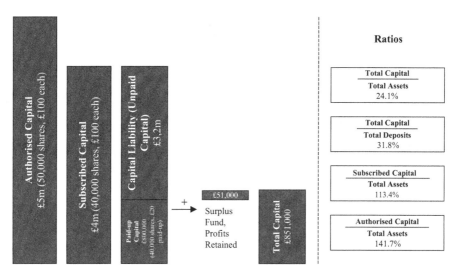

FIGURE 3.1 Capital structure of the London and Westminster Bank, 1844

The capital structure visualised in Figure 3.1 allows for the calculation of several ratios. Adding reserves and retained profits to the paid-up capital, one can calculate the total capital. Compared to total assets, capital stood at 24.1% (capital/assets ratio). The capital/deposits ratio was 31.8%. Total subscribed capital as a percentage of total assets was 113.4%. The dividends paid to shareholders were determined semi-annually and based on paid-up capital. In 1844, it was 6% of £800,000.

Figure 3.2 shows the capital/assets ratios (left axis) and the authorised capital (right axis) of the London and County Bank as well as the London and Westminster Bank from 1834 and 1837 to 1908. Both banks' capital/assets ratios reached their low points in the 1860s. The authorised capital was raised substantially twice in the mid-1860s and in 1878.

The two banks increased their capital in various ways. Firstly, they could call up further instalments from their shareholders and raise the fraction that was paid-up. Secondly, they sold additional shares from authorised capital that was not yet fully subscribed, which increased the paid-up capital. Furthermore, the reserves grew if investors bought shares with a premium. Thirdly, the authorised capital could be raised, which required the consent of shareholders.

3.2.2 Large Capital as a Distinguishing Feature of the Early Joint-Stock Banks

The London and Westminster opened its doors in 1834 with an authorised nominal capital of £5m, of which £1.7m was subscribed by proprietors (shareholders) in the first year of business. The paid-up capital stood at £182,000, representing 49.7% of total assets – well within

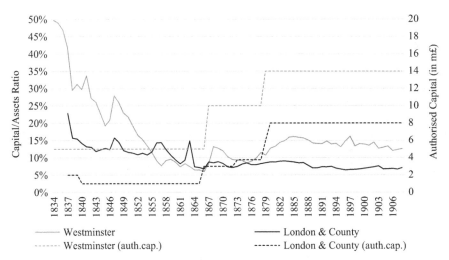

FIGURE 3.2 Capital/assets ratios and authorised capital in million £, Westminster Bank (1834–1908) and London and County Bank (1837–1908)[84]

Gilbart's 'one-third-requirement'.[85] The London and County Bank started operating three years later with an authorised nominal capital of £2m, of which also only a fraction was subscribed in the first year. The bank started with a paid-up capital of £24,000, representing a capital/assets ratio of 22.9%.

The fact that both Westminster and London and County started operating without having their authorised shares fully subscribed by shareholders was not unusual. The Country Bankers Act of 1826 allowed the establishment of joint-stock banks for the first time outside a 65-mile radius of London, but banks continued to be mostly unregulated.[86] The Act did not introduce a charter requirement or set standards for the organisation or management of banks. There was no minimum nominal capital and no rule that a certain number of shares would have to be paid up before a bank started its operation. Theoretically, banks could have commenced business with no shares subscribed at all.[87] A 'Secret Committee on Joint Stock Banks', tasked by

---

[84] Author's calculations. Data: Gregory, *Westminster Bank, Vol. 1*; Gregory, *Westminster Bank, Vol. 2*.

[85] For the annual reports of the first thirteen years, see James William Gilbart, *A Record of the Proceedings of the London and Westminster Bank, during the First Thirteen Years of Its Existence with Portraits of Its Principal Officers* (London: R. Clay, Bread Street Hill, 1847).

[86] *Country Bankers Act*, c. 46.

[87] Secret Committee on Joint Stock Banks, *Report from the Secret Committee on Joint Stock Banks: Together with the Minutes of Evidence, and Appendix*, 1838. The only step towards more regulation was the requirement to make a return to the Stamp Office, providing information about the company before commencing business; see *Country Bankers Act*, c. 46 Appendix, A & B.

TABLE 3.1   *Total capital resources (authorised capital and resources) in percent of total assets, Westminster Bank and London and County Bank, averages per decade, 1841–1910*[1]

	Westminster		London and County	
	Total Capital Resources/ Total Assets	C/A Ratio	Total Capital Resources/ Total Assets	C/A Ratio
1841–1850	137.8%	24.8%	77.5%	12.9%
1851–1860	54.0%	12.0%	25.1%	11.7%
1861–1870	35.3%	8.8%	17.0%	8.8%
1871–1880	39.7%	10.0%	19.1%	8.0%
1881–1890	53.1%	14.9%	25.4%	8.3%
1891–1900	50.2%	14.2%	20.2%	6.9%
1901–1910	47.2%	12.1%	18.8%	7.0%

[1]   Author's calculations. Data: Gregory, *Westminster Bank, Vol. 1*; Gregory, *Westminster Bank, Vol. 2*.

Parliament with analysing the effects of the 1826 Act in 1836, showed that only 15.8% of the nominal capital of English banks was paid up.[88] Setting the authorised capital very high and without any direct relation to expected business activities might have been done intentionally in many cases. On the one hand, it created an impression of ambition and high expectations for prospective shareholders. On the other hand, significant capital signalled strength to depositors.[89]

Table 3.1 shows the total capital resources (authorised capital and reserves) as a percentage of total assets. In the 1840s, Westminster's total capital resources were, on average, about 1.4 times the size of its balance sheet total.

Westminster's capital/assets ratio remained above 20% until 1850 and was still roughly within Gilbart's 'one-third-requirement'. As Gilbart himself outlined, having significant capital was one of Westminster's fundamental principles. The bank should be 'prepared at all times for a withdrawal of its deposits – to be able to give adequate accommodation to its customers – and to support public confidence in seasons of extreme pressure'.[90]

---

[88]   *Strictures on the Report of the Secret Committee on the Joint Stock Banks with an Appendix Containing Some Valuable Tables, Compiled from the Evidence* (London: Joseph Thomas, 1836), pp. 19–21.
[89]   Samuel Evelyn Thomas, *The Rise and Growth of Joint Stock Banking* (London: Sir I. Pitman & Sons, 1934), p. 222.
[90]   Gilbart, *Proceedings London and Westminster Bank*, p. 7.

However, operating with a high capital ratio was also a way of distinguishing the legal form of the bank from private banks. Gilbart argued that private banks did not 'carry on business with their own capital, but merely upon their credit'.[91] As Westminster stressed in its first prospectus for potential shareholders, the capital was one of the main advantages of joint-stock banks compared to private banks.[92] The future bank promoted that it should be established 'with such an extent of Capital as will ensure the perfect confidence and security of depositors, and the greatest practical accommodation and assistance to trade and commerce'.[93]

3.2.3   Conflicting Interests: Shareholders versus Depositors

In the years after the foundation of the Westminster Bank, its chairmen frequently justified capital increases as a way to foster public confidence – and, more specifically, depositors' confidence.[94] The bank was anxious to balance the interests of both shareholders and depositors. When shareholders questioned the increases of the reserve fund at general meetings, the board argued that no one should be able to accuse the bank of not augmenting the reserves 'whilst it went on increasing its dividends'.[95]

Similarly, in 1862, the Westminster Bank maintained that it wanted to pay high dividends but also emphasised that extensive reserves were required as a sign of 'prudence and safety' for depositors.[96] Five years later, the bank urged its shareholders once again to increase the capital, arguing that depositors should be offered more than the existing capital 'as an immediate security for the payment of their liabilities'. However, the bank promised to make the capital increase 'as advantageous as possible for the shareholders'.[97]

The London and County Bank used a similar line of argumentation to justify capital increases to its shareholders. By 1857, the bank had capital and reserves of £600,000 on its balance sheet. Their capital/assets ratio was 14.3%. At the annual

---

[91] Gilbart, *Proceedings London and Westminster Bank*, p. 6.

[92] 'The advantages of Joint Stock Banks are obvious: Their capital cannot be diminished by either deaths or retirements; their numerous Proprietors ensure to them confidence and credit, as well as ample business in deposits, loans, and discounts.' Gilbart, *Proceedings London and Westminster Bank*, p. 15.

[93] Gilbart, *Proceedings London and Westminster Bank*, p. 15.

[94] See Gilbart, *Proceedings London and Westminster Bank*, pp. 55: 'This increase of Capital will, in the opinion of the Directors, have a beneficial influence, as it gives the Bank an additional claim upon public confidence, and ensures the means of conducting, with satisfaction to its customers, a more extensive business.'

[95] The Bankers' Magazine, 'Reports of Joint-Stock Banks. London and Westminster Bank', 1857, 167–72 (p. 172).

[96] *The Bankers' Magazine*, 'Reports of Joint-Stock Banks. London and Westminster Bank', 1862, 90–5 (p. 92).

[97] *The Bankers' Magazine*, 'Reports of Joint-Stock Banks. London and Westminster Bank', 1867, 804–9 (p. 807).

meeting in 1857, London and County's chairman stated that the paid-up capital invested in the bank should be of 'fair proportion' and that this capital would have 'to carry the weight of the customers' balances'.[98] In 1862, another substantial increase of capital was necessary, according to the chairman of London and County, in order 'to be in the front rank of joint-stock banks'.[99] The chairman argued that the bank's growth, primarily driven by advances to railway companies, should not be financed with customers' deposits. At the same time, the chairman replied to criticism from the shareholders by emphasising that additional capital now would mean they would need to add less to the reserve fund in the future. Hence, London and County could share all its profits with the shareholders.[100]

As London and County raised additional capital in 1872, the chairman once again maintained that the relation of capital and reserves to liabilities should be 'fair'.[101] But how much did London and County's chairman consider to be fair or adequate? He referred to a target ratio of capital to liabilities of 10%.[102] Moreover, he commented that London and County had increased its capital in past years if the capital/liability ratio fell below 7%, and additional capital was necessary to 'keep up our position' compared to competitors.[103]

Compared to other large joint-stock banks, London and County's capital ratio (7.15%) was among the lowest. In 1872, Westminster had a capital/assets ratio of 9.4%, National Provincial had a ratio of 8.1%, and the London Joint Stock Bank had 8.2%. With that in mind, the chairman of London and County confirmed once again that a 10% ratio was considered a 'fair proportion' in 1873.[104] However, such ratios represented a significant shift in ideas among English banks, who had moved away from the initial idea of the 1820s and 1830s that joint-stock banks would need substantially high capital to distinguish themselves from private banks.

3.2.4   The City of Glasgow Shock

Despite frequent references to the importance of a high capital/liability ratio in gaining the trust of depositors, the capital/assets ratios of major English joint-stock banks had been falling since their establishment in the 1830s. The collapse

---

[98] *The Bankers' Magazine*, 'Reports of Joint-Stock Banks. London and County Bank', XVII (1857), 241–7 (p. 244).

[99] *The Bankers' Magazine*, 'Reports of Joint-Stock Banks. London and County Bank', 1864, 280–3 (p. 282).

[100] The Bankers' Magazine, 'Reports of Joint-Stock Banks. London and County Bank', *Reports of Joint-Stock Banks. London and County Bank*, pp. 282–3.

[101] *The Bankers' Magazine*, 'Reports of Joint-Stock Banks. London and County Bank', 1872, 788–94 (p. 792).

[102] Capital/assets ratio of 9.1%

[103] *The Bankers' Magazine*, 'Reports of Joint-Stock Banks. London and County Bank', *Reports of Joint-Stock Banks. London and County Bank*, p. 792.

[104] *The Bankers' Magazine*, 'Reports of Joint-Stock Banks. London and County Bank', 1873, 854–60 (p. 857).

of the City of Glasgow Bank in 1878 was a temporary turning point for the trend towards lower capital ratios. The reversal of the trend, however, did not last long.

Like most other banks at the time, the City of Glasgow Bank operated under unlimited liability, and its failure led to the bankruptcy of most of the shareholders.[105] Even though banks could register with limited liability from 1857 onwards, most banks continued to operate with unlimited liability until 1878, as unlimited liability was often seen as an essential guarantee for depositors.[106] Not surprisingly, contemporaries expected substantially higher capital ratios, as higher capital levels would replace unlimited liability. In an article titled 'The Great Addition About to Be Made to the Capital Employed in Banking Enterprise', *The Bankers' Magazine* argued that the ratio of capital to liabilities would be 'altered materially' with the introduction of limited liability. In fact, *The Bankers' Magazine* estimated that the new average capital/liability ratio would stand around 20%.[107]

Indeed, both Westminster and London and County increased their authorised capital in 1878. The two banks justified the increases as additional security needed for their depositors. Having abandoned unlimited liability, they did not want their stability to be questioned by customers.[108] At the same time – once again – the banks tried to find a 'good middle course as between the interests of the shareholders and the customers'.[109]

Besides Westminster and London and County, the National Provincial Bank also changed to limited liability and increased its capital. Lloyds and Midland, were already operating with limited liability before 1878 and did not issue additional capital. This behaviour is not surprising. Turner analysed a broader sample of sixty-three English banks for 1874 when some banks were already on limited liability and others were not. Turner shows that limited liability banks had higher capital ratios than those with unlimited liability in 1874.[110]

Turner provides a valuable contribution to the debate surrounding shareholder liability in British banking, highlighting that the debates focused on the credibility of unlimited liability regimes and the question of how

[105] Acheson and Turner, *The Death Blow to Unlimited Liability*. Sydney George Checkland, *Scottish Banking: A History, 1695–1973* (Glasgow: Collins, 1975), p. 471.
[106] Allen and others, *Commercial Banking Legislation And Control*, p. 232.
[107] *The Bankers' Magazine*, 'The Great Addition About to Be Made to the Capital Employed in Banking Enterprise', 1880, 28–9 (pp. 28–9).
[108] *The Bankers' Magazine*, 'Reports of Joint Stock Banks. London and Westminster Bank', 1880, 129–32 (p. 131). *The Bankers' Magazine*, 'Reports of Joint Stock Banks. London and County Bank', 1880, 230–3 (p. 232). This view is also supported by Turner, who attributes the late change to limited liability to concerns about the safety of depositors. Turner, *The Last Acre and Sixpence*, p. 124.
[109] Chairman of London and County at the annual meeting in 1880. The Bankers' Magazine, *Reports of Joint Stock Banks. London and County Bank*, p. 232.
[110] Turner, *Banking in Crisis*, p. 126.

depositors could be assured of bank safety once a bank changed from unlimited to limited liability.[111] He shows that William Clay, a member of Parliament from 1832 to 1857, had already outlined the relevant issues for discussing unlimited and limited liability in 1836. Clay argued that the change to limited liability would require forms of assurances to depositors concerning banking stability. The issues outlined by Clay were later discussed by banking experts, most notably Walter Bagehot and George Rae.[112] Resulting from this debate, the reserve liability was included in the Company Law in 1879.[113]

Figure 3.3 shows the capital/assets ratios of six joint-stock banks and the average ratio of all joint-stock banks from 1870 to 1914. By 1880, the capital/assets ratio stood at 17.5%. This level was considered the new standard by *The Bankers' Magazine* after eliminating unlimited liability. The new standard, however, deteriorated quickly. At the turn of the century, the capital/assets ratio stood at 11.6%. From 1880 to 1913, the capital/assets ratios of English joint-stock banks fell by 8.6pp.

3.2.5 The Twentieth Century View on Capital: Shareholders' Interests Prevail

After the failure of the City of Glasgow Bank, the public and bank managers viewed recapitalisations as a necessity to maintain public confidence.

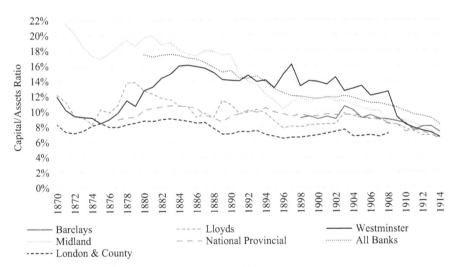

FIGURE 3.3 Capital/assets ratios, 1870–1914[114]

---

[111] Turner, *The Last Acre and Sixpence*, pp. 111–27.
[112] Turner, *The Last Acre and Sixpence*, pp. 115–21.
[113] See also Chapter 2.
[114] Data: 'The Economist Banking Supplement, Various, 1861–1946'.

Conversely, having too much capital was disparaged at the beginning of the twentieth century.

Once again, Westminster proves to be a case in point. The capital/assets ratio of the Westminster Bank was above the average of English joint-stock banks between 1895 and 1908 and was substantially higher than the ratio of any of its competitors shown in Figure 3.3. This high capitalisation was considered a problem at the Westminster Bank for many years.[115] Beyond the capitalisation itself, the structure of their capital was also viewed as problematic. Westminster's paid-up capital was twice as big as its reserves. Most other banks had reserves almost exceeding the paid-up capital. Consequently, given the high capital ratio, Westminster struggled to pay dividends as high as its competitors. And not only was the capital ratio high, but the proportion of paid-up capital within the company's total capital was considered high too.[116]

Westminster saw the merger with the London and County Bank in 1908 as a solution to that problem. At the extraordinary general meeting in 1908, Westminster's chairman Walter Leaf presented the bank's capital/liability ratio as one of the main reasons for the merger. Referring to Westminster's capital/liability ratio of 11% in 1907, Leaf argued that the ratio of London and County was below 5%, 'and it certainly could not be said that the larger figure [Westminster's] was necessary for the credit of their company'.[117] In a similar vein, *The Bankers' Magazine* commented that Westminster's capital was 'out of proportion' and that it would have been difficult to adjust the ratio if not through an amalgamation.[118] In contrast to previous discussions on the adequacy of the level of capital, neither the interests of depositors nor their confidence in the bank seemed to be of major importance anymore. Instead, Leaf remarked that their shareholders would be 'better protected by a reduced liability'.[119]

The newly established London County and Westminster Bank had a paid-up capital of £3.5m and reserves of £4.25m. London County and Westminster's capital/assets ratio stood at 9.2%, 3.3pp below the ratio of Westminster before the merger. With that, the capital structure of the 'new' Westminster converged towards that of its peers (see Figure 3.3).

Contemporary banking literature provides essential insights into the management of banks and their capital structure. Conflicting interests between shareholders and depositors with regard to the level of capital were frequently discussed in this literature. It was also a central topic within the management of

[115] Gregory, *Westminster Bank, Vol. 1*, p. 292.

[116] *The Bankers' Magazine*, 'The Important London Amalgamation', p. 349.

[117] *The Bankers' Magazine*, 'Reports of Joint Stock Banks. London and Westminster Bank', 1909, 438–9 (p. 439).

[118] *The Bankers' Magazine*, 'The Important London Amalgamation', p. 349.

[119] *The Bankers' Magazine*, 'Reports of Joint Stock Banks. London and Westminster Bank', *Reports of Joint Stock Banks. London and Westminster Bank*, p. 439.

English joint-stock banks from their emergence in the 1820s to the beginning of the twentieth century. At the beginning of English joint-stock banking, having significant capital seemed important. Furthermore, target capital ratios – such as Gilbart's 'one-third-requirement' – were used. The Westminster Bank seemed to follow that guideline until the 1850s. The London and County Bank communicated a capital/liability target ratio of 10% in the 1870s, which was probably the convention for joint-stock banks at the time. Capital considerations became more nuanced in subsequent years, stressing the required balance between shareholders' and depositors' interests. After the turn of the century, shareholders' interest in low capitalisation and high dividend payments seem to have prevailed, leading to even lower capital/assets ratios.

3.3 SWITZERLAND: TRANSPARENCY IN THE ABSENCE OF REGULATION

In the nineteenth century, many big Swiss banks publicly discussed their capital levels. The following analysis focuses mainly on Credit Suisse. Where possible, the discussion of capital adequacy is broadened to the whole group of big banks. However, in the absence of statutory accounting and publication standards, the availability of data and information remains fragmented.[120]

Founded in 1856 as 'Schweizerische Kreditanstalt', Credit Suisse is one of the oldest banks among the group of big banks. Credit Suisse was the most transparent bank during the nineteenth century, providing comprehensive information on the state of their business and regularly discussing reasons for changes in the capital structure. Credit Suisse has been ranked among the biggest banks in terms of total assets during its entire lifespan.[121] The bank gained considerable importance via financing railway projects and industrial finance during the last third of the nineteenth century.[122]

Credit Suisse was founded with a nominal capital of CHF 30m, of which CHF 15m was paid-up. Shareholders were not liable beyond the nominal capital.[123] The bank publicly discussed capital adequacy for the first time

---

[120] The only exception was minimum standards according to the Swiss Code of Obligations after 1883.

[121] Measured by total assets, Credit Suisse was usually the biggest or second biggest bank among the big banks (next to the Swiss Bank Corporation).

[122] Credit Suisse expanded domestically to become a universal bank in the 1930s. The bank also executed several major acquisitions in the 1990s (Bank Leu, 1990; First Boston, 1990; Swiss Volksbank, 1993; Winterthur Versicherungen, 1997). For the history of Credit Suisse, see Martin Esslinger, *Geschichte der Schweizerischen Kreditanstalt während der ersten 50 Jahre ihres Bestehens* (Zurich: Orell Füssli, 1907); Walter Adolf Jöhr, *Schweizerische Kreditanstalt: 1856–1956* (Zurich: Schweizerische Kreditanstalt, 1956); Joseph Jung, *Von der Schweizerischen Kreditanstalt zur Credit Suisse Group: Eine Bankengeschichte* (Zurich: NZZ Verlag, 2000).

[123] Esslinger, *Geschichte der Schweizerischen Kreditanstalt*, pp. 18–22.

when it issued additional stocks of a nominal CHF 5m in 1873. The issuance of new capital brought its capital/assets ratio back to the 30% level after it had fallen below that threshold two years earlier. Credit Suisse justified the issuance by referring to increasing business activities in Switzerland and abroad.[124] It has been stated that Credit Suisse profited from the strong economic activity in Switzerland, especially after the Treaty of Versailles in 1871.[125] Credit Suisse's board of directors emphasised the bank's international expansion and expectations of counterparties in foreign transactions.[126]

Credit Suisse issued additional capital in 1889 and 1897. The stock issuance in 1889 again led to an increase in the capital/assets ratio from 22.3% to 30.4%. Similarly, the issuance of additional capital in 1897 lifted the percentage from 25.9% to 34.1%.

The bank's 1889 annual report cited the findings of an internal study on the 'question of the equity capital increase'. This is the most extensive public elaboration by the bank on why it required additional capital. Credit Suisse's Board of Directors argued in favour of higher equity capital by mentioning the fast balance sheet expansion, the proportion of equity capital to liabilities, the risk of potential losses arising from accounts due from customers without collateral, the expected strong demand for credit as a result of an increase in business activities in the past, and the high (and increasing) dividend performances in the past for its investors. The bank also communicated that it wanted to return to the capital ratio it maintained after its last stock issuance in 1873.[127] This shows that Credit Suisse was aiming for a capital/assets ratio of around 30%, for which it issued new stocks.

These arguments were not uncommon among the big banks. The Swiss Bank Corporation (SBC) issued additional capital in the same years, highlighting the rapid total assets growth and the importance of its reputation. Moreover, the SBC's directors believed that customers could perceive other banks as serious competitors due to their high capital ratios. Thus, the bank would require more capital to keep its standing. In terms of its investors, the SBC assured them that the fresh capital was just the minimum needed for the bank's development and that the amount would ensure stable dividends in the future.[128]

In 1905, Credit Suisse commented on another stock issuance in its annual report, providing two arguments for raising its capital. Firstly, Credit Suisse was

---

[124] Schweizerische Kreditanstalt, *Jahresbericht Schweizerische Kreditanstalt 1973*, 1874, p. 3.

[125] Esslinger, *Geschichte der Schweizerischen Kreditanstalt*, p. 65.

[126] Schweizerische Kreditanstalt, *Jahresbericht Schweizerische Kreditanstalt 1973*, p. 3. Similarly, the bank commented in a later report that the issuance of additional stocks in 1873 was due to the additional capital requirements resulting from increasing commerce and manufacturing in Zurich, Switzerland, and abroad (Schweizerische Kreditanstalt, *Jahresbericht Schweizerische Kreditanstalt 1889*, 1890, p. 4.)

[127] Schweizerische Kreditanstalt, *Jahresbericht Schweizerische Kreditanstalt 1889*, pp. 4–5.

[128] Hans Bauer, *Schweizerischer Bankverein 1872–1972*, ed. Schweizerischer Bankverein (Basel, 1972), pp. 81–3.

taking over the 'Bank in Zurich' and the 'Oberrheinische Bank' in Basel and needed new shares for a share swap with existing shareholders.[129] Takeovers of other banks were an often-used reason for capital issuances among the big banks.[130] Secondly, the bank once again stressed that the capital/liability ratio should not fall below a 'certain' level. The board of directors suggested a ratio of 1:3 (capital/liability ratio: 33%; capital/assets ratio: 25%) and emphasised that such a ratio would still allow for achieving an 'adequate' return for its shareholders:

> The development of our institution during the last eight years was positive; it is however also an obligation, that given the risks of our business operation as a trading and financing institute, we need to make sure that the capital strength of our bank does not fall below a certain ratio as compared to the debt capital. Even though the current ratio of about 1:3 is not inappropriate, it seems to us that the requested increase of our capital is in the interest of the reputation, the credit and the productivity of our institute. Even with the capital increase, we believe we can communicate the expectation that we will be able to provide appropriate returns, which will not be below previous returns.[131]

After a capital increase in 1904, the leverage ratio grew to 25.3%. The bank increased its capital again in 1906. As on earlier occasions, Credit Suisse assured its investors that it would pay stable dividends in the future. However, Credit Suisse seemed to abandon its target capital ratio in the years leading up to the First World War; 1905 marked the last year the bank made a specific statement on the size of capital it aimed to maintain. From 1905 to 1914, capital/assets ratios decreased from 25.3% to 19.2%. The bank did not issue new shares until 1912, and only then as a result of the takeover of two banks.

A changing view on capital adequacy in later years was further demonstrated by Credit Suisse's capital increase in 1927. The bank refrained from mentioning specific ratios or discussing the capital situation in more detail. Instead, the bank only remarked in rather general terms that its own capital and the debt capital should be in a 'healthy proportion' to each other.[132]

Figure 3.4 shows Credit Suisse's capital/assets ratio as well as the total capital and reserves from 1857 to 1914. Until 1905, the bank issued new shares four times, usually when the capital/assets ratio fell below the 20% or 25% threshold. What is also apparent from Figure 3.4 is the importance of capital issuances not only for increasing the share capital but also for increasing the reserves. The premium between the nominal value and the share price was

---

[129] Schweizerische Kreditanstalt, *Jahresbericht Schweizerische Kreditanstalt 1904*, 1905, pp. 40–3.

[130] The Swiss Bank Corporation, for example, issued fresh capital when it took over the 'Bank in Basel' in 1906 as well as 'Speyr & Co.' and the 'Banque d'Escompte et de Dépôts Lausanne' in 1912. Schweizerischer Bankverein, *Jahresbericht Schweizerischer Bankverein 1906* (Basel, 1907); Schweizerischer Bankverein, *Jahresbericht Schweizerischer Bankverein 1912* (Basel, 1913).

[131] Schweizerische Kreditanstalt, *Jahresbericht Schweizerische Kreditanstalt 1904*, p. 43.

[132] Schweizerische Kreditanstalt, *Jahresbericht Schweizerische Kreditanstalt 1926*, 1927, p. 9.

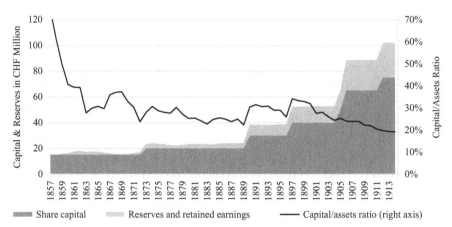

FIGURE 3.4 Share capital, reserves, and the capital/assets ratio of Credit Suisse, 1857–1914[133]

attributed to the reserves. During this period, it was mainly the premium on capital increases that led to growing reserves and not retained profits.

3.3.1   Swiss Banking Practice and the Role of 'Rules of Thumb'

The '1:3-rule' that was applied in Swiss banking practice was also promoted by James William Gilbart's *A Practical Treatise on Banking*, published in 1827. However, the Westminster Bank, of which Gilbart was the general manager from 1833 to 1860, abandoned that guideline in the 1850s. Did all Swiss banks nonetheless follow Gilbart's rule of thumb until the late nineteenth century, as the case of Credit Suisse would suggest?

It cannot be said that all Swiss banks followed Gilbart's principle. Most of the large joint-stock banks did, however, maintain capital/assets ratios above 20% until the end of the nineteenth century. Figure 3.5 shows the capital/asset ratios of the big banks from their establishment until 1914. The significant decreases in capital ratios at the beginning of the time series were because the founders were often ambitious regarding their business growth. Thus, capital ratios 'normalised' over time once a bank started making investments, granting loans, and attracting liabilities. As the banks grew, their capital/assets ratios fluctuated between 20% and 40%.

Until the 1940s, the big banks had considerably higher capital ratios than other bank groups in Switzerland. By 1914, the average capital/assets ratio of the big banks stood at 20.1%. Cantonal banks had a capital/assets ratio of 12.1% and Raiffeisen banks a ratio of 3.3%. In earlier years, this discrepancy

---

[133] Author's calculations. Data: Schweizerische Kreditanstalt, *Jahresberichte Schweizerische Kreditanstalt 1857–1914*, 1914.

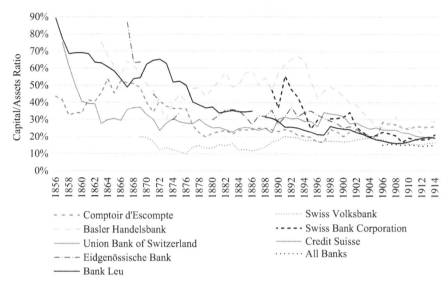

FIGURE 3.5 Capital/assets ratios, big banks, Switzerland, 1856–1914[134]

was even more prominent. Consequently, if Gilbart's ideas regarding capital (capital/liability ratio of 1:3) were present in Switzerland, only one group of banks had adopted them. All other groups would have disregarded it, which is unlikely.

3.3.2 The Business Models of the big banks

What else explains the big banks' persistently high capital/assets ratios? The answer lies in the business models of the big banks and how the banks themselves perceived the risks associated with their business. Credit Suisse referred to the riskiness of its business operations as an argument in favour of a high capital ratio, maintaining that the high risks required more capital. What exactly did this mean? Big banks such as Credit Suisse and SBC offered a variety of banking services for industrial and commercial companies, leading to a high loan exposure and often also to securities investments on the asset side. Engaging in business activities bearing high risk would require more capital. Other banking groups, such as regional, savings, Raiffeisen, and cantonal banks, focused mainly on deposits and mortgages for private customers. The mortgage business was considered less risky.[135]

---

[134] Author's calculations. Data: Annual reports of the respective banks.

[135] Thomas Husy, *Die eigenen Mittel der schweizerischen Banken*, Betriebswirtschaftliche Studien (St. Gallen: Fehr, 1946), p. 38.

TABLE 3.2 *Share of securities and unsecured loans in percent of total assets, big banks, 1870–1910*[1]

	1870	1880	1890	1900	1910
Securities	13.9%	11.9%	10.2%	8.0%	8.7%
Unsecured loans	n.a.	21.5%	23.0%	24.0%	16.9%

[1] Author's calculations. Data: Individual Annual Reports. Notes: The following banks are missing for 1870: Swiss Bank Corporation (SBC), Union Bank of Switzerland (UBS), Comptoir d'Escompte de Genève (CEG), Bank Leu. Missing for 1880: UBS and CEG. Missing for 1890 and 1900: UBS. Data on unsecured loans is only available from Credit Suisse, SBC, and Bank Leu.

Table 3.2 provides insights into the asset structure of the big banks in 1870, 1880, 1890, 1900, and 1910. At the time, investing in securities and providing unsecured commercial loans were two key pillars of the big banks' business. The table presents these two asset items as a percentage of total assets.

The share of unsecured loans to commercial customers fluctuated between 16.9% and 24.0%. It seems that the amount of unsecured loans as a percentage of total assets dropped at the beginning of the twentieth century. Similar to the unsecured loans, the share invested in securities also fell over time. By 1910, banks were investing 8.7% of their assets in securities on average. In 1870, the percentage had stood at 13.9%.

One might also ask how well-diversified the securities portfolios were. There was a high sectoral dependence on investments in railway companies. In the case of Credit Suisse, for example, around 40–60% of the stocks held between 1870 and 1910 were in railway companies. The largest amount was invested in the 'Nordostbahn'.[136] The 'Nordostbahn' was run by Alfred Escher, who was also the president of the board of Credit Suisse.[137] Credit Suisse also invested in a variety of foreign securities. Overall, the bank followed a somewhat speculative business model until the 1880s.[138]

The lower shares of securities and unsecured loans in the balance sheets in 1910 indicate that banks had reduced the risks of their assets, which would allow for a lower capital ratio. Furthermore, another emerging business model among the big banks impacted the composition of their securities portfolio when they, together with the cantonal banks, established a monopoly in issuing government securities.

The underwriting business of the big banks had been growing since their establishment. In 1897, Credit Suisse started a cartel with the SBC and the

[136] Schweizerische Kreditanstalt, *Jahresbericht Schweizerische Kreditanstalt 1870*, 1871; Schweizerische Kreditanstalt, *Jahresbericht Schweizerische Kreditanstalt 1890*, 1891; Schweizerische Kreditanstalt, *Jahresbericht Schweizerische Kreditanstalt 1910*, 1911.
[137] Escher was president of the board from 1856 to 1877 and from 1880 to 1882.
[138] Jöhr, *Schweizerische Kreditanstalt*, pp. 89–92.

Union Financière de Genève. More banks joined in the following years, forming the 'cartel of the big banks'.[139] The cartel contract stated that all government bond issues of more than CHF 2m that a cartel member handled had to be forwarded to the cartel. The cartel members then shared the placement and its profits.[140] The power of the big banks grew further when their cartel joined forces with the Association of Cantonal Banks in 1911. Government financing on the federal and cantonal levels, as well as the emission of bonds for the by then nationalised Swiss railway, became impossible without the support of the big banks and the cantonal banks.[141] Some of these securities were kept in the banks' balance sheets. The available data in the annual reports of the big banks indicates that the share of government bonds increased slightly in the years before the First World War.

Overall, three effects had altered the business models of the big banks by 1914. Firstly, the big banks had reduced the share of unsecured loans. Secondly, the share of securities had decreased. Thirdly, the banks had engaged in the underwriting business. These three changes lowered the overall risks of the banks and their balance sheets and might have justified lower capital ratios.

The perception of what amount of capital should be considered adequate has changed over time. Banks followed specific benchmarks of about 25% until the late nineteenth century. Most large joint-stock banks in Switzerland showed similar behaviour, as they frequently issued new stocks to restore their target capital/assets ratio. This behaviour seems to have changed during the decade leading up to the First World War, when capital issuances became less frequent. The riskiness of their business was an often-cited reason for issuing fresh capital, and banks compared their standing with that of their competitors. Yet the variation of the capital ratios decreased over time. Stable dividends for investors were given high importance in the statements made by banks, which is unsurprising given that investors had to approve capital issuances. The trade-off that defined an adequate capital ratio for the Swiss big banks was usually one between the risk of the business model and shareholders' interests.

---

[139] The first episode of a cartel among the big banks can be traced back to 1863 when Credit Suisse and the Basler Handelsbank agreed on a cartel contract in order to jointly organise the takeover and placement of shares and bonds. The two banks were joined by the Banque Commerciale Genevoise in the same year. The cooperation only lasted until 1867. See Esslinger, *Geschichte der Schweizerischen Kreditanstalt*, p. 173.

[140] One reason for the establishment of the cartel was that banks faced increased competition for domestic government issues from French banks. The French banks profited from abundant domestic capital at low interest rates and were essential financiers of the Swiss government. By 1907, the capital supply from France dried up, and the Cartel of the big banks became increasingly influential. Linder, *Die schweizerischen Grossbanken*, p. 110; Esslinger, *Geschichte der Schweizerischen Kreditanstalt*, p. 175.

[141] Linder, *Die schweizerischen Grossbanken*, p. 110.

3.4   UNITED STATES: CAPITAL REQUIREMENTS FROM THE VERY BEGINNING

The US banking market offers numerous examples for analysing the foundation of banks and their capital policies. Compared to the evolution of banking in the United Kingdom and Switzerland, the development of banking in the United States was turbulent. Striking features of the US banking market were frequent crises, a high number of small banking units, many market entries and exits, varying regulatory regimes (on the federal and state levels), several supervisory agencies, and – in the context of capital policies, the most relevant difference – the right to issue banknotes.

The period leading up to the twentieth century in US banking can be broadly divided into three periods: the early years of American banking until 1837, the era known as free banking from 1837 to 1863, and the national banking era from 1863 to 1913.[142] Different regulatory and supervisory systems and agencies emerged during these periods, which also had implications for regulating capital in banking.

Banking regulation and supervision were left to the individual states throughout the free banking period. Banks could obtain a charter and enter the market freely if they could raise a certain amount of capital. Bank regulation and supervision varied according to the different states. The national banking period covers the period from the establishment of nationally chartered banks to the creation of the Federal Reserve (FED). The Banking Acts of 1863 and 1864 provided the regulatory framework for that period and led to the emergence of the first federal banking supervisory agency: the Office of the Comptroller of the Currency (OCC). Among the OCC's tasks were the chartering and supervision of national banks. From 1913, the OCC shared its supervisory responsibility for national banks with the FED. Additionally, the FED had supervisory authority over state banks that chose to become members of the Federal Reserve System. A third federal bank supervisory agency finally emerged in 1934. The Federal Deposit Insurance Corporation (FDIC) was charged with administering the deposit insurance programme and had supervisory authority over national banks and state banks that opted for federal deposit insurance.

The first commercial banks in the United States and the leading banks from New York City serve as examples of capital policies in the eighteenth and nineteenth centuries. Given the fragmentation of the US banking market, the domestic relevance of the New York City–based banks measured by market shares, for example, cannot be compared to that of the large banks in England or Switzerland. However, the prominent banks of New York took central

---

[142] Colonial banking in the United States is not covered. For a discussion of the role of capital in colonial banking, see George Taylor Harris, *The Capital Structure in American Banking*, unpublished dissertation (The University of Iowa, 1953), pp. 67–72.

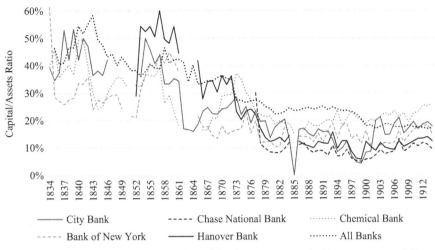

FIGURE 3.6 Capital/assets ratios, selected banks in New York City, 1834–1914[143]

importance in the US banking market. They were located in the country's leading financial centre, were among the largest banks in the country, and were of vital relevance as much of the reserves of banks in the United States were placed in New York City banks.

Figure 3.6 shows the capital/assets ratios of five prominent New York City banks from 1834 to 1914: The Bank of New York (founded 1784, now commonly known as BNY Mellon), City Bank (1812, now Citigroup), Chase National Bank (1877, now JP Morgan Chase), as well as the Chemical Bank (1823), and Hanover Bank (1873), which both became part of JP Morgan Chase over time.

The capital/assets ratios of the five New York banks remained above the 20% threshold for most of the time until the 1870s and ranged roughly between 10% and 20% throughout the following years leading up to 1914. Compared to all banks in the United States, the five banks tended to have lower capital/assets ratios.

---

[143] Data: All banks (United States): United States, Bureau of the Census, *Historical Statistics of the United States. Colonial Times to 1970*; Bank of New York/Chemical Bank/Hanover Bank: 1834–61: Warren E. Weber, 'Antebellum US State Bank Balance Sheets', *Federal Reserve Bank of Minneapolis, Research Division*, 2018; 1865–1911: Office of the Comptroller of the Currency, 'Annual Report of the Comptroller of the Currency, Various Years'; 1912–14: Rand McNally and Company, 'Rand McNally Bankers Directory, Various Years' (Rand McNally); City Bank: 1834–64: Harold Van B. Cleveland and Thomas F. Huertas, *Citibank 1812–1970* (Cambridge: Harvard University Press, 1985); 1865–1914: Office of the Comptroller of the Currency, *Annual Report of the Comptroller of the Currency, Various Years*; Chase National Bank: 1877: John Donald Wilson, *The Chase* (Harvard Business School, 1986); 1878–1911: Office of the Comptroller of the Currency, *Annual Report of the Comptroller of the Currency, Various Years*; 1912–14: Rand McNally and Company, *Rand McNally Bankers Directory, Various Years*.

3.4.1 How to Get Something for Nothing: The Dubious Quality of Capital in the Early US Banking Period

The United States' first commercial banks were already founded by the 1780s. The Bank of North America was established in 1781, the Bank of Massachusetts and the Bank of New York in 1784. Following Alexander Hamilton's initiative (the first secretary of the US treasury), the federal government made its first steps towards central banking in 1791 with the creation of the Bank of the United States, known as the First Bank of the United States. The First Bank of the United States was also active as a commercial bank, accepting deposits and providing loans to the public. It operated until 1811 and was succeeded by the Second Bank of the United States in 1816. The Charter of the Second Bank ended in 1836, initiating the free banking era.

Bank capital was an essential concern in all of these new banking establishments, and was often of dubious quality. Similar to English joint-stock banks, a feature of US banking was that the authorised capital stipulated in the bank charter deviated strongly from the paid-up capital. Raising capital for a bank was a gradual process in which shareholders subscribed capital in several instalments. A case in point is the First Bank of the United States, with an authorised capital of $10m, of which the federal government subscribed $2m. As Hamilton realised that it was impossible to fund such an amount with specie (gold or silver) in a period where precious metals were scarce, the charter stipulated that only one-fourth of the remaining $8m had to be paid in specie. Shareholders could pay the remaining $6m with government securities.[144]

After the first instalment by the shareholders, the First Bank of the United States started operating with only $400,000 paid up. As the federal government could not provide $2m for its subscribed shares, the bank, now able to create money, provided a loan to the government at an interest rate of 6%. The government used the loan to pay for the shares, for which it then received dividends from the bank.[145]

A build-up of capital through several instalments of shareholders and a substantial deviation between authorised and actual capital was representative of many bank foundations that followed. Banks often started operating after one instalment, representing as little as 5% to 15% of the authorised capital. A second issue frequently criticised by contemporaries concerned banks' lack of specie money. In many cases, the foundation of later banks with a lower standing involved speculative schemes. Shareholders used the shares they received after the first instalment as collateral for a loan from the same bank. They then paid for the second

---

[144] Dewey, *State Banking Before the Civil War*, p. 5; Gallatin, *Considerations on the Currency and Banking*, p. 97; Gouge, *A Short History of Paper Money and Banking in the United States*, p. 72.

[145] Gouge, *A Short History of Paper Money and Banking in the United States*, p. 72.

instalment with the money received from the bank as a loan.[146] It was essentially a bet by shareholders on the bank's survival and ability to pay a dividend above the loan's interest rate or, in William Gouge's words, 'hocus-pocus'.[147] The use of bank loans for buying additional stock was widespread, and some states passed laws prohibiting or at least limiting the practice from the late 1820s. Overall, banking provisions became stricter towards the end of the free banking era.[148]

3.4.2   The First Capital Adequacy Ratios: Limiting Note Issuance

The Bank of New York (founded in 1784) and one of its founding fathers, Alexander Hamilton, took a less speculative stance on banking policy. During the first seven years of its existence, the bank operated without a charter, and its owners were subject to unlimited liability. The paid-up capital was $500,000. The Bank of New York received its charter from the State of New York after several attempts in 1791. By then, New York was only the second state in the United States to charter a bank, and the bank charter also constituted a first step towards banking provisions.

The 1791 Bank of New York charter stipulated a capital of $900,000, but, more importantly, it also introduced a formal debt/capital ratio to control the note issuance. The charter limited the amount of debt to a maximum of three times the capital subscribed.[149] The debt/capital ratio of 1:3 in 1791 – or a capital/debt ratio of one-third – was probably one of the first capital adequacy rules in the United States.[150]

As noted earlier, the idea for limiting note issuance likely originated from old note-issuing banks in Europe.[151] The charter of the First Bank of the United States in 1791 included – indirectly – a note-issue limitation too. The amount of debt was not to exceed the bank's authorised capital of $10m.[152] A similar 1:1 ratio was applied to the Second Bank of the United States, limiting the amount of debt to the bank's capital of $35m.[153]

The charter of the Bank of New York served as a blueprint for many subsequent bank charters, and the limitation of note issue was a frequent

---

[146] Dewey, *State Banking Before the Civil War*, p. 6. For discussions of contemporaries, see Erick Bollmann, *Paragraphs on Banks* (Philadelphia: C. & A. Conrad & co., 1811); Lord, *Principles of Currency and Banking*; Gouge, *A Short History of Paper Money and Banking in the United States*.

[147] Gouge, *A Short History of Paper Money and Banking in the United States*, p. 71.

[148] Dewey, *State Banking Before the Civil War*, p. 154.

[149] Allan Nevins, *History of the Bank of New York and Trust Company, 1784 to 1934* (New York: Bank of New York and Trust Company, 1934), pp. 20–1.

[150] Harris, *The Capital Structure in American Banking*, p. 73.

[151] Tucker, *The Theory of Money and Banks Investigated*, p. 210.

[152] Dewey, *State Banking Before the Civil War*, p. 53.

[153] Ralph Charles Henry Catterall, *The Second Bank of the United States* (Chicago: The University of Chicago Press, 1903), p. 483.

charter provision.[154] Limiting the debt – or, more narrowly, note-issue – to bank capital became a standard rule in US state banking until the Civil War. The requirements varied across states and became stricter between the 1830s and the 1860s.[155] During the national banking era, the note issue was regulated, too: The National Banking Acts of 1863 and 1864 limited note issues to a national bank's capital stock.[156]

While such limits probably avoided the over-issue of notes in individual cases and in the early banking period in the United States, they had little effect on the average national bank during the national banking era. The total banknote volume never grew close to the capital stock of national banks between 1863 and 1914. The banknotes-to-capital ratio was about 60% on average in the respective period – far from reaching the 1:1 limit.[157] Thus, the amount of capital was not a limiting factor for most of the national banks.

3.4.3 Building Up Capital Through Retained Earnings

Retained earnings were the primary source for the growing capital stock of banks. Issuing new shares was rather infrequent. A case in point is that the paid-up capital among New York City–based banks was remarkably stable over time. During the beginning of the national banking era, the paid-up capital of the banks had reached $5.3m, and reserves stood at $2.5m. By 1914, the five banks had accumulated reserves of $72.9m and paid-up capital reached $38.0m. The National Banking Act of 1864 also supported the trend of retaining profits to increase capital. The Act required that national banks retained profits until the reserves reached 20% of the subscribed capital. Such rules also found their way into many banking provisions at the state level.[158]

The subscribed capital of the Bank of New York, for example, remained almost constant between 1791 and 1853.[159] The bank had even urged the legislator to change its charter and increase the capital several times in the previous decades. Aiming for a capital increase of $1m in 1835, the Bank of New York argued that business in New York City had grown rapidly while the bank's capital had not grown much. Moreover, the bank referred to the

[154] Nevins, *History of the Bank of New York and Trust Company, 1784 to 1934*, p. 20.
[155] Gouge, *A Short History of Paper Money and Banking in the United States*, p. 51; Dewey, *State Banking Before the Civil War*, pp. 53–63. William John Shultz and M. R. Cain, *Financial Development of the United States* (New York: Prentice-Hall, 1937), p. 247.
[156] *National Banking Act*.
[157] Author's calculations. Data: Office of the Comptroller of the Currency, *Annual Report of the Comptroller of the Currency 1931*, pp. 1021–2, Tab. 95. 1932–9: Office of the Comptroller of the Currency, *Annual Report of the Comptroller of the Currency 1939*, p. 301, Tab. 59.
[158] Frank P. Smith and Ralph W. Marquis, 'Capital and Surplus as Protection for Bank Deposits', *The Bankers Magazine*, 1937, 215–26 (p. 217).
[159] The subscribed capital was increased from $900,000 to $950,000 in 1832.

competition from banks located in Connecticut and Massachusetts.[160] Another reason was probably the Bank of New York's competitive position in New York City: banks established in the years after the Bank of New York were substantially better capitalised. Aaron Burr's rivalling Manhattan Company raised $2m in 1799, the Merchants' Bank followed in 1803 with a capital of 1.25m (with Articles of Association drafted by Alexander Hamilton), and the City Bank of New York, founded in 1812, had an authorised capital of $2m.

The Bank of New York finally increased its capital to $2m in 1853 when it rechartered under New York's Free Banking Act of 1838 and was thus regulated by the general banking laws of the State of New York. Another increase to $3 m followed in 1859. Yet another direction was taken in 1873 due to the financial panic of that year. Being faced with reduced earnings and having to pay taxes on its capital stock, the bank decided to reduce its subscribed capital from $3m to $2m.[161] The bank did not change its nominal capital again until 1921.

Other relevant New York City banks also maintained relatively stable paid-up capital: the Chemical Bank's paid-up capital remained constant at $300,000 until 1906 when it increased its capital to $3m. Significant changes in the capital structures of the Hanover Bank and City Bank did not occur until 1899. Hanover increased its capital from $1m to $3m and City Bank from $1m to $10m.

3.4.4   From Notes to Deposits: The 10% Capital/Deposits Ratios as a Yardstick in Banking Supervision

During the national banking era, issuing notes became a less important liability item for national banks. Measured against the total assets, close to 20% of the total liabilities consisted of banknotes in 1867. This constituted the high point in the period between 1864 and 1913. By 1913, 6.5% of the total liabilities were made up by notes. However, the amount of deposits grew substantially compared to total liabilities. In 1867, the deposits/liabilities ratio was 45.9%. In 1913, the ratio reached 73.8%.[162] Deposits, therefore, became the major funding source. Thus, the protection of depositors rather than noteholders received more attention. Minimum capital requirements in absolute numbers (for example, depending on a city's population) and capital/notes ratios lost their importance.

Capital/deposits requirements found their way into banking supervision as a rule of thumb at the federal level and as formal or informal provisions at the

---

[160] Henry Williams Domett, *A History of the Bank of New York, 1784–1884: Compiled from Official Records and Other Sources at the Request of the Directors*, 4th ed. (Cambridge, MA: The Riverside Press, 1922), p. 83; Nevins, *History of the Bank of New York and Trust Company, 1784 to 1934*, p. 51.

[161] Nevins, *History of the Bank of New York and Trust Company, 1784 to 1934*, p. 84.

[162] Author's calculations. Data: United States. Bureau of the Census, *Historical Statistics of the United States. Colonial Times to 1970*, Series 635/648/653.

state level towards the end of the nineteenth century. One of the first statutory capital/deposits requirements was probably in the Iowa Savings Bank Law of 1874.[163] The law limited the deposits to a maximum of ten times the capital.[164] Several other states introduced formal capital/deposits requirements in the following decades. An overview of 1935 indicated that sixteen states formally limited capital to deposits at the time. Statutory capital/deposits ratios by then often ranged between 4% and 10%.[165] Beyond statutory requirements, contemporaries assumed that by the 1930s, many state banking supervisors also used capital/deposit ratios as guidelines.[166]

On the federal level, national banks never had to meet statutory capital/ deposit requirements. However, the OCC used the ratio in supervisory practice. By 1914, the Comptroller of the Currency, John Skelton Williams, even proposed a legal 10% or 12.5% capital/deposits requirement for national banks to the United States Congress.[167] The Comptroller made several similar suggestions in later years, but Congress never introduced a formal capital requirement. The OCC's clear public stance also officialised the use of the guideline in banking supervision.[168]

The OCC applied the capital/deposits ratio in banking supervision probably until the 1930s. In 1948, the OCC reviewed its past capital policies, stating that 'Up to less than a quarter century ago there was a general feeling that, subject to exceptions, a ratio of $1 of capital structure to $10 of deposits was about "right"'. Skelton described the capital/deposits ratio as a 'rough method for gauging a relationship of a bank's capital cushion to the amount of its loans and investments'.[169] A similar statement was made in 1940 by the Superintendent of Banks for the State of New York, William R. White, who referred to the 10% rule as an 'elastic administrative principle'.[170]

The banking crisis of the 1930s also led to (a last) application of capital/ deposit ratios by the two other federal bank supervisory agencies. The Federal Reserve used the 10% capital/deposits ratio as a condition for state banks to

[163] Harris, *The Capital Structure in American Banking*, p. 170.

[164] Howard H. Preston, *History of Banking in Iowa, The Rise of Commercial Banking* (Iowa: The State of Iowa Historical Society, 1922), p. 139. Robinson mentions the California State Bank Act of 1909 as one of the first applications of a 10% capital/deposits ratio. Roland I. Robinson, 'The Capital-Deposit Ratio in Banking Supervision', *Journal of Political Economy*, 49.1 (1941), 41–57 (p. 42).

[165] Smith and Marquis, *Capital and Surplus as Protection for Bank Deposits*, p. 222.

[166] Robinson, *The Capital-Deposit Ratio in Banking Supervision*, p. 47. Robinson assumed that many more states were using the 1:10 capital/deposits ratio in supervisory practice.

[167] Office of the Comptroller of the Currency, 'Annual Report of the Comptroller of the Currency 1914', 1914, pp. 21–2.

[168] Howard D. Crosse, *Management Policies for Commercial Banks* (Englewood Cliffs, NJ: Prentice-Hall, 1962), p. 162.

[169] Office of the Comptroller of the Currency, 'Annual Report of the Comptroller of the Currency 1948', 1949, pp. 3–4.

[170] Harris, *The Capital Structure in American Banking*, p. 169.

join the Federal Reserve System between 1933 and 1935.[171] Similarly, the newly established FDIC applied the 10% rule to banks who applied for admission to the (by then) Temporary Federal Deposit Insurance Fund in 1934. The FDIC slightly adapted the 1:10 rule, deducting assets classified as worthless or doubtful from a bank's total capital. The FDIC defined this as 'net sound capital'.[172] The FDIC further developed the definition of capital over time by adjusting it with various assumptions. To calculate the 'net sound capital' (after 1943 called 'adjusted capital accounts'), the FDIC took the book value of total capital accounts, added the value of assets not shown on the books (hidden reserves), and deducted the value of overvalued assets and liabilities that were not shown on the books.[173]

The FDIC confirmed this policy in its 1935 annual report, expressing concerns over banks' capital and its importance for protecting depositors, and stating that 'no bank should be operated without a net sound capital equal to at least 10 percent of its deposits'.[174] The FDIC made one of the last references to the 10% capital/deposits ratio in 1937.[175] In the following years, all three federal bank supervisory agencies were about to shift their focus from deposits to assets when assessing capital adequacy. More specifically, the perception that adequate capital should depend on the assets' risk started to develop. Such new approaches would also allow for individual assessment as the asset composition of banks became more heterogeneous over time.[176] The idea was accelerated by growing government debt levels in the banks' balance sheets.

3.5 CONCLUDING REMARKS

Early banking literature of the late eighteenth and nineteenth centuries established several basic ideas about bank capital, many of which are still valid today. Firstly, the authors of publications on banking and banking practitioners had a common understanding of the purpose of capital to cover losses and induce trust for various bank stakeholders, such as shareholders, depositors, and – if applicable – noteholders. With regard to the trust function, banks also used their capital to publicly signal stability and ambition. Trust was critical in an environment where joint-stock banks were a relatively new concept. In England, the new joint-stock banks of the 1830s had to differentiate themselves from the dominant private banks. In Switzerland, large joint-stock banks financing infrastructure and industry were a new

[171] Robinson, *The Capital-Deposit Ratio in Banking Supervision*, p. 44.
[172] FDIC, 'Annual Report of the Federal Deposit Insurance Corporation 1934', 1935, p. 16.
[173] FDIC, 'Annual Report of the Federal Deposit Insurance Corporation 1945', p. 21.
[174] FDIC, 'Annual Report of the Federal Deposit Insurance Corporation 1935', 1936, p. 28.
[175] FDIC, 'Annual Report of the Federal Deposit Insurance Corporation 1936', 1937, p. 27.
[176] Robinson, *The Capital-Deposit Ratio in Banking Supervision*, p. 50.

concept in the second half of the nineteenth century. And in the United States, the first decades of the nineteenth century brought up many speculative schemes that undermined public trust in banking. The fact that capital was essential for building trust and communicating responsible banking practices is underlined by the fact that almost every bank advertisement in magazines or newspapers of any of the three countries during the nineteenth century highlighted a bank's capital and reserves.

Bank capital ratios in England, Switzerland, and the United States show some common features too. They were high in the banks' first years of establishment and subsequently fell. This evolution was natural, as banks started with a higher amount of capital, anticipating a certain volume of business in the future. Moreover, capital ratios converged over time among the leading banks in the respective countries.

Low or high capital ratios create incentives for specific stakeholders, such as shareholders, depositors, or bank managers. Choosing an adequate capital ratio was and still is a trade-off between those interests. However, serving shareholders' interests was certainly strongly reflected in banks' decision-making. A case in point is the frequent assurances of bank managers to their shareholders that dividends remained stable despite a capital issuance. In England, the main discussion dealt with the interests of shareholders and depositors. Banks often justified the decision to issue additional capital as a necessary compromise between safety for depositors and stable and attractive returns for investors. In Switzerland, the trade-off was more about dividends for investors versus the risk of the business models. The banks seemed to be eager to publicly signal trustworthy and responsible behaviour in their business, being aware that their activities involved a comparably high risk. In the United States, the trade-off for most of the nineteenth century was mainly between shareholders and noteholders. The focus shifted to depositors' interests only from the beginning of the twentieth century. In contrast to England and Switzerland, the US regulators and supervisors actively influenced the limits of leverage through formal and informal capital requirements. The strong government involvement in capital requirements initially originated from concerns regarding an over-issue of banknotes.

Writers on banking and practitioners of the nineteenth century had an understanding of the relation between risk and return: a risky business model required a higher capital ratio. Prudent bankers adjusted their capital policies to the riskiness of their business model. However, there are also examples during the early period of US banking wherein bankers intentionally set up speculative schemes that created opportunities for shareholders to invest in equity with very little equity.

What changed gradually throughout the nineteenth century was the understanding of risk. Authors of banking literature, banking practitioners, and supervisors had increasingly sophisticated views of risk as knowledge accumulated. The real bills doctrine set the spotlight on the maturity of assets.

Short-term assets were perceived as low risk, as banks could liquidate them quicker. However, the idea of what liquidity meant changed from the second half of the nineteenth century. The relevance of markets to sell assets – also assets with longer maturities – was acknowledged. Moreover, an asset's collateral and the counterparty's quality received attention. Loans secured by mortgages and loans to a government are the most prominent examples. The latter – lending to governments – would receive significant attention during the twentieth century and fundamentally changed the capital adequacy assessment in banking.

4

Two World Wars

Overturning Conventions

The two World Wars mark turning points in the evolution of capital/assets ratios and the perception of capital adequacy. During the First and Second World Wars, three major factors contributed to a further leveraging of the banking system: government financing, inflation, and the generally unfavourable political and legal environment for the capital issuances of banks. Each of these factors on its own influenced the capital/assets ratios. During wartime, these drivers jointly accelerated the further deterioration of capital levels.

The capital/assets ratios of banks in Switzerland, the United Kingdom, and the United States fell substantially during the two World Wars. Figure 4.1 shows the banks' capital ratios from 1910 to 1950. In the United Kingdom, the capital ratios were already at a low level in 1914. During the First World War, the capital/assets ratios fell from 8.3% to 5.5%. The Second World War brought another decline of 2.5pp for British banks, falling to as little as 3.0% in 1945.

The Swiss and the US banks showed a similar deterioration in capital/assets ratios, albeit at a higher level. Capital/assets ratios stood at 15.0% (Switzerland) and 17.0% (United States) by 1914. They fell by 1.9 and 3.7pp, respectively, during the First World War. During the Second World War, the capital/assets ratios fell by 1.6pp in Switzerland and 5.3pp in the United States. In Switzerland, the group of the big banks experienced an even more pronounced decline. Their capital ratios fell by 5.2pp during the First and 4.4pp during the Second World War (see Table 4.1).

The two wars had fundamentally shifted conventions on what was deemed adequate capital. At the beginning of the twentieth century, the big banks in Switzerland followed a target capital/assets ratio of about 25%. For British joint-stock banks, the conventional capital/assets ratio fluctuated around 10%. In the United States, the supervisory practice of federal bank supervisors focused on a capital/deposits ratio of about 10% until the 1930s.

TABLE 4.1 *Capital/assets ratios during the First and Second World Wars*[1]

	1914	1918	Change in pp	1939	1945	Change in pp
Switzerland	15.0%	13.1%	−1.9	12.0%	10.4%	−1.6
– big banks	*20.1%*	*14.9%*	*−5.2*	*15.4%*	*11.0%*	*−4.4*
United Kingdom	8.3%	5.5%	−2.8	5.5%	3.0%	−2.5
United States	17.0%	13.3%	−3.7	12.0%	6.7%	−5.3

[1] Data: see footnote 1.

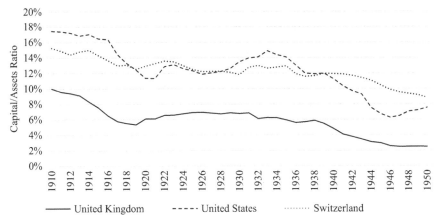

FIGURE 4.1 Capital/assets ratios, United Kingdom, United States, and Switzerland, 1914–50[1]

The idea that the share of required capital should relate to the risk inherent in a bank's balance sheet existed already in the nineteenth century, but the recognition of risks developed over time. At first, the focus was on the duration of assets, whereby banks and their managers preferred short-term over long-term assets. However, the growth of government debt in banks' balance sheets during the First and Second World Wars shifted the attention to the default risk of assets.

The economic dynamics of war financing were very similar in the United Kingdom, Switzerland, and the United States: government debt grew, inflation rates were high, and banks became involved in securing capital for the state. The three countries primarily differed in the amount of government

[1] Author's calculations. Data: Swiss National Bank, *Die Banken in der Schweiz (annual issues 1906–2015)*; 'The Economist Banking Supplement, Various, 1861–1946'; Sheppard, *The Growth and Role of UK Financial Institutions*. United States, Bureau of the Census, *Historical Statistics of the United States: Colonial Times to 1970*.

debt accumulated during the two wars and banks' exposure to government debt. The massive build-up of government debt in banks' balance sheets initiated the demise of old capital adequacy guidelines – and gave rise to approaches considering the riskiness of assets when measuring capital adequacy.

Another dimension where the three countries deviated from the beginning of the First until the end of the Second World War was the organisation of bank supervision. In the United States, the Office of the Comptroller of the Currency (OCC) was established in 1863, the Federal Reserve (FED) in 1913, and the Federal Deposit Insurance Corporation (FDIC) in 1933. While the US central bank did have some supervisory responsibility for member banks of the Federal Reserve System, there were also two other federal agencies with supervisory responsibilities and, additionally, many state banking supervisory agencies. In Switzerland, the banking supervisor – the Federal Banking Commission (FBC) – was established in 1934. The Swiss National Bank (SNB), founded in 1906, only had limited macroprudential supervisory authority for banks. In the United Kingdom, banking supervision and monetary policy were both conducted by the Bank of England (BoE), and monetary goals were the primary concern that guided banking supervision.

4.1   WARTIME DYNAMICS OF BALANCE SHEETS

Banks play a central role in times of war as an integral part of the economy and a facilitator of credit. Thus, banks' balance sheets are a mirror of monetary and fiscal policy in wartime. During the First and Second World War, bank balance sheets in Switzerland, the United Kingdom, and the United States showed very similar characteristics.

Banks became crucial providers of government debt in all three countries by pooling deposits and investing in government bills and bonds. The share of government investment increased substantially compared to other assets, leading to a structural change on the asset side. Inflation rates and the velocity of money were high during both World Wars. The balance sheet items most affected by the rising price level were deposits. Moreover, the 'liquidity preference' of the public in uncertain times further contributed to the deposits' growth. Customers switched to financial products with shorter maturities, such as accounts payable at short notice or on demand.

Inflation also undermines the value of paid-up equity capital. The paid-up capital's value is fixed and increases when a bank issues new capital. In real terms, the value of the paid-up capital is reduced by inflation. Besides the devaluation of the paid-up capital, the process of raising fresh capital was hampered in wartime by formal and informal constraints. In Great Britain, for example, capital issuances had to be approved by a committee. In Switzerland, similar regulations did not exist, but bankers deemed it inappropriate to issue capital and compete with the state for the scarce resource of capital. In the United States, federal bank supervisory agencies suspended disciplinary measures against banks with deteriorating capital ratios. The combination of formal and informal restrictions on capital issuances, the devaluation of paid-up capital in real terms, and balance sheet expansion contributed substantially to the decline of capital/assets ratios.

Figures 4.2 and 4.3 show two key aggregates of the economic policies between 1910 and 1950: government debt and inflation rates. Figure 4.2 highlights the substantial growth of the total government debt in the three countries during the two World Wars. British government debt grew strongly during wartime. In 1918, it reached £5.9bn – more than 8.3 times larger than by the end of 1913. The US government debt grew to $12.5bn in 1918 (10.4 times larger than before the war). The United States officially declared war during the First World War in 1917 and was actively involved in the war for nineteen months only. Nevertheless, the economic mobilisation – as in Switzerland – was extensive.

Government debt grew substantially during the Second World War, but growth rates were lower than from 1914 to 1918. The US federal government had a total of $258.7bn in debt outstanding in 1945, which was almost seven times the amount before the war. In the United Kingdom, government debt almost tripled during the Second World War. Switzerland was not directly involved in either of the two wars through warfare.[2] Nevertheless, government debt doubled in both war periods. The Swiss government (at all government levels) had CHF 3.9bn debt outstanding in 1918 and CHF 15.4bn in 1945.

In all three countries, government debt grew beyond the GDP, underlining the significant amount of outstanding debt. Debt/GDP ratios in 1945 were 235.4% in the United Kingdom, 116.0% in the United States, and 103.9% in Switzerland.[3]

---

[2] For the involvement of Swiss banks in the Second World War, see Barbara Bonhage, Marc Perrenoud, and Hanspeter Lussy, *Nachrichtenlose Vermögen bei Schweizer Banken: Depots, Konten und Safes von Opfern des nationalsozialistischen Regimes und Restitutionsprobleme in der Nachkriegszeit.*, ed. Unabhängige Expertenkommission Schweiz – Zweiter Weltkrieg (UEK) (Zurich: Chronos, 2001), xv. For a broader overview, see Hans Ulrich Jost, *Politik und Wirtschaft im Krieg: die Schweiz 1938–1948* (Zurich: Chronos, 2016).

[3] Data: United Kingdom: Bank of England, 'A Millennium of Macroeconomic Data. A30a. Government Debt 1727–2016', 2016: www.bankofengland.co.uk/statistics/research-datasets (accessed 6 June 2018). Switzerland: Government debt includes debt on a federal, cantonal, and municipal level. Author's calculations. Data: HSSO, 'Historische Statistik der Schweiz Online, Tab. Q.6a.', 2012: www.hsso.ch/2012/q/6a. HSSO, 'Historische Statistik der Schweiz Online, Tab. Q.16a.', 2012: www.hsso.ch/2012/q/16a. HSSO, 'Historische Statistik der Schweiz Online, Tab. U.45.', 2012: www.hsso.ch/2012/u/45 (accessed 10 December 2014). United States: Richard Sutch, 'Gross Domestic Product: 1790–2002, Table Ca10', in *Historical Statistics of the United States, Earliest Times to the Present*, ed. Susan B. Carter, Scott Sigmund Gartner, Michael R. Haines, et al. (New York: Cambridge University Press, 2006): http://dx.doi.org/10.1017/ISBN-9780511132971.

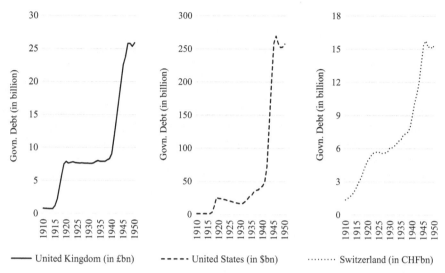

—— United Kingdom (in £bn)   - - - - United States (in $bn)   ········· Switzerland (in CHFbn)

FIGURE 4.2 Gross government debt in Switzerland (in CHFbn), the United Kingdom (in £bn), and the United States (in $bn), 1910–50[4]

The United Kingdom, the United States, and Switzerland followed an expansionary monetary policy during the two wars. Figure 4.3 shows the inflation rates of the three countries from 1910 to 1950. The changes in the consumer price indices have similar patterns: inflation rates reached their high point in 1917/18 at around 25%. The First World War followed a deflationary period from 1921 to 1923/4. The Second World War was marked again by a period of high inflation, albeit on a comparatively lower level. The inflation rates during the Second World War peaked between 15% and 16% in 1940/1 (United Kingdom, Switzerland) and 1947 (United States).

4.1.1 Assets Side: Financing Wars

Banks' contributions to financing governments can be traced by analysing the asset side of balance sheets. Such investments are usually in the form of direct

[4] Data: United Kingdom: Bank of England, 'A Millennium of Macroeconomic Data. A29. The National Debt', 2016: www.bankofengland.co.uk/statistics/research-datasets (accessed 6 June 2018). Switzerland: HSSO, *Historische Statistik der Schweiz Online, Tab. U.45*. The data for Switzerland consists of government debt from all three governmental levels (federal, cantonal, municipal). United States: John Joseph Wallis, 'Federal Government Debt, by Type: 1791–1970, Table Ea650', in *Historical Statistics of the United States, Earliest Times to the Present*, ed. by Susan B. Carter, Scott Sigmund Gartner, Michael R. Haines, et al. (New York: Cambridge University Press, 2006): http://dx.doi.org/10.1017/ISBN-9780511132971.

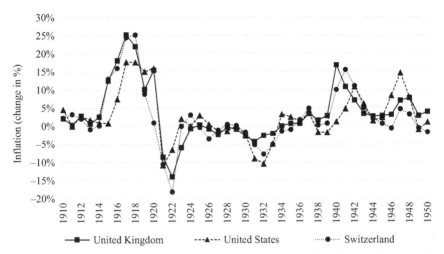

FIGURE 4.3 Inflation (change of consumer price index) in the United Kingdom, the United States, and Switzerland, 1910–50[5]

loans to governments or investments in government securities, which are part of a bank's investment portfolio. While finding data on bank loan composition is challenging, data on banks' investment portfolios are available in many cases.

Figure 4.4 shows the government securities at face value that banks held as a percentage of the total gross government debt. For the United Kingdom and the United States, data is available from 1910 to 1950. Data on Swiss banks and their government investments are available after 1924. All three data sets have various shortcomings. The amount of British treasury bills is based on estimates.[6] The US data covers federal government debt only, leaving states aside. The Swiss data includes bonds only. Short-term debt instruments, more specifically treasury bills ('Schatzanweisungen') and

[5] Data: United Kingdom: Bank of England, 'A Millennium of Macroeconomic Data. A47. Wages and Prices 1209–2016', 2016: www.bankofengland.co.uk/statistics/research-datasets (accessed 6 June 2018). Switzerland: HSSO, 'Historische Statistik der Schweiz Online, Tab. H.39.', 2012: www.hsso.ch/2012/h/39 (accessed 10 December 2014). United States: Peter H Lindert and Richard Sutch, 'Consumer Price Indexes, for All Items: 1774–2003, Table Cc1-2', in *Historical Statistics of the United States, Earliest Times to the Present*, ed. by Susan B. Carter, Scott Sigmund Gartner, Michael R. Haines, et al. (New York: Cambridge University Press, 2006): http://dx.doi.org/10.1017/ISBN-9780511132971.
[6] For the First World War, the amount of treasury bills cannot be found in the statistics of *The Economist* and the *Bankers' Almanac* published at the time. The volume of treasury bills in the balance sheets of British banks from 1910 to 1950 is based on estimates by Sheppard, *The Growth and Role of UK Financial Institutions*, pp. 116–17.

rescriptions ('Reskriptionen'), could not be considered.[7] Direct loans to the Swiss government are neglected even though they were an important funding source.[8]

Nevertheless, Figure 4.4 serves as a reference point for banks' key position in financing government debt. British banks held up to 29% of the total British government debt during the First World War. This share dropped substantially in subsequent years. It rose again during the Great Depression and further increased after 1939. British banks' share of government debt reached about 16% during the Second World War.

Government debt in US banks' balance sheets grew rapidly during the First World War but was outpaced by the rapid increase of the total government debt, of which substantial parts were allocated outside the banks' balance sheets. Until 1917, banks held about two-thirds of federal government debt. The banks' share in government debt fell substantially in 1918, to about one-fourth. The share of government debt increased again from 1921 onwards. As a result of the Great Depression, US banks provided more than 50% of US government debt in 1936. In 1941, 48% of federal government debt was in the books of US banks.

In Switzerland, banks were also crucial lenders to the government.[9] Besides the commercial banks, the SNB was also a central creditor. It held most of the rescriptions during the First World War.[10] The SNB directly financed the government, which was not the case to such a large extent by the Second

---

[7] 'Schatzanweisungen' were short-term securities (3–24 months) issued by the Swiss government's treasury department and placed only at banks. Rescriptions were securities issued by the government and financed by the SNB. These securities could then be sold by the SNB to the market and were important during the First and Second World Wars. See also Patrick Halbeisen and Tobias Straumann, 'Die Wirtschaftspolitik im internationalen Kontext', in *Wirtschaftsgeschichte der Schweiz im 20. Jahrhundert*, ed. Patrick Halbeisen, Margrit Müller, and Béatrice Veyrassat (Basel: Schwabe Verlag, 2012), pp. 983–1075 (p. 997).

[8] A part of the loans was registered in the debt registry of the federal government. Switzerland's first War Loan, issued in September 1936, for example, was not structured as a bond but based on entries in the debt registry. The use of a debt registry had various advantages compared to an ordinary security. Instead of holding a security, lenders could treat the loan as a receivable and would not need to value the investment in their balance sheet based on a market value. Moreover, the government as a borrower could control who owned its debt (as opposed to ordinary bonds traded on a market). See also *Bundesgesetz über das eidgenössische Schuldbuch vom 21. September 1939*, 1939.

[9] Malik Mazbouri, Sébastien Guex, and Rodrigo Lopez, 'Finanzplatz Schweiz', in *Wirtschaftsgeschichte der Schweiz im 20. Jahrhundert*, ed. Patrick Halbeisen, Margrit Müller, and Béatrice Veyrassat (Basel: Schwabe Verlag, 2012), pp. 468–518 (p. 484). For an overview of the role of the banks during the two wars, see also: Malik Mazbouri and Marc Perrenoud, 'Banques suisses et guerres mondiales', in *Kriegswirtschaft und Wirtschaftskriege*, ed. Valentin Groebner and Sébastien Guex (Zurich: Chronos, 2008), pp. 233–53.

[10] In 1918, CHF 312m of CHF 492m rescriptions were held by the SNB; the rest was placed on the market. Eveline Ruoss, *Die Geldpolitik der Schweizerischen Nationalbank 1907–1929: Grundlagen, Ziele und Instrumente* (Zurich, 1992), p. 92; Hermann Schneebeli, *Die Schweizerische Nationalbank 1907–1932* (Zurich, 1932), p. 469.

World War. The engagement of Swiss banks in public debt rose sharply in 1941, and by 1944 Swiss banks held about 17% of all government securities. This number, however, understates the actual contribution of Swiss banks to government financing. Considering all debt instruments (loans, treasury bills, rescriptions), the Swiss banks funded about a quarter of Switzerland's government debt by 1945.[11]

What was the effect of government securities on banks' balance sheets? Figure 4.5 shows the percentage of government securities compared to banks' total assets in the United Kingdom, the United States, and Switzerland. In all three countries, banks were vital lenders to the government during wartime and – in the United Kingdom and the United States – also in the 1930s. By 1944,

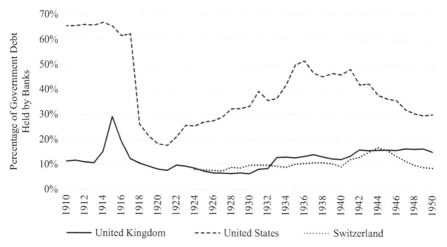

FIGURE 4.4 Percentage of gross government debt held by banks, United Kingdom (1910–50), United States (1910–50), and Switzerland (1924–50)[12]

[11] Author's calculations. The total face value of the bonds was CHF 2.4bn. Additionally, the Swiss banks had invested CHF 871m in rescriptions and CHF 606m in direct loans to the federal government, cantons, and municipalities. The total government debt held by banks in 1945 amounted to CHF 3.87bn. Data: Swiss National Bank, 'Das Schweizerische Bankwesen 1945' (Zurich: Orell Füssli, 1946), p. 43. Another important government lender was the life insurance companies, which held 5.4% of the government debt in 1945. They were important for the bond issues of the central government, taking over on average about one-sixth of all government bonds. Peter König, 'Der Anteil der Lebensversicherungsgesellschaften an der Finanzierung des Geldbedarfes des Bundes 1939–1945', *Schweizerische Zeitschrift für Volkswirtschaft und Statistik*, 1947, 560–9.

[12] Author's calculations. Data: United Kingdom: Bank of England, *A Millennium of Macroeconomic Data. A30a. Government Debt 1727–2016*; Sheppard, *The Growth and Role of UK Financial Institutions*; HSSO, *Historische Statistik der Schweiz Online, Tab. U.45*; Swiss National Bank, *Die Banken in der Schweiz (annual issues 1906–2015)*. United States: United States, Bureau of the Census, *Historical Statistics of the United States: Colonial Times to 1970*, Tables 640, 662. Wallis, *Federal Government Debt, by Type: 1791–1970, Table Ea650*.

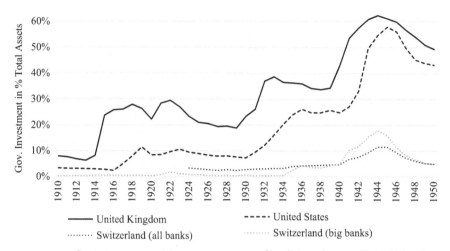

FIGURE 4.5 Government securities as a percentage of banks' total assets, United Kingdom, United States, and Switzerland, 1910–50[13]

62.2% of the total assets of British banks consisted of government debt. In the United States, this ratio peaked at 57.8% in 1945.

The total assets of Swiss banks consisted of 11.5% government bonds in 1945. Considering all debt types (loans, rescriptions, bills) would increase the ratio to 18.5%.[14] Figure 4.5 also displays the share of government securities in the big banks' balance sheets in Switzerland.[15] The big banks held comparatively more government debt on their balance sheets than other banks (17.8% in 1944).[16]

Apart from being lenders to the government, the big banks were also involved in underwriting government securities. They formed a cartel with the Association of Cantonal Banks. Excluding the first war loan in 1914, the cartel

[13] Authors' calculations. Data: Switzerland: Swiss National Bank, *Die Banken in der Schweiz (annual issues 1906–2015)*. Big banks 1910–24: Data collected by the author from the annual reports of the following banks: Basler Handelsbank, Eidgenössische Bank, Comptoir d'Escompte de Genève, Schweizerische Volksbank, Schweizerische Kreditanstalt, Schweizerische Bankgesellschaft, Schweizerischer Bankverein, Bank Leu; United States: United States, Bureau of the Census, *Historical Statistics of the United States: Colonial Times to 1970*, Tables 581, 640, 662; United Kingdom: Sheppard, *The Growth and Role of UK Financial Institutions*.

[14] Author's calculations. See footnote 11.

[15] Before 1924, the only source of information is the annual reports of individual banks. Many banks voluntarily published an overview of their investments. Some banks even published the individual titles held by the bank; others published information on an aggregated level, showing the different asset classes. Therefore, the portfolio composition of the group of the eight big banks was collected. The eight big banks represent about 30% of the Swiss banking market from 1910 to 1923.

[16] If all forms of debt are considered for the big banks, 27.0% of the total assets of the big banks were invested in the Swiss government debt in 1945. Author's calculations. Data: See footnote 11.

was involved in all the government issuances during the First World War. In most cases, the cartel provided a firm commitment of underwriting. Thus, the banks were responsible for the risk of selling federal and cantonal bonds and bills to customers or other banks. The total volume underwritten by the cartel between 1914 and 1921 was about CHF 3bn.[17]

The high ratios of government investments in all three banking systems show that banks were crucial lenders to the government. This raises the question of how banks increased their government debt exposure. From an accounting perspective, there are two ways: firstly, banks can reallocate assets. In that case, banks would have divested some assets and increased their exposure to government investments. Secondly, banks can increase total assets through investments in government debt, which also requires an increase on the liability side.

A reallocation effect on the asset side did not occur on a larger scale in the United Kingdom, the United States, or Switzerland. One of the largest balance sheet items on the asset side in all three banking systems was amounts due to customers, such as loans and advances. In wartime, the amounts due to customers usually increased, which supported the supply of capital for the war economy. However, government debt growth outpaced the growth of amounts due to customers substantially in all three countries during the two wars.

Within the short-term assets, however, there were some reallocation effects. In Switzerland, there was a rapid decline in foreign commercial paper investments. Treasury bills quickly replaced commercial papers during the First World War.[18] Similar effects were observed in London, where the declining share of commercial papers and the drop of investments in foreign credit went in hand with the growth of treasury bills during both World Wars.[19]

4.1.2 Liabilities Side: Deposits and Capital Issuances

How was the enormous growth of government debt in bank balance sheets financed? On the liabilities side, customers' deposits (due from customers) were the most relevant funding source. In the United Kingdom, deposits contributed almost 90% of the balance sheet total from 1910 to 1950. About 65–70% of the total liabilities in Switzerland and the United States came from customers.[20] The United Kingdom's higher share relates to statistical differences (no separate data on government deposits and interbank borrowing).

---

[17] Hermann Kurz, *Die schweizerischen Grossbanken: Ihre Geschäftstätigkeit und wirtschaftliche Bedeutung* (Zurich: Orell Füssli, 1928), p. 288.
[18] Swiss National Bank, 'Das Schweizerische Bankwesen 1916' (Bern: Buchdruckerei Stämpfli & Cie, 1918), p. 6.
[19] 'Banking Supplement 1940', *The Economist* (London, 18 May 1940), p. 4.
[20] Excluding interbank deposits and government deposits.

Table 4.2 shows the changes in volumes and percentages of the two most important items of the banks' balance sheets during the two World Wars (1914–18/1939–45): deposits (liabilities) and government securities (assets). In all three countries, customers' deposits grew substantially during the two wars and outpaced the growth of the balance sheet total. In terms of volume, the deposits grew more than the total of government securities. In the United Kingdom, for example, government securities held by banks grew by £391m during the First World War and £2.3bn during the Second World War. The deposits increased by £774m and £2.5bn, respectively.

The high share of deposits on the liabilities side and the rapid growth of deposits (in volume and per cent) highlight the crucial role of deposits when it comes to the balance sheet expansion during the two wars.

TABLE 4.2 *Changes in percent (nominal changes) and volume (in million domestic currency) of amounts due to customers, domestic government securities, and total assets, United Kingdom, United States, and Switzerland, 1914–18 and 1939–45*[1]

		Change in	1914–1918	1939–1945
	Customers' deposits (liability)	% (p.a.)	14.4%	11.3%
		£m	774	2,543
	Government securities (asset)	% (p.a.)	53.8%	22.9%
		£m	391	2,293
		% (p.a.)	13.3%	10.8%
United Kingdom	Total assets	£m	782	2,547
	Customers' deposits (liability)	% (p.a.)	10.0%	14.4%
		$m	12,538	92,128
	Government securities (asset)	% (p.a.)	32.9%	27.9%
		$m	2460	76947
		% (p.a.)	9.5%	13.3%
United States	Total assets	$m	14,994	94,439
	Customers' deposits (liability)	% (p.a.)	7.0%	2.4%
		CHFm	2,554	2,537
	Government securities (asset)	% (p.a.)	n/a	16.9%
		CHFm	n/a	1,585
		% (p.a.)	5.9%	1.9%
Switzerland	Total assets	CHFm	3,116	2,631

[1] Data: United Kingdom: Sheppard, *The Growth and Role of UK Financial Institutions.* Switzerland: Swiss National Bank, *Die Banken in der Schweiz (annual issues 1906–2015).* United States: United States. Bureau of the Census, *Historical Statistics of the United States. Colonial Times to 1970,* tables 581, 585, 640, 662.

Why did customers' deposits grow to such a large extent during the two wars? The high inflation rates during wartime, shown in Figure 4.3, substantially depreciated the value of money. Banks mainly deal with nominal financial instruments. Exceptions on the asset side are, for example, direct holdings of bank premises or real estate. The payments related to nominal financial instruments are fixed in nominal amounts. An increase in the expected inflation raises nominal interest rates, which translates into a change in the nominal value of a financial instrument.[21] Therefore, nominal balance sheet items adjust to inflation.

One of the drivers of inflation during the wars was the velocity of money. These effects were already understood and described during the First World War. *The Economist* outlined the driving forces behind the deposit growth in 1916: namely, four processes that can contribute to the increase of deposits: first, deposits grow if the country's stock of gold is increasing and the gold is brought to the banks. This increases the cash on the asset side and deposits on the liabilities side. Second, deposits grow if the stock of paper currency is increased and the currency is paid in. Third, banks can create money by giving discounts, loans, and advances, which then create deposits. The fourth and last channel runs from banks buying securities to deposit growth. As banks invested in government securities, cash was transferred from the BoE to the government. British banks, therefore, held securities instead of cash. The government drew on the balance at the BoE and invested this capital in the economy. The companies that had received capital were depositing it into their accounts, which increased the volume of deposits.[22] *The Economist* heavily criticised the expansionary monetary policy of the government and the BoE and argued that private individuals would have to start investing in government securities more substantially to reduce inflation.[23] The role of inflation as a driver of deposit growth during the two wars was also discussed in Switzerland.[24]

Besides inflation, various other reasons were frequently mentioned in the context of growing deposits. Both in the United Kingdom and Switzerland, it was argued that the public had a 'liquidity preference' during the two World Wars. In times of uncertainty and depressed securities prices, bank customers shifted their long-term investments into deposits, making their wealth more

---

[21] Irving Fisher, *The Theory of Interest: As Determined by Impatience to Spend Income and Opportunity to Invest It* (New York: Macmillan, 1930).

[22] For an overview of drivers of deposit growth during the First World War, see also E. Victor Morgan, *Studies in British Financial Policy, 1914–25* (London: Macmillan, 1952), p. 242.

[23] 'Banking Supplement 1916', *The Economist* (London, 21 October 1916), pp. 701–2; 'Banking Supplement 1945', *The Economist* (London, 29 December 1945), p. 2.

[24] Jöhr, *Schweizerische Kreditanstalt*, p. 238; Swiss National Bank, 'Das Schweizerische Bankwesen 1917' (Bern: Buchdruckerei Stämpfli & Cie, 1919), p. 5; Swiss National Bank, 'Das Schweizerische Bankwesen 1942' (Zurich: Orell Füssli, 1943), p. 11.

readily available.[25] Other domestic effects, such as the liquidation of inventories at the beginning of the wars, might have also impacted the growth of deposits.[26]

Another relevant driver of deposits' growth in Switzerland was foreign capital inflows. The SNB mentioned the stream of capital from abroad many times in its annual statistical publications during the First and Second World Wars. Whereas capital inflows were directly referred to as 'tax flight capital' during the First World War, such specific remarks were not made in later years.[27] The SNB simply referred to it as 'foreign capital inflows'.[28] No figures available provide insights into the volume of foreign deposits during the two wars, even though the Independent Commission of Experts Switzerland attempted to make such estimates when examining Switzerland's role during the Second World War.[29] Switzerland was a stable financial hub in the turmoil of war, which was the basis for large financial transactions. The Swiss franc was a stable currency and the only currency in Europe which was almost freely convertible. Indeed, Swiss banks also participated in purchases of Nazi gold and provided credit to Germany, Italy, and the Allies. Moreover, banking secrecy – codified in the Banking Act of 1934 but already rooted in the Swiss banking sector since the end of the nineteenth century – certainly also attracted foreign funds.[30]

Changes in two components can lead to a rise of equity capital. New shares might be issued, or reserves increased. Figures 4.6, 4.7, and 4.8 show the paid-up capital and the reserves of Swiss, British, and US banks.

Swiss banks were hesitant with new capital issuances in the early years of the First World War. There were almost no recapitalisations from the summer of 1914 to 1916. The capital increases shown in Figure 4.6 are mostly related to banks that were newly included in the SNB statistics. It was only in 1916 that a more considerable amount of capital was issued (CHF 25m). The reasons

[25] 'Banking Supplement 1941', *The Economist* (London, 20 November 1941), p. 5; Swiss National Bank, 'Das Schweizerische Bankwesen 1918' (Bern: Buchdruckerei Stämpfli & Cie, 1920), p. 4.

[26] Swiss National Bank, 'Das Schweizerische Bankwesen 1918', p. 3; Swiss National Bank, 'Das Schweizerische Bankwesen 1942', p. 11.

[27] Swiss National Bank, 'Das Schweizerische Bankwesen 1918', p. 4.

[28] Swiss National Bank, 'Das Schweizerische Bankwesen 1940' (Zurich: Orell Füssli, 1941), p. 8.

[29] The Independent Commission of Experts Switzerland analysed Switzerland's role during the Second World War. One part of the investigation focused on foreign capital at Swiss banks in the form of deposits, securities accounts, and safes that have not been claimed by someone after the war. The availability of the sources, however, did not allow the authors to make an estimate about the volume of these assets. Bonhage, Perrenoud, and Lussy, *Nachrichtenlose Vermögen bei Schweizer Banken: Depots, Konten und Safes von Opfern des nationalsozialistischen Regimes und Restitutionsprobleme in der Nachkriegszeit*. For a broader analysis of assets under management, see Christophe Farquet, *Histoire du paradis fiscal suisse* (Paris: SciencesPo les presses, 2018).

[30] Sébastien Guex, 'The Origins of the Swiss Banking Secrecy Law and Its Repercussions for Swiss Federal Policy', *Business History Review*, 2000, 237; Robert Vogler, 'The Genesis of Swiss Banking Secrecy: Political and Economic Environment', *Financial History Review*, 8.1 (2001), 73–84.

mentioned for these issuances were the positive development of the economy after 1916 as well as growing deposits.[31] These capital increases had little effect on the capital/assets ratio.

The first years of the Second World War in Switzerland are comparable to the period of 1914 to 1916. Only two cantonal banks issued fresh capital in 1941. The big banks did not issue capital at all during the war. There were no formal constraints with regards to capital issuances during both wars. Especially during the Second World War, however, there was a widespread conception that banks should not lock up capital that could be used for sovereign debt. As an observer at the time put it: 'Issuing capital during the war forbade itself'.[32]

Whereas almost no capital was issued in Switzerland during wartime due to informal constraints, the same happened in the United Kingdom due to formal restrictions. During the First World War, capital issuances had to be approved by the Treasury. In January 1915, the Treasury announced that 'in the present crisis all other considerations must be subordinated to the paramount necessity of husbanding the financial resources of the country with a view to the

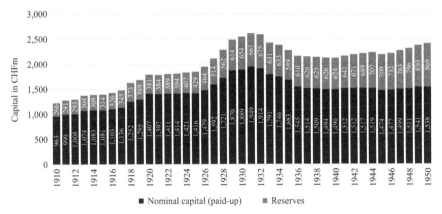

FIGURE 4.6 Nominal capital (paid-up) and reserves in CHF millions, Swiss banks, 1910–50[33]

---

[31] Swiss National Bank, 'Das Schweizerische Bankwesen 1916', p. 2. For an overview of Switzerland's monetary policies during the First World War, see Ruoss, *Die Geldpolitik der Schweizerischen Nationalbank 1907–1929*; Sébastien Guex, *La politique monétaire et financière de la Confédération suisse: 1900–1920* (Lausanne: Payot, 1993). For an overview of monetary policy during the First and Second World Wars, see Michael Bordo and Harold James, 'Die Nationalbank 1907–1946: Glückliche Kindheit oder schwierige Jugend?', in *Schweizerische Nationalbank, 1907–2007*, ed. Schweizerische Nationalbank SNB (Zurich: Verlag Neue Zürcher Zeitung, 2007), pp. 29–118. Tobias Straumann, *Fixed Ideas of Money: Small States and Exchange Rate Regimes in Twentieth Century Europe*, Studies in Macroeconomic History (Cambridge: Cambridge University Press, 2010).

[32] Jöhr, *Schweizerische Kreditanstalt*, p. 476.

[33] Swiss National Bank, *Die Banken in der Schweiz (annual issues 1906–2015)*.

successful prosecution of the war' and that 'it feels it imperative in the national interest that fresh issues of capital shall be approved by the Treasury before they are made'.[34]

The control of capital issuances was only one dimension of wartime control of financial resources. The export of capital was also severely restricted.[35] The Treasury's embargo had a substantial impact on the British financial market. In 1914, £512.6m were issued in the United Kingdom, of which £180.1m was not for the government. In 1916, £585.6m were issued, with only £31.5m left for non-government issuances. The figures diverged even more in 1917, with total issues of £1.3bn – of which all but £40.9m were government securities.[36] After the war, the government attempted to maintain this capital control policy. However, a less restrictive regulation was eventually introduced, forbidding only capital issuances that could contribute to foreign capital purposes.[37] The government withdrew the domestic ban on capital issuances in March 1919.[38]

During the Second World War, the British government again controlled private capital operations. Based on a Treasury Memorandum of Guidance that was issued on 12 September 1939, capital issuances were to be restricted to production and services related to defence, essential services (such as transport and food supplies), and export purposes.[39] Moreover, the BoE asked banks to focus their lending on defence production, exports, coal mining, and agriculture. After the war, in May 1945, new capital issuances were allowed again, but only for reconstruction purposes.[40]

Figure 4.7 shows the paid-up capital and reserves of British banks from 1910 to 1950. During these four decades, there was only one major increase of capital, in 1919 and 1920.

In the United States, the amount of bank capital in the banking system was much more volatile than in the United Kingdom and Switzerland. The changing capital was partly related to market entries and exits, and banks could still increase their capital. Figure 4.8 shows the capital and reserves in US banking from 1910 to 1950. During the First World War, capital and reserves gradually grew, at around 2.3% and 3.4%. The number of banks grew at about the same

---

[34] 'Passing Events', *The Investors' Review* (London, 23 January 1915), XXXV, No. 890 edition, p. 76.

[35] Henry Francis Grady, *British War Finance: 1914–1919* (New York: Columbia University Press, 1927), pp. 59–61.

[36] Richard Sidney Sayers, *The Bank of England 1891–1944* (Cambridge: Cambridge University Press, 1976), pp. 79–83.

[37] Regulation 30F. Grady, *British War Finance*, p. 63.

[38] Susan Howson, *Domestic Monetary Management in Britain: 1919–38*, Occasional Paper/ University of Cambridge, Department of Applied Economics (Cambridge: Cambridge University Press, 1975), p. 10. For an overview of British monetary and financial policy during the First World War, see also Morgan, *Studies in British Financial Policy, 1914–25*.

[39] Richard Sidney Sayers, *Financial Policy, 1939–45* (London: Her Majesty's Stationery Office, 1956), p. 165.

[40] Susan Howson, *British Monetary Policy 1945–51* (Oxford: Clarendon Press, 1993), p. 38.

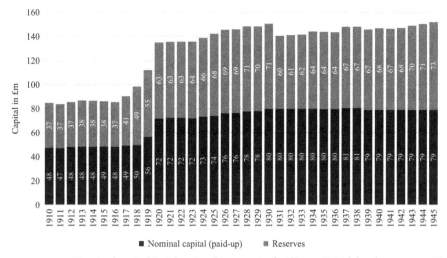

FIGURE 4.7 Nominal capital (paid-up) and reserves in £ millions, British banks, 1910–45[41]

pace. The situation during the Second World War was different. The nominal capital remained stable, but the reserves grew steadily, averaging 5.1% yearly.

Despite the increase in bank capital, capital/ratios deteriorated, given the substantial growth of total assets during wartime. War financing was prioritised over capital adequacy. Adhering to strict capital ratios would have restricted war financing.[42] Therefore, the supervisors decided to suspend the use of capital ratios in 1942. The Comptroller of the Currency, the FDIC, the Board of Governors of the Federal Reserve System, and the Executive Committee of the National Association of Supervisors of State Banks issued a joint statement assuring banks that they would not take action against them due to investments in government securities or short-term loans to customers to purchase government bonds.[43] The FDIC was even more specific, stating that banks with deteriorating capital ratios due to war financing would not be sanctioned.[44]

The war years were a period of extraordinary conditions, which left their mark on banks' balance sheets in the United States, the United Kingdom, and Switzerland. Contemporaries in all three countries argued that balance sheets – and, with them, capital ratios – would return to 'normal' in peacetime. On a broader level, there was also the idea of returning to the pre-war economic system, most prominently represented by the gold standard.

[41] Author's calculations, the Bank of England was excluded. Data: 'The Economist Banking Supplement, Various, 1861–1946'.
[42] Crosse, *Management Policies for Commercial Banks*, p. 164.
[43] FDIC, 'Annual Report of the Federal Deposit Insurance Corporation 1942', 1943, p. 55.
[44] FDIC, 'Annual Report of the Federal Deposit Insurance Corporation 1942', p. 5.

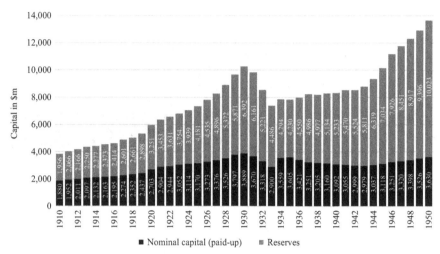

FIGURE 4.8 Nominal capital (paid-up) and reserves in $ millions, US banks, 1910–50[45]

A normalisation in the banking sector meant that government debt and deposits would contract again. However, a transition to pre-war balance sheets and to a pre-war macroeconomic environment did not happen after either of the two wars or in either of the three countries. An economic recession followed the First World War. After the Second World War, Great Britain first dealt with reconstructing and reorganising the economy, while the United States and Switzerland rapidly entered a period of economic expansion.

4.2 BRITISH BANKING AND CAPITAL: THE ABSENCE OF A TOPIC

By the beginning of the twentieth century, bank capital was no longer a central topic in British banking. Referencing Gilbart's 1:3 rule stipulated in 1827, *The Bankers' Magazine* noted in 1914 that 'this practice is now but a matter of history'.[46] Instead, the magazine praised the advantages of short-term securities, which allow for lower capital ratios.[47]

One of the key references on England's amalgamation movement, Joseph Sykes, argued that capital adequacy did not receive serious attention in England

---

[45] Office of the Comptroller of the Currency, *Annual Report of the Comptroller of the Currency 1931*, Tab. 96; Office of the Comptroller of the Currency, *Annual Report of the Comptroller of the Currency 1939*, Tab. 57; Office of the Comptroller of the Currency, 'Annual Report of the Comptroller of the Currency 1951', 1952, Tab. 44.

[46] *The Bankers' Magazine*, 'The Progress of Banking in Great Britain and Ireland During 1913', 1914, 850–70 (p. 860).

[47] *The Bankers' Magazine*, 'The Progress of Banking in Great Britain and Ireland During 1913', p. 860.

until 1918.[48] This view is undoubtedly accurate from the 1880s to 1918. The collapse of the City of Glasgow Bank in 1878 briefly triggered a reassessment of capital liability and capital policies in banking. After that, little was said about capital. And if bank capital was discussed, at least bankers seemed to view it as a necessary evil. Several large mergers of banks took place in 1917 and 1918. With the discussions of these mergers – or, more specifically, the growing market power of the merged banks – capital briefly resurfaced as a topic. One might add to Sykes's statement that capital adequacy largely disappeared from the public discourse after 1920, and it disappeared entirely as a topic until the late 1960s.

4.2.1 Amalgamations Movement in England

From 1914 to 1918, the First World War led to an expansion of the balance sheet totals. Combined with the loss in the real value of the paid-up capital, it put the capital/assets ratio under pressure. Even though the macroeconomic environment was an essential driver of the capital ratios, it was not this process that raised interest in the capital of English banks in 1918. Instead, the rapidly growing market concentration of English banking – the amalgamation movement – led to inquiries about the adequacy of banks' capital.

After the first establishment of joint-stock banks in England in the 1820s, the number of joint-stock banks grew rapidly for about six decades, reaching its high point in the 1880s with around 110 joint-stock banks.[49] From the 1880s onwards, the structure of the banking system changed as larger banks started to take over smaller, mostly local or provincial and private banks. The characteristics of bank sizes of the merged banks changed with time, mainly because the number of small local banks diminished, and private banks based on a partnership model became almost extinct. From 1910 to 1918, larger banks started to merge among themselves. These banks often did not operate in different geographical locations, as had been the case before, but in the same overlapping regions. The concentration process culminated in a series of large mergers. In 1917, the National Provincial Bank amalgamated with the Union of London and Smiths Bank. In March 1918, Westminster amalgamated with Parr's Bank. During the summer of 1918, London City and Midland merged with the London Joint Stock Bank, Lloyds amalgamated with the Capital and Counties Bank, and Barclays with the London Provincial and South Western Bank. In 1918, there were only twenty-six joint-stock banks left in England.[50]

---

[48] Joseph Sykes, *The Amalgamation Movement in English Banking, 1825–1924* (London: P. S. King & Son, Ltd., 1926), p. 102.

[49] Scottish and Irish joint-stock banks (about twenty) not included. See 'The Economist Banking Supplement, Various, 1861–1946'.

[50] 'The Economist Banking Supplement, Various, 1861–1946'.

Five major banks emerged from the amalgamation period: Barclays Bank, the London County Westminster and Parr's Bank, Lloyds Bank, the London Joint City and Midland Bank, and the National Provincial and Union Bank of England. In 1918, these Big Five combined held more than four-fifths of the total assets of all banks in England and Wales.[51] Overall, nineteen amalgamations, involving thirty-eight banks, took place in 1917 and 1918.[52] With these large amalgamations, public opinion became increasingly critical towards the concentrated market and requests in favour of a regulatory intervention were voiced. Generally, there was a lack of trust towards the oligopolistic banking structure, which was usually referred to as the 'Money Trust'.[53]

In February 1918, the Chancellor of the Exchequer appointed a Committee on Bank Amalgamations, also known as the Colwyn Committee.[54] The committee was assigned to consider the effects of amalgamations and discuss potential legislation on this matter.[55] The Colwyn Committee finished its report in May 1918 and outlined the advantages and disadvantages of amalgamations.[56] One of the key findings of the report dealt with capital adequacy:

The proportion of capital to deposits is now so small in the case of English joint stock banks – even excluding the temporary war increase in the amount of deposits – that any further shrinkage of Bank capital is clearly undesirable, in the interest of depositors, if it can be avoided. Attention has been drawn to the fact that amalgamation schemes usually mean a reduction in the total paid-up capital and uncalled liability of the two pre-amalgamation units.[57]

---

[51] Author's calculations based on individual balance sheet data. For the whole banking market, see Sheppard, *The Growth and Role of UK Financial Institutions*.

[52] Sykes, *The Amalgamation Movement*, p. 74.

[53] For example, the *Daily Express* noted on 4 February 1918 that the amalgamation of the London County and Westminster with Parr's Bank was just another step towards 'money power in a few hands', and went on to argue that the consolidation process, which had already begun with the takeover of small local banks and private banks and had brought banking based on personal relationships to an end, eliminated competition. The article called on the Board of Trade to step in and end the 'Money Trust' system (*Daily Express*, 1918, from the British National Archives: T 1/12431/52485). See also Committee on Bank Amalgamations, 'Report of the Treasury Committee on Bank Amalgamations. Treasury Minute Dated 11th March 1918', 1918, The National Archives, T 1/12325/20697. Sykes, *The Amalgamation Movement*, p. 74.

[54] The Committee's chairman was Lord Colwyn.

[55] The Committee held eight meetings and questioned twenty-two witnesses, among them also the influential bankers of the time, such as Walter Leaf, chairman of the London County Westminster and Parr's Bank; Lord Inchcape, director of the National Provincial and Union Bank of England; and Sir Edward Holden, chairman and managing director of the London City and Midland Bank.

[56] Committee on Bank Amalgamations, *Report Committee on Bank Amalgamations, BNA*, T 1/12325/20697.

[57] Committee on Bank Amalgamations, *Report Committee on Bank Amalgamations, BNA*, T 1/12325/20697.

Banks reduced their capital through mergers when shares of a bank were paid in cash. In such a process, the shares of one of the two banks were cancelled. Other takeovers were achieved by paying old shareholders with fewer but more valuable shares of the surviving bank. The liabilities were then transferred, leading to a further leveraging of the new entity.[58]

The statement quoted earlier shows that the committee was aware of the problems of low bank capital. In addition, it emphasised the conflicting interests of depositors in safety versus shareholders in high dividends, confirming the view that capital was seen as a form of insurance for depositors. The Colwyn Committee also took a critical standpoint towards the reduction of uncalled liability. In an internal circular summarising the committee's provisional impressions, this opinion became even more evident: the cancellation of uncalled liability was thought to reduce the security of depositors. According to the committee, further large amalgamations were not in the interest of the public – the only interests such amalgamations would have served were those of shareholders.[59]

In its official report, the committee was more diplomatic and stated that arguments against further mergers outweighed those in favour. It proposed legislation that required governmental approval for amalgamations by the Board of Trade and the Treasury, which should be advised by a Statutory Committee. Regarding larger amalgamations of banks with overlapping territories, the committee suggested prohibiting such mergers.[60] Despite these proposals, a law on bank amalgamations was never introduced, even though a bill was forwarded to Parliament in 1919.[61] The government opted for informal arrangements with the banks instead of introducing statutory banking legislation.[62]

However, the informal approach to convince banks of the importance of higher capital levels was successful. The fact that the government appointed a new Advisory Committee in the summer of 1918 to analyse pending mergers certainly helped.[63] The committee did not have legal power, but the government

---

[58] *The Bankers' Magazine*, 'The Progress of Banking in Great Britain and Ireland During 1918', 1919, 381–90 (pp. 382–3); *The Bankers' Magazine*, 'Progress of Banking in Great Britain and Ireland during 1944', 1945, p. 241.

[59] Committee on Bank Amalgamations, 1918, Provisional Impressions: British National Archives, T 1/12431/52485. Barclays abolished the uncalled liability in 1921, while the other four of the Big Five did so between 1956 and 1958. See Turner, *Banking in Crisis*, pp. 131–2.

[60] Committee on Bank Amalgamations, *Report Committee on Bank Amalgamations, BNA, T 1/12325/20697*.

[61] A draft of the bill can be found in the British National Archives: T 1/12325/20697.

[62] Moreover, Sayers mentions that a more general regulation of mergers (not only banking) was discussed at the time and that the president of the Board of Trade changed from Albert Stanley to Auckland Geddes in May 1919. Stanley was one of the central opponents of bank amalgamations. Sayers, *The Bank of England*, p. 241.

[63] The advisory committee consisted of Lord Inchcape, Lord Colwyn, and C. L. Stocks as secretary. See British National Archive: T 1/12431/52485

could provide de facto power to the committee based on the embargo for capital issuances introduced at the beginning of the First World War.[64]

The clear stance of the Amalgamations Committee – and later also the Advisory Committee – against further leveraging through mergers triggered bankers to strengthen their capital position.[65] The fact that a war-related increase in deposits had led to an additional leveraging of the banking sector further raised awareness among bankers.

In 1919 and 1920, the paid-up capital of English banks grew by about £20m, reaching £72m by the end of 1920. In 1920, *The Economist* noted that 'the danger of allowing this ratio [capital/deposits] to fall to so low a figure is being realised by bank directors'. One year later, *The Economist* stated:

> It should be pointed out that some of this increase in capital is due to the rearrangement of capital necessitated by amalgamations and alliances. At the same time, tangible evidence has been given that banks' directors have become alive to the fact that the ratio of capital and reserves to deposits had shrunk during the war to an abnormally low figure.[66]

Despite these increases in the paid-up capital, the capital ratios grew only moderately. In 1918, the capital/assets ratio was 5.8%. The ratio grew slightly to 6.4% in 1920, even though the total assets also grew. During the second half of the 1920s, the ratio remained at the 7% level. However, this was primarily due to the contracting balance sheets of the British banks between 1920 and 1925. The capital/assets ratio never returned to pre-war levels above 10%.

4.2.2   During and After the Second World War: Banking Without Capital

> Nowadays, in England at least, capital has ceased to be necessary.[67]

Economist and historian Richard Sidney Sayers wrote this sentence in one of the most popular banking textbooks of the twentieth century. *Modern Banking* was first published in 1938 and issued in several editions up to the 1970s. Sayers argued that English banks had a long track record of stability and had built up substantial hidden reserves. If it came to the capital, the author was more concerned about foreign than domestic banks:

> In some other countries, where the banks are less firmly established and public confidence could be more easily shaken, the capital of banks naturally retains its requirement relating the minimum capital to the deposit liabilities of a bank.[68]

---

[64] Sayers, *The Bank of England*, pp. 79–83.
[65] Sykes notes that the Committee on Financial Facilities after the war was also against low levels of capital. Sykes, *The Amalgamation Movement*, p. 142.
[66] 'Banking Supplement 1921', *The Economist* (London, 21 May 1921), p. 1034.
[67] Richard Sidney Sayers, *Modern Banking, Sixth Edition* (Oxford: Clarendon Press, 1964), p. 30.
[68] Sayers, *Modern Banking, Sixth Edition*, p. 30.

These sentences were printed in the sixth edition of *Modern Banking,* published in 1964. In the first edition of the textbook in 1938, Sayers avoided the topic of capital altogether.[69] He viewed liquidity as the primary source of stability in banking. This view was representative of the perception of liquidity and solvency after the Second World War.

The topic of capital and capital adequacy also received little attention in the media. Both *The Economist* and *The Bankers' Magazine* had frequently discussed such topics before the war. Building up capital was seen as part of the progress of the British banking system, enhancing its resilience. The annual article in *The Bankers' Magazine* discussing the evolution of the capital/deposits ratio was no longer published after the war, having until then been published for more than four decades. Later articles in *The Bankers' Magazine* on the capitalisation of banks were mostly descriptive, simply announcing changes in the structure of the capital or capital issuances. The same applied to articles published in *The Economist* and, in contrast to the aftermath of the First World War, the idea of returning to pre-war capital ratios was not expressed in either of these two key publications.

Scholars' lack of interest in the topic of solvency, as well as the lack of media coverage, have to be viewed against the policy environment at the time. As discussed, the amount of government debt was high, and so was the share of government debt in the banks' balance sheets. One of the central goals of monetary policy after the Second World War was to ensure capital supply for government debt. Therefore the banks, as sources of finance for the government, were highly affected by the government's repressive monetary policy.[70]

Instead of statutory regulation – as, for example, in Switzerland and the United States – British banking regulation was exercised informally and flexibly through the BoE. This informal supervision was guided by moral suasion and the 'Governor's eyebrows'.[71] Cash and liquidity ratios were the crucial tools in the BoE's supervisory practice. The cash ratio ensured that banks held a certain amount of their deposits at the BoE. The liquidity ratio forced banks to hold large amounts of cash, money at call, bills of exchange, and British government bills. This led to a high share of short-term government debt in banks' balance sheets. The cash ratio was set at 8% and had to be adhered to daily between 1946 and 1971, while the liquidity ratio ranged around 30%.[72]

With such a focus on liquidity, there was little room for capital requirements. The goal of monetary policy to ensure demand for short-term government debt,

---

[69] Sayers briefly discussed the role of capital in the context of American banking: Richard Sidney Sayers, *Modern Banking, First Edition* (London: Oxford University Press, 1938), pp. 42–43.

[70] Turner, *Banking in Crisis,* p. 181.

[71] See, for example, Forrest Capie, *The Bank of England: 1950s to 1979,* Studies in Macroeconomic History (Cambridge: Cambridge University Press, 2010), pp. 587–643; Turner, *Banking in Crisis,* pp. 181–6; Michie, *British Banking,* pp. 173–81.

[72] Turner, *Banking in Crisis,* p. 181.

enforced through informal control and liquidity ratios, was often believed to conflict with capital requirements.[73] It was not surprising that no capital issuances took place in such an environment. No bank raised new capital during the Second World War, even though the capital/assets ratio fell from 5.7% to 3.0%. By 1953/4, capitalisation reached a low point at 2.3%. Barclays and Midland had even lower capital/assets ratios (1.9% and 2.1%, respectively, without hidden reserves).

Capital ratios were rapidly shrinking at the beginning of the 1950s. Were the banks reckless, not worrying about the deterioration of their capital resources? After all, banks frequently referred to shareholders' and depositors' interests when issuing capital until the First World War. Moreover, there seemed to be an agreement that banks would need to strengthen their capital position between 1918 and 1920. Was the depletion of capital a sign that all these ideas had disappeared?

Some banks had already expressed concerns about their capital position before the Second World War. In 1937, for example, the Westminster Bank considered its capital too low. Comparing ratios with the other Big Five banks, the General Manager of Westminster Bank (Sir Charles Lidbury) noted internally that their own capital/deposits ratio was lower than that of the other big banks and that Westminster paid comparatively higher dividends. On the one hand, Lidbury pointed out that banks should issue capital in periods of 'cheap money' and, therefore, the time was right to issue capital. On the other hand, he also referred to various problems arising from a possible capital issuance. In his view, it seemed difficult to adequately compensate new shareholders without 'watering down' the 'preferential position' of existing shareholders. Westminster eventually decided against a capital increase.[74]

During the Second World War, several banks attempted to raise new capital. Between September and December 1943, the National Provincial, Midland, and Lloyds Bank all approached the Governor of the Bank of England, Montagu Norman, to discuss capital issuances. The governor replied to National Provincial that they 'must abandon the idea'. Norman argued that if '£5/6 million were needed for one bank, the total for all banks might be £40 million or £50 million', adding that 'it seems impossible that a proposal of this kind could be allowed for a single bank'.[75] The argument that the capital issuance of one bank would trigger the other banks to recapitalise was frequently used in

---

[73] *Clearing Banks – Capital Increases, Internal Note*, Banking and Banking Practice: Clearing Bank Capital (London, 5 November 1959), Bank of England Archive, C40/102. In order to maintain the demand and supply for government debt, the goal was to keep interest rates stable. On the monetary policy, see, for example, D. C. Rowan, 'The Monetary System in the Fifties and Sixties', *The Manchester School of Economic & Social Studies*, 41.1 (1973), 19–42.

[74] Charles Lidbury, 'Internal Note', 1934, Archive of the Royal Bank of Scotland, Edinburgh, WES/1174/206.

[75] *Clearing Banks' Capital*, Banking and Banking Practice: Clearing Bank Capital (London, 6 February 1959), Bank of England Archive, C40/102.

later years. It was always presented along with a brief calculation showing the total amount of capital that would be tied up by all the banks if they were to capitalise. The BoE would not have allowed such resources to be withdrawn.

Further attempts to raise capital and reorganise their capital structure were made after the war by the National Provincial (1946), District Bank (1946, 1949), Barclays (1948, 1949, 1953), Martins Bank (1953), and Midland (1958). The banks usually argued that capital was needed to protect depositors. In order to demonstrate the need for additional capital, they compared their capital with the fixed assets (premises, investments in subsidiaries and associated companies) they held. A frequently made argument with which the BoE did agree was that fixed assets should not exceed the capital.[76] The difference between capital and fixed assets was later known as 'free resources'. The ratio between 'free resources' and deposits was called the 'free resources ratio'. Thus, a new ratio emerged from the supervisory practice of the 1950s. The previously used capital/deposits ratio had lost importance in discussions between the BoE and the banks.

According to the BoE, issuing new capital in the post-war period 'was completely out of the question under existing conditions'.[77] 'Existing conditions' referred to the credit squeeze of the 1950s. In the view of the BoE, capital should be used for the 'productive' industry.[78] Moreover, the BoE considered liquidity to be much more important than capital from a depositor's point of view.[79] The bank also noted that depositors did not seem to worry about low capital/deposits ratios:

It cannot be said that depositors really look on the share Capital of the Clearing Banks as providing any significant protection for their deposits. The experience of the last few years, when depreciation of banks' investments made heavy inroads on shareholders' capital, underlines this; and if the safety of deposits were ever in doubt, it is, in any case, to liquidity that the depositors should rather look.[80]

Despite postponing new capital issuances by the banks, the BoE was not completely ignorant of the importance of capital. In 1946, the bank told the Committee of London Clearing Bankers that they should be prepared to raise

---

[76] See, for example, *Letter from Barclays Chairman to Governor of the Bank of England*, Banking and Banking Practice: Clearing Bank Capital (London, 12 February 1959), Bank of England Archive, C40/102; *Martins Bank*, Banking and Banking Practice: Clearing Bank Capital (London, 5 December 1958), Bank of England Archive, C40/102; *Lloyds Bank Limited*, Banking and Banking Practice: Clearing Bank Capital (London, 18 April 1962), Bank of England Archive, C40/102.

[77] *Clearing Banks' Capital.*

[78] *Clearing Banks – Capital Increases, Internal Note.*

[79] *Barclays Bank Capital*, Banking and Banking Practice: Clearing Bank Capital (London, 10 April 1958), Bank of England Archive, C40/102.

[80] *London Clearing Banks' Capital, Internal Note*, Banking and Banking Practice: Clearing Bank Capital (London, 8 October 1958), Bank of England Archive, C40/102.

capital once the time was right.[81] The time for capital issuances came in 1958, when all of the Big Five were finally allowed to raise capital.[82] As a result, the average capital/assets ratio grew from 2.6% in 1957 to 3.2% in 1959.

The BoE also discussed the importance and role of capital internally. It was clear that priority was given to liquidity ratios. On the issue of solvency, however, there was a range of opinions. In 1958, the bank's Chief Cashier surmised that 'even in the Bank of England we are beginning to believe that Capital plays little or no part in a soundly based banking structure'.[83] At the same time, internal reports at the bank discussed that long-run targets for capital/deposits ratios should be between 5% and 7%.[84] However, such deliberations never materialised as formal or informal minimum capital standards. Instead, the British system continued on a path of informal supervision with a clear focus on liquidity.

4.3   SWITZERLAND: THE DEMISE OF GUIDELINES – AND THE RISE OF RULES

In contrast to the British banking market, in Switzerland capital adequacy was a relevant topic during and after both World Wars. After the First World War, Swiss banks aimed to restore previous capital ratios and return to the old capital policy conventions. However, banks' total assets did not contract, even though many contemporaries had expected it, as deposits continued to grow. The situation after the Second World War was different. Informal conventions that guided capital policies were no longer present, as the crisis of the 1930s triggered the introduction of minimum capital ratios. With that, the focus was on maintaining statutory capital requirements, and self-reflections of banks on what was an adequate capital for them disappeared from the public discourse.

4.3.1   After the First World War: Back to Normal?

Towards the end of the First World War, there was a widespread sentiment in Switzerland that economic conditions – and, with that, banks' balance sheets – would return to pre-war conditions once the war was over. By 1918, the SNB expected that deposits would contract and that 'the [capital/liability] ratios should, therefore, perhaps improve again by themselves over time'.[85]

---

[81] *Barclays Bank Capital. Committee of the London Clearing Bankers Minute Book 1946–1954*, British Bankers' Association (London, 7 November 1946), London Metropolitan Archives, CLC/B/029/MS32006/009.

[82] *Clearing Banks – Capital Increases, Internal Note.*

[83] *London Clearing Banks' Capital, Internal Note by the Chief Cashier*, Banking and Banking Practice: Clearing Bank Capital (London, 13 October 1958), Bank of England Archive, C40/102.

[84] *London Clearing Banks' Capital, BOEA, C40/102; Internal Note by the Chief Cashier – Secret*, Banking and Banking Practice: Clearing Bank Capital (London, 21 March 1961), Bank of England Archive, C40/102.

[85] Swiss National Bank, 'Das Schweizerische Bankwesen 1917', p. 8.

Contemporaries took a similar perspective and referred to the abnormally inflated balance sheets of banks as a result of the war economy.[86] And two of the big banks – Credit Suisse and the Swiss Bank Corporation – commented in their annual reports of 1917 that their large total assets and deposits were only a temporary phenomenon and would soon be shrinking again.[87]

Once the war was over, it became clear that macroeconomic conditions would not normalise immediately. The post-war economic depression reached its high point in Switzerland in 1922 with high deflation and high unemployment rates. Moreover, asset prices had been falling and capital markets were not able to absorb large capital issuances at the time, which restricted Swiss banks' capacity to refinance through capital issuances.[88]

At the international level, the monetary disorders after the war had consequences for the Swiss financial centre, leading to large-scale foreign capital inflows in Switzerland. Against expectations and the adverse domestic economic development, the balance sheet totals and deposits of Swiss banks did not contract after the First World War. Total assets grew by 6.6% between 1918 and 1922 (1.6% p.a.). Deposits even increased by 15.6% (3.4% p.a.). This growth reinforced the belief among the Swiss banking sector that capital issuances could not be postponed any further, given 'the unfavourable capital/ liability ratio', as concluded by the SNB.[89] Moreover, the SNB noted that 'the uncertain outcome of the current depression and the need to counter it as a precaution really cannot be stressed enough'.[90]

The Swiss banks started issuing capital once they realised that their balance sheets would not contract but grow due to foreign capital inflows.[91] Between 1918 and 1922, Swiss banks increased their paid-up capital substantially, by CHF 389.3 m (+20%). The capital was increased despite difficult economic conditions, and even though distressed prices at capital markets led to very low share premia. In addition to the nominal capital raised, only CHF 13.3m could be added to the reserves as premia.[92]

---

[86] Werner Hügi, *Ökonomische Eigenarten im schweizerischen Bankgewerbe* (Bern: P. Haupt, 1927), p. 85.

[87] Kurz, *Die schweizerischen Grossbanken*, p. 25. Schweizerischer Bankverein, *Jahresbericht Schweizerischer Bankverein 1918* (Basel, 1919), p. 26.

[88] Husy, *Die eigenen Mittel*, p. 57.

[89] Swiss National Bank, 'Das Schweizerische Bankwesen 1920' (Art. Institut Orell Füssli, Zurich, 1921), p. 15.

[90] Swiss National Bank, 'Das Schweizerische Bankwesen 1920', p. 15.

[91] Jöhr, *Schweizerische Kreditanstalt*, p. 279. Linder, *Die schweizerischen Grossbanken*, p. 203. Herbert Raff, *Schweizerische Bankgesellschaft: 1862, 1912, 1962* (Zurich: Schweizerische Bankgesellschaft, 1962), p. 96.

[92] Author's calculations. Data: Swiss National Bank, 'Das Schweizerische Bankwesen 1918', p. 34; Swiss National Bank, 'Das Schweizerische Bankwesen 1919' (Bern: Buchdruckerei Stämpfli & Cie, 1921), p. 40; Swiss National Bank, 'Das Schweizerische Bankwesen 1920', p. 87; Swiss National Bank, 'Das Schweizerische Bankwesen 1921' (Art. Institut Orell Füssli, Zurich, 1923), p. 69; Swiss National Bank, 'Das Schweizerische Bankwesen 1922' (Art. Institut Orell Füssli, Zurich, 1924), p. 65.

Even though capital increases after the First World War were substantial in absolute terms, they had little impact on capital/assets ratios. The average capital/assets ratio of all Swiss banks grew from 13.1% in 1918 to 13.6% in 1922. For the big banks, the impact was more substantial. Their ratio increased from 14.8% to 17.5%. However, it was only a short-term recovery. The rapid growth of deposits as a key component of liabilities also continued in later years. From 1922 to 1929, the deposits of Swiss banks grew on average by 6.6% per year. The deposits of the big banks even increased by an average of 10.5% p.a. Foreign capital inflows were a substantial driver of this growth.

There are no exact figures for the volume of foreign deposits transferred to Switzerland during and after the First World War. Contemporaries estimated that about half of the deposits flowing to the Swiss banks in 1929 were transferred from abroad (about CHF 440m).[93] Gottlieb Bachmann, Head of Department I of the SNB from 1925 to 1939, estimated the total volume of foreign funds by the end of 1929 to be between CHF 1-1.3bn.[94] Domestic and foreign deposits in Swiss banks reached a volume of CHF 9.4bn in 1929.[95] Foreign capital inflows led to a further increase in the total assets, which in turn contributed to the deterioration of the capital/assets ratio. In 1929, the capital/assets ratio of all Swiss banks was 12.1%, while the ratio of the big banks fell to 14.0%.

Compared to the period before the First World War, these ratios were substantially lower. The perception of 'adequate capital' had changed substantially. Before the war, a capital/liability ratio of about 30% (c/a ratio = 23%) was considered adequate for the big banks.[96] After the First World War, contemporaries viewed a capital/liability ratio of about 20% as

---

[93] Rudolf Erb, *Die Stellungnahme der schweizerischen Grossbanken zu den bank- und währungspolitischen Problemen der Kriegs- und Nachkriegszeit* (Zurich: A.-G. Gebr. Leemann & Co, 1931), p. 15.

[94] Bernard Worner, *La Suisse, centre financier européen* (Argenton: Impr. de Langlois, 1931), p. 101. For an overview of sources discussing foreign capital inflows during and after the First World War, as well as the foreign investments of the Swiss banks, see Mazbouri, Guex, and Lopez, *Finanzplatz Schweiz*, pp. 484-6, and Yves Sancey, *Quand les banquiers font la loi: Aux sources de l'autorégulation bancaire en Suisse et en Angleterre, de 1914 aux années 1950*, Histoire et société contemporaines (Lausanne: Ed. Antipodes, 2015), pp. 371-410. For estimates about tax flight from Germany after the First World War, see Christophe Farquet, 'Quantification and Revolution: An Investigation of German Capital Flight after the First World War', *EHES Working Paper*, 2019.

[95] Switzerland was also the fourth largest creditor behind the United Kingdom, France, and the Netherlands in the period from 1924 to 1930. Katherine Watson and Charles H. Feinstein, 'Private International Capital Flows in Europe in the Inter-War', in *Banking, Currency, and Finance in Europe Between the Wars*, ed. Charles H. Feinstein (Oxford: Oxford University Press, 1995), pp. 94-130 (p. 116).

[96] Swiss National Bank, 'Das Schweizerische Bankwesen 1920', p. 32.

the new standard for the big banks.[97] The standard ratio for banks focusing on savings and mortgages was in between 9% and 10%.[98] The SNB was not worried about these new conventions, highlighting that the reserves had increased substantially since the end of the war and that the Swiss banks held more liquid assets, which would require less capital.[99]

4.3.2 The Importance of Formal Capital Requirements

The early 1950s mark the end of two conventions that had directed the capital policies of Swiss banks for a long time. Firstly, the group of the big banks no longer had the highest capital ratio of all the banking groups in Switzerland.[100] Traditionally, the argument had been that the big banks conducted comparatively (to other banks) riskier business and therefore required more capital. However, with high shares of government papers in their balance sheets and sharply increasing amounts of deposits during and after the war, the business model of the big banks had changed. Moreover, the importance of direct industrial investments decreased. Secondly, and certainly related to that, the rules of thumb that had been used as a reference for capital adequacy were abandoned. Before the First World War, the big banks had frequently issued new capital in order to maintain a certain capital ratio. After the First World War, a capital/liability ratio of about 20% for big banks was accepted by the SNB. In 1945, the capital/assets ratio of the big banks was 11.0%; it had dropped by 4.4pp during the war. The combined capital/assets ratio of all banks stood at 10.5%.

After the Second World War, the idea of returning to pre-war capital levels did not exist. In contrast to the aftermath of the First World War, the economic conditions were fundamentally different. Switzerland was in an economic upswing and the balance sheets of the Swiss banks grew rapidly. Between 1945 and 1950, the average annual growth rate of the balance sheet totals was 5.5%, while the economy grew on average by 8.0% p.a.[101] Despite these economically favourable conditions, there were very few capital issuances in the post-war years. Between 1945 and 1950, Swiss banks issued new nominal

[97] Erb, *Stellungnahme der schweizerischen Grossbanken*, p. 79; Schweizerische Volksbank, *Denkschrift der Schweizerischen Volksbank zur Feier ihres 50jährigen Bestandes – 1869–1919* (Bern, 1919), p. 59.

[98] Ernst Wetter, *Bankkrisen und Bankkatastrophen der letzten Jahre in der Schweiz* (Zurich: Orell Füssli, 1918), p. 207. Such capital levels were also considered as adequate for German mortgage banks. See von Bissing Wolfgang Moritz Freiherr, 'Die Schrumpfung des Kapitals und seine Surrogate', in *Untersuchung des Bankwesens 1933 I. Teil*, ed. Untersuchungsausschuß für das Bankwesen 1933 (Berlin: Heymanns, 1933), p. 77.

[99] Swiss National Bank, 'Das Schweizerische Bankwesen 1920', p. 32.

[100] Swiss National Bank, 'Das Schweizerische Bankwesen 1951' (Zurich: Orell Füssli, 1952), p. 17.

[101] Data on GDP growth: HSSO, *Historische Statistik der Schweiz Online*, Tab. Q.6a.; HSSO, *Historische Statistik der Schweiz Online*, Tab. Q.16a.

capital of only about CHF 110m (7% of the paid-up capital). The two largest big banks at the time – the Swiss Bank Corporation and Credit Suisse – did not increase their nominal capital in the years after the war at all.[102] Why did banks not consider a return to pre-war capital levels?

Firstly, the legacy of the Great Depression still influenced the post-war banking structure. The Second World War brought the period of restructuring and consolidation among the big banks to a halt. This process, which also affected the capital structure of the banks, had been triggered by the Great Depression. Once the war was over, one of the first items on the agenda of the banks was to deal with the legacies of the 1930s.

The Swiss Volksbank had to be rescued by the federal government in 1933.[103] The government held 50% of the Volksbank's capital. Not long into the war, however, the bank considered its capital to be too high and aimed to pay back the government's capital. However, the Volksbank postponed the transaction until after the war.[104] The Volksbank's primary goal after the war was to become independent again and to start reducing the Swiss government's capital share, which happened between 1947 and 1949.[105] By 1945, the bank's capital/assets ratio was 10.5%. In 1950, the ratio was 7.6%.[106] Being the outcome of a long-planned capital reorganisation, it can be assumed that the management of Volksbank perceived a capital/assets ratio of roughly 7% to 8% as adequate.

Another bank from the group of big banks, Bank Leu & Co., had to be restructured in 1936 and again after the war. The bank reduced its capital and re-issued new shares in 1945. The increase of the capital was related to the write-down of foreign investments made before the war. Two other banks, the Basler Handelsbank and the Eidgenössische Bank, were also heavily invested in German loans and securities during the 1930s and never fully recovered from their losses. The Basler Handelsbank was taken over by the Swiss Bank Corporation in 1945.[107] The Eidgenössische Bank was taken over by the Union Bank of Switzerland (UBS) in the same year. UBS increased its nominal capital for that purpose by CHF 10m to CHF 50m.[108] Nevertheless, the capital/

---

[102] Swiss National Bank, 'Das Schweizerische Bankwesen 1951', p. 17.

[103] Jan Baumann, 'Bundesinterventionen in der Bankenkrise 1931–1937: Eine vergleichende Studie am Beispiel der Schweizerischen Volksbank und der Schweizerischen Diskontbank' (unpublished doctoral dissertation; University of Zurich, 2007).

[104] Ernst Schneider, *Die schweizerischen Grossbanken im zweiten Weltkrieg 1939–1945* (Zurich: Brunner & Bodmer, 1951), p. 101.

[105] Neue Zürcher Zeitung, 'Schweizerische Volksbank, Delegiertenversammlung' (Zurich, 24 February 1947), section Handelsteil, p. 3. The *Neue Zürcher Zeitung* also noted that 'During the uncertain war years, the Volksbank attached great importance to maintaining its comparably high equity capital.'

[106] Author's calculations, based on annual reports.

[107] Schneider, *Die schweizerischen Grossbanken im zweiten Weltkrieg 1939–1945*, p. 103.

[108] Swiss National Bank, 'Das Schweizerische Bankwesen 1945', p. 13.

assets ratio of the Union Bank of Switzerland fell to 7.1% in 1950, and the ratio of the Swiss Bank Corporation to 7.6%.

Another legacy of the Great Depression and the war years was the low dividends for shareholders. Traditionally, Swiss banks aimed for stable dividends. The target dividend was usually met by augmenting or releasing internal or published reserves.[109] A case in point is Credit Suisse, which paid a dividend of 8% from 1895 to 1933.[110] The 'traditional 8%' became a benchmark for the big banks. Besides Credit Suisse, Bank Leu & Co., the Swiss Bank Corporation, the Eidgenössiche Bank, and the Basler Handelsbank all paid a dividend of 8% in 1930. The Union Bank of Switzerland paid 7% and the Swiss Volksbank 5%.[111] The losses of the 1930s forced banks to cut their dividends to between 0% and 5% (1935). A sharp reduction in foreign business in 1939 led banks to lower dividends even further – on average, by another percentage point.[112] It was not until 1952 that Credit Suisse and the Swiss Bank Corporation reached the 8% level again. The Union Bank of Switzerland paid 8% from 1956 onwards, and the Swiss Volksbank paid 8% only after 1960.

Given the low dividends after the war, it seems that the banks either opted in favour of their shareholders' interest or thought that they could not place enough shares in the market given the low dividends. Instead of issuing shares, the banks increased dividends first. This process would have certainly been more difficult, if not impossible, the other way around.

Secondly, hidden reserves reduced the need for immediate capital issuances after the war. While capital ratios might not have been growing, hidden reserves (not represented in public figures) probably were. The extent of the hidden reserves after the war is unknown. It is likely that the Great Depression diminished most of the hidden reserves since only two of the big banks – Credit Suisse and the Swiss Bank Corporation – managed to get through the crisis without being forced to reduce their nominal capital. Many other banks used most of their hidden reserves and large parts of their published reserves.[113] As asset prices increased after the war, hidden reserves started to accumulate substantially.[114] The actual capital rose with the increase of the hidden reserves. This build-up of hidden reserves cannot be detected in published accounts, but it certainly strengthened the solvency of the banks.

---

[109] Linder, *Die schweizerischen Grossbanken*, pp. 132–3. Schneider, *Die schweizerischen Grossbanken im zweiten Weltkrieg 1939–1945*, p. 108.

[110] Jöhr, *Schweizerische Kreditanstalt*, p. 270.

[111] See annual reports for dividend data.

[112] Rudolf Speich, *75 Jahre Schweizerischer Bankverein: 1872–1947. Vergangenheit und Gegenwart: Ansprache* (Basel: Schweizerischer Bankverein, 1947), p. 57; Schneider, *Die schweizerischen Grossbanken im zweiten Weltkrieg 1939–1945*, pp. 258–62.

[113] Husy, *Die eigenen Mittel*, p. 61; Schneider, *Die schweizerischen Grossbanken im zweiten Weltkrieg 1939–1945*, pp. 258–62.

[114] Jöhr, *Schweizerische Kreditanstalt*, p. 476.

Thirdly, new regulation replaced existing conventions on capital ratios. Bank capital was first regulated on a national level in Switzerland in 1934/5 with the Banking Law and the Banking Ordinance. According to the Banking Law, a bank's capital would have to be in an 'appropriate' proportion to its liabilities.[115] The Banking Ordinance further specified minimum capital requirements.[116]

The introduction of written rules certainly contributed to the demise of informal conventions on what amount of capital was perceived as adequate. The optimal amount of capital was discussed at times in the annual reports of banks and regularly in the statistical publications of the SNB. After the 1930s, however, the topic was not covered as frequently anymore. If capital was mentioned in the annual reports of banks or by the SNB, it was only in the form of a short note that the banks met the capital requirements.[117]

Another vital part of the capital legislation was that it allowed lower capital requirements for liabilities invested in mortgages and government debt. This rule shows that the regulators aimed to adjust capital requirements to the credit risk of the assets. The more nuanced view on capital and risk coincided with structural changes in banks' balance sheets at the time. During the war, the share of government debt in balance sheets grew. After the war, the big banks substantially increased their share in short-term loans to companies and later in mortgages. Short-term loans bore less risk than direct holdings of companies. Moreover, holding direct investments in companies had lost importance during the inter-war years.[118] The geographic diversification of loans also increased. Foreign investments had been particularly skewed towards Germany until the 1930s. As for mortgages, these were thought to be of low risk as the land was collateralised.[119] Overall, lower risks through shorter maturities, diversification, and secured assets meant that a bank would require comparably less capital – and both regulators and banks were aware of that.

The SNB also did not seem to be concerned by the falling capital/assets ratio, outlining that the structure of the assets had changed, and the fact that both the liquidity and the capital ratios of the big banks were substantially above the statutory requirements.[120]

---

[115] See Art. 4, *BankG 1934*.

[116] See Art. 12, *Vollziehungsverordnung zum Bundesgesetz über die Banken und Sparkassen vom 26. Februar 1935*, 1935.

[117] See respective annual reports by the Schweizerische Nationalbank SNB, 'Das Schweizerische Bankwesen', various years. In the annual reports of UBS, the Swiss Bank Corporation, and Credit Suisse, capital adequacy was no longer discussed. The banks only mentioned the amount of capital and announced capital increases. Occasionally, banks would refer to the fact that they had met the capital requirements.

[118] For an overview of investments by the big banks in other companies before and after the Second World War, see Linder, *Die schweizerischen Grossbanken*, pp. 101–4; Schneider, *Die schweizerischen Grossbanken im zweiten Weltkrieg 1939–1945*, pp. 179–209.

[119] Jöhr, *Schweizerische Kreditanstalt*, p. 476.

[120] Swiss National Bank, *Das Schweizerische Bankwesen 1951*, p. 17.

4.4   THE UNITED STATES: THE BIRTH OF RISK-WEIGHTED ASSETS

The government debt of the United States grew rapidly in 1917/18, the 1930s, and during the Second World War. The large shares of government debt in the balance sheets of US banks had also changed the practice of assessing capital adequacy by the three federal bank supervisory agencies. A minimum capital/deposits ratio of 10% was the common supervisory practice in the United States until the Second World War. The bank supervisory agencies abandoned the traditional capital/deposits as a result of the fundamental change in the banks' asset structure. A good example is the statement by the FDIC in 1945: 'Enforcement of the traditional 10 per cent overall capital ratio would not be wise at this time because the increase in bank assets over the past few years has occurred largely in the non-risk category.'[121] Capital ratios of US banks had been falling since 1931. In 1941, the average capital/deposit ratio of banks in the United States hit the 10% threshold. The capitalisation of the large New York City banks was even more pronounced. Among seven large New York banks (Bank of New York, Chase, Chemical, City, Hanover, JP Morgan, Manufacturers) four had missed the 10% capital/deposits ratio in 1935. By 1941, the average capital/deposits ratio of these banks stood at 6.8%.

The trend towards lower capital ratios and higher shares of government debt in banks' balance sheets was preceded by an increasingly nuanced view towards risk – or, more specifically, potential losses – in banking and the need for capital to cover such losses. The banking literature had established already in the nineteenth century that capital requirements should relate to a bank's risk. Moreover, it was clear that a uniform capital/deposits ratio of 10% did not reflect the different asset compositions among US banks.[122] The late 1930s and 1940s produced a series of proposals by practitioners and academics for alternatives to the 10% capital/deposits requirement in the United States. Some of these suggestions aimed to modify the existing capital/deposits ratio by deducting risk-free cash from the amount of deposits.[123] Other ideas aimed to introduce additional reserves to strengthen capital through retained profits above a certain return threshold, to be defined for each asset class.[124] The most widespread opinion, however, was clearly that the time had come to change the focus from deposits to assets when determining the required amount of capital.[125]

The transition to risk-based approaches are well documented by the communications of the three federal bank supervisory agencies. By the late 1930s, they had arrived at a system that classified assets of different risk into

---

[121] FDIC, *Annual Report of the Federal Deposit Insurance Corporation 1945*, pp. 8–9.

[122] Robinson, *The Capital-Deposit Ratio in Banking Supervision*, p. 50.

[123] Suggestion made by the chairman of the board of directors of the Bank of Manhattan Company, J. Stewart Baker. See Robinson, *The Capital-Deposit Ratio in Banking Supervision*, p. 53.

[124] J. Harvie Wilkinson, *Investment Policies for Commercial Banks* (New York: Harper, 1938).

[125] Crosse, *Management Policies for Commercial Banks*, pp. 165–73.

four groups. The 1940s and 1950s brought several proposals on how such categories could be related to a sufficient capital. One of them, the Federal Reserve's ABC formula, eventually became one of the conceptual forerunners of the Basel I framework, introduced in the late 1980s.

4.4.1   From Deposits to Assets: A New Supervisory Focus

The FDIC was the last federal bank supervisory agency to highlight the relevance of the 10% capital/deposit ratio in its annual report in 1936. In the same year, the FDIC also stressed that a sufficient capital should have 'due regard for the quality and character of the assets' in 1937.[126] The FDIC repeated the statement regarding the quality of assets in various ways in the following years. In 1938, the FDIC referred for the first time to a capital/liabilities ratio of 10% as a 'working rule', rather than a capital/deposits ratio.[127]

After 1938, the FDIC shifted its focus to the so-called 'quality of assets'. It was the first of the three supervisory agencies to change from deposits to assets. The FDIC provided a nuanced view on sufficient capital by deducting cash and government debt from the banks' total assets when discussing capital adequacy during the 1930s and 1940s. The ratio of capital to these adjusted assets was commonly known as the capital/risk-assets ratio. However, the FDIC was careful not to term this comparison a ratio and hesitant to refer to a specific minimum requirement. The FDIC was concerned that banks could use the new capital ratio as an argument against necessary capital increases.[128] Thus, the term 'risk assets' was publicly avoided until 1945, even though the FDIC considered the riskiness of assets.[129]

The Comptroller of the Currency and the Board of Governors of the Federal Reserve seemed to go through a similar evolution as the FDIC, but adopted the idea of 'risk assets' much quicker. Throughout the Second World War, both agencies had acknowledged the growth of deposits and the change in the asset structure among banks, and had introduced an alternative measure for sufficient capital. The Federal Reserve was the first of the three supervisory agencies to use the term 'risk assets' in its 1943 annual report. It calculated risk assets by deducting cash, reserves, amounts due from banks, and government securities. The FED argued that the capital/risk-assets ratio was higher than it was before the war, and, thus, the banks were well capitalised.[130] The OCC started using the term 'risk assets' publicly in 1944. Similar to the statements by the FED, the OCC referred to the falling capital/deposits ratio and underlined

---

[126] FDIC, 'Annual Report of the Federal Deposit Insurance Corporation 1936', p. 27.

[127] FDIC, 'Annual Report of the Federal Deposit Insurance Corporation 1937', 1938, p. 15.

[128] FDIC, 'Annual Report of the Federal Deposit Insurance Corporation 1942', p. 5.

[129] FDIC, 'Annual Report of the Federal Deposit Insurance Corporation 1945', p. 9.

[130] Federal Reserve, 'Annual Report of the Board of Governors of the Federal Reserve System 1943', 1943, p. 30.

that this picture changes once the risks of the assets are considered. By the end of the Second World War, all three federal agencies used a capital/risk-assets ratio.

Despite developing a new methodology for capital adequacy, the federal agencies were concerned about the evolution of capital in banking given that the war was coming to an end. The OCC stated that 'more capital is one of the primary needs of the banking system' and that it would be necessary to 'protect the further expansion of liabilities and of risk assets which can be foreseen in the postwar period'.[131] Once the war was over, the FED and the OCC urged banks to re-examine their capital situation. It was expected that deposits and holdings of government securities would decline, which would require additional capital.[132]

In reviewing its policy towards capital adequacy, the OCC announced in 1949 that it had placed more emphasis 'on capital in relation to several factors, particularly competence of management, and volume and quality of assets'. As a rule of thumb, the Comptroller used a ratio of 'capital funds to loans and investments other than United States government securities'. The Board of the Federal Reserve, too, referred to a capital/risk-assets ratio when assessing the capital of banks.

4.4.2   Categorising Assets According to Risk

Even though all three agencies used capital/risk-assets ratios from the late 1930s, they did not publicly communicate specific quantitative capital requirements. Initially, the federal bank supervisory agencies considered a minimum capital/risk-assets ratio of 20% as sufficient.[133] After the Second World War, supervisors often used benchmarks for comparing capital ratios of banks. Such benchmarks could consist of certain bank types or banks in a certain region. Banks below such averages would receive more attention from bank examiners.[134] Such an approach is – of course – problematic if the average of the benchmark is constantly falling.

One of the weaknesses of the capital/risk-assets ratio was certainly its inability to account for different degrees of risk: the two categories were either no risk (government securities, cash) or risk (everything else). Bank supervisors and other experts were well aware of this deficiency. By 1945, for example, the FDIC had discussed various factors that should be considered

---

[131] Office of the Comptroller of the Currency, 'Annual Report of the Comptroller of the Currency 1944', 1945, p. 2.

[132] Office of the Comptroller of the Currency, 'Annual Report of the Comptroller of the Currency 1945', 1946, p. 2; Federal Reserve, 'Annual Report of the Board of Governors of the Federal Reserve System 1946', 1946, p. 49.

[133] Crosse, *Management Policies for Commercial Banks*, p. 164.

[134] Harris, *The Capital Structure in American Banking*, p. 242. Barron H. Putnam, 'Early Warning Systems and Financial Analysis in Bank Monitoring', *Economic Review*, Federal Reserve Bank of Atlanta, 54.11 (1983), 6–12 (p. 8).

when assessing capital adequacy, most notably the types of assets and their expected losses. But the FDIC noted that 'it has not been found practicable to devise a formula which would take into account all these factors'.[135] Yet such a formula emerged in the following years.

In supervisory practice, however, bank examiners had already developed more sophisticated approaches to assess asset quality. Moreover, federal and state banking supervisors held various conferences between 1934 and 1938 – often at the request of the Secretary of the Treasury – aiming to create uniform standards for banking supervision. Two vital subjects were the definition of capital and the valuation and classification of assets. Already early on in 1934, the supervisors agreed on a concept for classifying loans into four different risk categories.[136] The guidelines for loans were further developed and extended to securities in 1938, and led to a joint statement by the Secretary of the Treasury, the FED, the FDIC, and the OCC. The agreement defined four different securities groups:[137] Group I was dedicated to 'obligations in which the investment characteristics are not distinctly or predominantly speculative'. Obligations with 'distinctly or predominantly speculative characteristics' were assigned to Group II. Group III covered obligations in default and group IV concerned stocks.

Beyond the different risk groups, the 1938 joint agreement also defined how the securities were to be valued by bank examiners. One key issue at the time was that fluctuating bond prices would have a negative impact on the so-called 'net sound capital' ratio of a bank if such bonds were valued at market prices. Before 1938, the net sound capital was usually calculated by deducting the difference between the value of a security in the bank's book from the market price. This approach led to a high volatility in the capital ratios of banks, which bank supervisors at the time wanted to avoid. The problem was solved by allowing banks to value group I securities (government securities or obligations with high ratings) at book value or at cost, as they were not purchased for speculative reasons. For Group II, an 18-month average of the market price was used. Only securities in Groups III and IV were valued at market prices.[138]

The evolution of new measurements for capital adequacy was also accompanied by various publications of academics. One of the leading voices in academia on capital in banking was Roland Robinson, professor of finance at Northwestern University and president of the American Finance Association in 1953. In 1941, Robinson reviewed the evolution of the capital/deposit ratio as a supervisory requirement in an article in the *Journal of Political Economy*. His article provided several suggestions and became a reference for many later

---

[135] FDIC, 'Annual Report of the Federal Deposit Insurance Corporation 1945', p. 9.
[136] Harris, *The Capital Structure in American Banking*, p. 156 ff.
[137] FDIC, 'Annual Report of the Federal Deposit Insurance Corporation 1938', 1939, pp. 61–78.
[138] FDIC, 'Annual Report of the Federal Deposit Insurance Corporation 1938', pp. 66–7.

publications. Robinson criticised the capital/deposits ratio by referring to the role of capital as a protection against asset losses. The probability of such losses would depend on the quality of assets and have no connection to the deposits. Moreover, Robinson concluded that the risk of assets varies to a great degree, from riskless cash to risky loans, and he argued that capital ratios for a bank mostly active in the money market should be different to those for provincial banks with a high undiversified credit risk to agriculture and industry. Robinson's main contribution was to suggest different capital requirements for each asset category on a bank's balance sheet.[139] The idea, however, must have already circulated earlier: John T. Madden, director of the Institute of International Finance of New York University, went in a similar direction in 1940.[140]

Discussions on how to measure capital adequacy continued into the 1950s. Contributions on the topic usually focused on three questions: (i) should there be one uniform capital/risk-assets ratio for all banks?; (ii) who should determine the risk of an asset (banks independently or supervisors); (iii) what kind of ratios could be used in practice?[141]

In 1952, the Illinois Bankers Association suggested a further developed version of the capital/risk-assets ratio. The proposal was based on a report by Gaylord Freeman, a banker and later chairman of the First National Bank of Chicago. Freeman argued that each bank would have to list all its assets and simulate the crisis of the 1930s. A deviation of the price from the price in the bank's book would then be deducted from the bank's capital. The proposal also came with several categories of assets and their potential losses, based on the experience of the Great Depression. Loans, for example, had a potential loss of 10%, municipal bonds of 20%.[142]

Another suggestion in 1952 was brought forward by the New York FED. It suggested six risk categories for assets. Each category was assigned a certain percentage of required capital. No capital was required for the riskless category I (cash, government securities with a maturity less than five years and other 'secure' assets). Category II required 5% capital, category III 12%, category IV 20%, category V (defaulted bonds, stocks) 50%, and category VI (fixed assets) 100%. Assigning weights to all these categories leads to a required capital,

[139] Robinson, *The Capital-Deposit Ratio in Banking Supervision*, pp. 49, 56.
[140] Institute of International Finance, New York University, 'Problems of Capital-Deposit Ratio', *The Bankers Magazine*, 1940, 537–8.
[141] Tynan Smith and Raymond E. Hengren, 'Bank Capital: The Problem Restated', *Journal of Political Economy*, 55.6 (1947), 553–66; Roland I. Robinson, 'Bank Capital and Dividend Policies', *Harvard Business Review*, 1948, 398–409; Helen J. Mellon Cooke, 'Significance of Bank Capital Ratios', *Journal of Political Economy*, 57.1 (1949), 75–7.
[142] Crosse, *Management Policies for Commercial Banks*, p. 166; Sandra L. Ryon, 'History of Bank Capital Adequacy Analysis', ed. FDIC Division of Economic Research, *FDIC Working Paper*, 1969, pp. 16–19.

which could then be compared to a bank's actual capital. Each bank should hold between 100% and 125% of the required capital.[143]

The most advanced model of the 1950s was developed by the Board of Governors of the Federal Reserve. The 'Form for Analyzing Bank Capital' became known as the ABC formula and was used into the 1970s.[144] Similar to the approach by the New York Federal Reserve Bank, the ABC formula categorised assets into different groups. These groups ranged from cash to high-risk securities. The FED already differentiated between credit risk and market risk, assigning weights to different asset classes for each risk category.[145] The sum of these risk-weighted assets (a term not used at the time), led to the required capital, which could then be compared to the actual capital of a bank.[146] The expected range of that ratio was 80–120%. If a bank fell below the 80% threshold, the Federal Reserve would further examine it. Compared to earlier proposals, the ABC formula featured several novelties: it considered the relationship of assets (correlations) and a potential lack of diversification. The ABC form also assessed the liquidity of a bank and specified higher capital requirements for banks with inflows and outflows of deposits. Additionally, the form considered potential liabilities for a bank active in trust activities.[147]

4.5 CONCLUDING REMARKS

Rapidly growing balance sheets coupled with high inflation rates during the two World Wars led to substantially lower capital ratios. The growing shares of government debt in banks' balance sheets led to a fundamental reassessment of what adequate capital in banking meant. This gave rise to the concept of risk-assets in the United States. Risk-assets were defined as assets minus cash and government securities. A first adjustment of assets by risk (or, to be more specific, no risk or risk) led to a new measurement of capital adequacy: the capital/risk-assets ratio.

The invention of risk-based approaches to capital requirements cannot entirely be attributed to the US bank supervisory agencies. The idea that the amount of capital should relate to risk existed already in the nineteenth century. It was discussed in the literature, and bank managers knew the trade-offs that came with high or low leverages. Moreover, Switzerland's banking legislation of 1934 also provides an example of a first attempt for a simple risk-weighting

---

[143] Crosse, *Management Policies for Commercial Banks*, p. 169; Ryon, *History of Bank Capital Adequacy Analysis*, pp. 22–3.

[144] For an example of the ABC form, see Yair E. Orgler and Benjamin Wolkowitz, *Bank Capital* (New York: Van Nostrand Reinhold, 1976), pp. 86–7.

[145] Orgler and Wolkowitz, *Bank Capital*, pp. 71–2.

[146] The capital was adjusted by classified assets (assets with a high likelihood of loss, as assessed by the bank examiner).

[147] Crosse, *Management Policies for Commercial Banks*, pp. 178–79.

by defining two different asset categories. Nevertheless, three specificities of the US system created a logical avenue for the thought process on capital adequacy: high government debt, the existence of bank supervising agencies, and the frequent public discussion of policies on bank supervision.

The share of government debt in US banks' balance sheets was high. During the Second World War, many banks could no longer meet the 10% capital/deposits ratio. This forced the US supervisory agencies to reconsider their informal guidelines for capital requirements. War financing was prioritised, and bank supervisors suspended the use of capital/deposits ratios. All three federal bank supervisors publicly discussed their (discretionary) policies on capital adequacy publicly. The shift towards new, risk-based approaches is, therefore, well documented.

Government financing was the priority in Switzerland and the United Kingdom too, but bank regulation and supervision differed from the United States. Capital requirements and a bank supervising agency, the Federal Banking Commission, were introduced in Switzerland in 1934. Before 1934, a market-based consensus emerged that a capital/liabilities ratio of about 20% was appropriate. The new banking regulation of 1934 implemented a statutory minimum capital/liabilities ratio. The requirement was too low to impede war-related financing in Switzerland. Moreover, banking regulation was 'light touch', and the newly established Federal Banking Commission was a weak supervisor with unclear competencies.[148] The effect of the statutory capital regulation in Switzerland was that discussions on the riskiness of business models in banking and capital adequacy disappeared from the public discourse. Instead, banks, the supervisor, and the SNB only commented on whether or not banks met the capital requirements. Conventions that had developed informally were replaced by rules written down in exact numbers.

In the United Kingdom, monetary and financial policies were both under the authority of the BoE. The Second World War gave rise to a repressive monetary policy. Moreover, the informal banking supervision of the BoE was oriented towards liquidity targets rather than solvency targets. In the view of the BoE, liquidity ratios ensured that a rapid demand for deposits could be met with the sale of liquid assets and the discounting of securities at the BoE. The Bank was convinced that banking stability was based on liquidity rather than solvency. The historical track record of the 1930s, in which the British system had not experienced a banking crisis, certainly reinforced this view. Capital/assets ratios in the United Kingdom reached a striking low point at the beginning of the 1950s with 2.6%. Feeling uncomfortable with such a low level of capitalisation, banks even asked the BoE before, during, and after the Second World War to raise additional capital. The BoE opposed these attempts until the late 1950s. The restrictive, non-statutory financial policy was subjected to monetary policy.

---

[148] Bernhard Müller, 'Die Entwicklung der Bankenaufsicht in der Schweiz', *Schweizerische Aktiengesellschaft: Zeitschrift für Handels- und Wirtschaftsrecht*, 1 (1977), 1–13.

Similar to the United States, capital requirements for banks in the United Kingdom were rooted in informal guidelines instead of strict rules, providing discretionary power to bank supervisors. However, the United States had several federal and many state banking supervisors – and the United Kingdom had one. Moreover, there was no public discourse on the topic of adequate capital in the United Kingdom. In the United States, bank supervisors publicly commented on their changes in supervisory practices. Besides the fact that financial and monetary policies were more separated in the United States, another reason was probably the structure of the banking market. In the United Kingdom, communicating with only a few banks could be done privately. It was efficient and the likelihood that private information was shared publicly by one of the banks was low. In the United States, it was different. Communicating to thousands of banks privately required much more resources. Moreover, given the large number of entities involved, the chances that information (on capital guidelines, for example) would have become public was very high.

The United Kingdom, the United States and Switzerland left the post–Second World War period on very different tracks. In the United States, a country with a long tradition of informal capital adequacy guidelines in supervision, the methodology for assessing adequate capital was substantially revised during the war. However, the country continued to operate without statutory minimum capital ratios. On the British side, there was an informal system in which the supervisor paid little importance to solvency. In Switzerland, there was a formal system with statutory minimum capital ratios.

5

How Banking Crises Drive Capital Regulation

Changes in banking regulation are often the outcome of financial crises. In the United States, the United Kingdom, and Switzerland, both domestic and international financial instability spurred a series of regulatory reforms in banking during the second half of the twentieth century. Discussions affecting the measurement of capital took place within these countries, and from the 1970s also in international working groups.

In the United Kingdom and the United States, considerations on adequate capital materialised as a result of domestic turbulences. In the United Kingdom, the secondary banking crisis of the 1970s led to a fundamental review of banking regulation. In 1979, statutory banking legislation replaced the previous system based on informal control by the Bank of England. In the United States, the two largest bank failures since the Great Depression in 1973 and 1974 alerted bank supervisors, initiating a shift of their focus on identifying potential 'problem banks'. Financial ratios, such as capital adequacy ratios, received more attention again. In Switzerland, statutory banking legislation and minimum capital ratios had already been introduced much earlier, in 1934, as a result of the Great Depression.

However, the main driver of changes in the banking markets and banking regulation was the globalisation of finance. This increased banking instability, changed the competitive environment of banks, and led to high growth rates among multinational banks. Moreover, global markets triggered the harmonisation of capital adequacy rules through Basel I in 1988. With that, capital adequacy had become one of the key themes in banking regulation.

Figure 5.1 shows the evolution of capital/assets ratios in the United Kingdom, Switzerland, and the United States from 1940 to 1990. The period from the late 1960s was marked by diminishing capital ratios. The capital/assets ratio of US banks shows a steady decline since the 1960s and a rapid deterioration between 1971 and 1973. The Swiss banks' average capital/assets

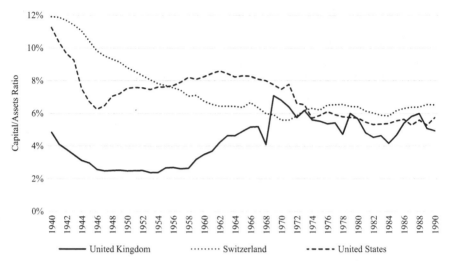

FIGURE 5.1 Capital/assets ratio, United Kingdom, United States, and Switzerland, 1940–90[1]

ratio halved between 1940 and 1970 and then ranged between 6% and 7% until 1990. The aggregated national average, however, conceals the fact that the capital strength of the big banks rapidly deteriorated. British banks' capital/assets ratio fluctuated between 2.4% and 3.0% from 1945 to 1958 and recovered substantially in subsequent years. The sudden increase in capital ratios in 1969 to 7.4% was mostly due to the disclosure of hidden reserves. Not included for British banks is non-paid capital by shareholders, which would increase the 'total capital strength' until the beginning of the 1960s by more than two percentage points.[2]

This chapter focuses on the evolution of capital regulation in the United Kingdom, the United States, and Switzerland up to the 1980s. The financial history literature provides good coverage of the emergence of the Basel Accord in 1988 and the convergence of capital regulation. Perhaps the seminal work in this field is Goodhart's history of the Basel Committee on Banking Supervision (BCBS).[3] Several scholars address the history of the BCBS, placing it into the

---

[1] Data Switzerland: Swiss National Bank, *Historical Time Series*. Data United Kingdom: 1880–1966, all banks: Sheppard, *The Growth and Role of UK Financial Institutions*; 1967–78: Data obtained from individual annual reports of Big Four/Big Five due to lack of data availability in official statistics (official statistics included subordinated debt as capital); 1979–83, clearing banks: Revell, *Costs and Margins in Banking: Statistical Supplement*; 1984–2008, all banks: OECD, *Income Statement and Balance Sheet Statistics*.

[2] See Section 2.5.1.

[3] Charles A. E. Goodhart, *The Basel Committee on Banking Supervision: A History of the Early Years, 1974–1997* (Cambridge: Cambridge University Press, 2011).

broader perspective of regulatory and supervisory evolution, or provide case studies that aid an understanding of the process of financial globalisation and banking supervision.[4] Moreover, several contributions examine the history of the BCBS from political science or international relations perspectives. One of the first to discuss the Basel Accord was Ethan Kapstein, in 1989 and 1994.[5] Many publications that followed used Kapstein's narrative as a starting point. Moreover, a stream of literature covers the evolution of national regulatory frameworks. In contrast to the existing literature, this chapter focuses mostly on the evolution of capital regulation, how and why capital regulation changed over time, and the use of capital ratios in supervisory practice. Before turning to the national narratives, the changing international landscape as well as the emergence of Basel I is discussed.

5.1 THE INTERNATIONAL ENVIRONMENT AND REGULATORY CONVERGENCE

The macroeconomic and financial sphere was redefined with the end of Bretton Woods at the beginning of the 1970s. The European currencies had already returned to convertibility back in 1958. The balance sheets of the major banks in the United Kingdom and Switzerland expanded rapidly from the 1950s onwards and the financial centres in the respective countries gained in importance. New York was the most relevant financial centre. London established itself as a hub for the Eurodollar market towards the end of the

---

[4] See, for example, Piet Clement, 'The Missing Link: International Banking Supervision in the Archives of the BIS', in *State and Financial Systems in Europe and the USA: Historical Perspectives on Regulation and Supervision in the Nineteenth and Twentieth Centuries*, ed. Stefano Battilossi and Jaime Reis (Farnham/Burlington, VT: EABH/Ashgate, 2010), pp. 167–75; Catherine R. Schenk, 'Summer in the City: Banking Failures of 1974 and the Development of International Banking Supervision', *The English Historical Review*, 129.540 (2014), 1129–56; Gianni Toniolo and Eugene N. White, *The Evolution of the Financial Stability Mandate: From Its Origins to the Present Day* (Cambridge, MA: National Bureau of Economic Research, January 2015); Christopher Kobrak and Michael Troege, 'From Basel to Bailouts: Forty Years of International Attempts to Bolster Bank Safety', *Financial History Review*, 22.2 (2015), 133–56; Alexis Drach, 'Liberté surveillée: supervision bancaire et globalisation financière au Comité de Bâle, 1974–1988', Histoire (Rennes: Presses universitaires de Rennes, 2022).

[5] Ethan B. Kapstein, 'Resolving the Regulator's Dilemma: International Coordination of Banking Regulations', *International Organization*, 43.2 (1989), 323; Ethan B. Kapstein, *Governing the Global Economy: International Finance and the State* (Cambridge, MA: Harvard University Press, 1994); Tony Porter, *States, Markets and Regimes in Global Finance*, International Political Economy Series (New York/London: St. Martin's Press/Palgrave Macmillan, 1993); Steven Solomon, *The Confidence Game: How Unelected Central Bankers Are Governing the Changed Global Economy* (New York: Simon & Schuster, 1995); Thomas Oatley and Robert Nabors, 'Redistributive Cooperation: Market Failure, Wealth Transfers, and the Basle Accord', *International Organization*, 1998, 35; Duncan Wood, *Governing Global Banking: The Basel Committee and the Politics of Financial Globalisation*, Global Finance Series (Aldershot: Ashgate, 2005); Tarullo, *Banking on Basel*.

1950s, and the financial hub in Switzerland attracted large-scale capital inflows, of which substantial volumes were invested abroad. In the 1960s, the top three financial centres in terms of global importance were New York, London, and Switzerland.[6]

A series of events between the 1960s and 1980s questioned the stability of the monetary system and, with that, the stability of financial markets. The Euro-currency markets grew rapidly after the late 1950s. The unregulated offshore market for short-term funds in US currency – the Eurodollar market – increasingly undermined the Bretton Woods system of pegged exchange rates and questioned the monetary control of central banks.[7] By 1971, the US government had decided to terminate the convertibility of US dollars to gold, which initiated the transition to a system of flexible exchange rates. The end of Bretton Woods, together with the oil crisis of 1973, led to increasing financial instability, coupled with inflation and diverging interest rates around the world.[8]

The failure of two banks in 1974 triggered the reassessment of risk, regulation, and supervision in banking on an international level. The Franklin National Bank collapsed in May 1974 in the United States. In Germany, the small German Bank Herstatt failed due to speculation on foreign exchange markets.[9] The collapse of Herstatt, in particular, and the disturbances on foreign exchange markets fuelled concern about financial stability and led to the creation of two initiatives to foster international cooperation in the 1970s: the Basel Committee of Banking Supervision at the Bank of International

[6] Youssef Cassis, 'Commercial Banks in the 20th-Century Switzerland', in *The Evolution of Financial Institutions and Markets in Twentieth-Century Europe*, ed. Youssef Cassis, Gerald D. Feldman, and Ulf Olsson (Aldershot: Scolar Press, 1995), pp. 64–77 (p. 71).

[7] On the emergence of the Eurodollar market, see, for example, Catherine R. Schenk, 'The Origins of the Eurodollar Market in London: 1955–1963', *Explorations in Economic History*, 35.2 (1998), 221–38; Stefano Battilossi, 'Introduction: International Banking and the American Challenge in Historical Perspective', in *European Banks and the American Challenge: Competition and Cooperation in International Banking Under Bretton Woods*, ed. Youssef Cassis and Stefano Battilossi (Oxford: Oxford University Press, 2002), pp. 1–36; Ioan Balaban, 'International and Multinational Banking under Bretton Woods (1945–1971): The Experience of Italian Banks' (unpublished thesis, European University Institute, 2021). Ioan Achim Balaban, 'Banking and Eurodollars in Italy in the 1950s', *Enterprise & Society*, 2022, 1–25.

[8] For an overview on Bretton Woods, see, for example: Michael D. Bordo, 'The Bretton Woods International Monetary System: A Historical Overview', in *A Retrospective on the Bretton Woods System*, ed. Michael D. Bordo and Barry Eichengreen (University of Chicago Press, 1993), pp. 3–108; Bordo, *The Bretton Woods International Monetary System*; Barry Eichengreen, *Globalizing Capital: A History of the International Monetary System* (Princeton: Princeton University Press, 1998), pp. 93–128. For an outline of the international environment from the 1950s to the 1980s and the development of international organisations, see also Youssef Cassis, *Crises and Opportunities* (Oxford: Oxford University Press, 2011), pp. 121–30.

[9] On the effects of banking failures – more specifically, those of Herstatt, Lloyds Lugano, and the Israel-British Bank – on the evolution of the financial system see Schenk, *Summer in the City*.

Settlements (BIS) and the Committees of the European Economic Community (EEC).

First to emerge was an ad-hoc working group established in 1969 by supervisors of the EEC member countries to discuss a potential harmonisation of banking legislation. In 1972, the 'Groupe de Contact' became a permanent place for supervisors to discuss various issues that had surfaced in the context of the internationalisation of finance.[10] Among these issues were, for example, common publication standards for banks, cross-border examinations of banks' foreign subsidiaries, the Euro-currency markets, and the measurement of solvency and liquidity in the respective countries.[11] Many of these discussions were taken up by the European Commission, which produced a first Draft Directive for the coordination of banking legislation in 1972. The proposed paper was an all-encompassing framework that would have regulated all credit institutions and managerial competences, as well as solvency and liquidity.[12] However, the far-reaching regulatory ambitions for the Directive were lowered once the United Kingdom joined the EEC in 1972.[13] The European attitude towards regulation was in stark contrast to the discretionary approach in the United Kingdom. Nevertheless, the First Banking Directive by the European Commission, as well as the establishment of official working groups, had pushed the development of concepts to measure capital adequacy forwards.

The EEC members adopted the First Banking Directive in 1977. The key feature of the Directive was that each member state needed to have an authorisation procedure for credit institutions.[14] The capital requirements stated that institutions 'must possess adequate minimum own funds' when applying for authorisation and that a supervisor could withdraw the authorisation if an institution 'no longer possesses sufficient own funds'.[15] Article 6 also stated that domestic authorities should establish liquidity and solvency ratios for monitoring purposes. In order to harmonise solvency and liquidity definitions, a special Advisory Committee should 'decide on the various factors of the observation ratios'.[16]

---

[10] The Groupe consisted of officials from the supervisory authorities of the by then six EEC member countries: Belgium, France, Germany, Italy, Luxembourg, and the Netherlands.

[11] Goodhart, *The Basel Committee on Banking Supervision*, pp. 19–22.

[12] See Capie, *The Bank of England*, p. 600.

[13] Kapstein, *Governing the Global Economy*, p. 134.

[14] Peter W. Cooke, 'Self-Regulation and Statute – the Evolution of Banking Supervision', in *UK Banking Supervision*, ed. Edward P. M. Gardener (London: Allen & Unwin, 1986), pp. 85–98 (p. 89).

[15] Council of the European Communities, *First Council Directive on the Coordination of Laws, Regulations and Administrative Provisions Relating to the Taking up and Pursuit of the Business of Credit Institutions*, 1977, Art. 3 & 8.

[16] Council of the European Communities, *First Council Directive on the Coordination of Laws, Regulations and Administrative Provisions Relating to the Taking up and Pursuit of the Business of Credit Institutions*, Art. 6.

The Advisory Committee did not propose minimum capital requirements, but, rather, four different ratios for observational purposes: a risk-assets ratio (own funds/risk assets), a gearing ratio (own funds/other liabilities), a fixed assets ratio (own funds/fixed assets), and a large exposures ratio (own funds/ total large exposures).[17] The members of the committee defined 'own funds' as paid-up capital, reserves, and provisions that were made for unexpected losses, and therefore had the character of reserves. With regards to subordinated debt, the committee opted for two definitions of 'own funds': one which included and one which excluded subordinated debt. This distinction reflected the diverging views on the definition of capital in the different EEC member countries.

For the 'risk assets ratio', the Advisory Committee defined three categories with which to weight assets. Zero weighting was given to assets guaranteed by institutions of the EEC or guaranteed by an EEC member country and a specific list of countries (referred to as the 'preferential zone').[18] Assets of credit institutions (and assets with guarantees from such institutions) from the preferential zone were assigned a 20% weight. All other assets were weighted with 100% (e.g. domestic credit to the private sector, assets from the non-preferential zone). For loans covered by 'real estate or marketable securities', the national supervisors could make their own weighting decisions.[19] The EEC's framework did not stipulate a minimum capital requirement but presented a reliable framework for assessing capital adequacy.

In 1989, the European Commission adopted the Second Banking Coordination Directive, introducing the Single Banking Licence in Europe.[20] This 'single passport' allowed banks from the EEC member states to establish subsidiaries and provide services throughout EEC countries. More important with regards to capital adequacy were the 'Own Funds Directive' and the 'Solvency Ratio Directive' in 1989.[21] These two directives, however, did not build directly on the proposals by the EEC's own Advisory Committee

---

[17] Commission of the European Communities, Advisory Committee on Banking Coordination, *Notice on the Calculation of Observation Ratios for Assessing Bank Solvency*, Committee of London Clearing Bankers. Capital and Liquidity Adequacy of Banks' (London, 1 May 1980), London Metropolitan Archives, CLC/B/029/MS32152B/004.

[18] The countries were the EEC members and Australia, Austria, Canada, Finland, Iceland, Japan, New Zealand, Norway, Portugal, Spain, Sweden, Switzerland, and the United States. Commission of the European Communities, Advisory Committee on Banking Coordination, *Calculation Observation Ratios*, LMA, CLC/B/029/MS32152B/004, pp. 7–8.

[19] Commission of the European Communities, Advisory Committee on Banking Coordination, *Calculation Observation Ratios*, LMA, CLC/B/029/MS32152B/004, p. 10.

[20] Council of the European Communities, *Second Council Directive 89/646/EEC of 15 December 1989 on the Coordination of Laws, Regulations and Administrative Provisions Relating to the Taking up and Pursuit of the Business of Credit Institutions, 89/646/EE*, 1989.

[21] Council of the European Communities, *Council Directive 89/299/EEC of 17 April 1989 on the Own Funds of Credit Institutions, 89/299/EEC*, 1989; Council of the European Communities, *Council Directive 89/647/EEC of 18 December 1989 on a Solvency Ratio for Credit Institutions, 89/647/EEC*, 1989.

developed in the 1970s. Instead, the EEC mostly translated Basel I into the European legal framework.

At the BIS, the BCBS had started working on capital adequacy shortly after the EEC's Advisory Committee went to work. In September 1974, the central bank governors at the BIS had decided to establish a 'Standing Committee on Banking Regulations and Supervisory Practices', later termed the 'Basel Committee for Banking Supervision'. The aim of the BCBS was to 'intensify the exchange of information between central banks on the activities of banks operating in international markets and, where appropriate, to tighten further the regulations governing foreign exchange positions'.[22] While this statement in the press release was fairly broad, the internal understanding of the BCBS and its goals was much clearer. George Blunden, the first chairman of the BCBS, noted that 'our main objective is to help ensure the solvency and liquidity of banks'.[23]

The BCBS advanced several suggestions that became cornerstones of banking regulation and supervision. It promoted the concept of home country control, which established that every financial institution, including foreign subsidiaries, is supervised by its national supervisor. The first step in this direction was the BCBS's proposal in 1978 to use consolidated balance sheets and income statements in supervisory practice[24] – a topic, incidentally, which had already been being discussed by the EEC's 'Groupe de Contact' since 1972.[25]

The topic of the soundness and safety of the financial system gained further significance with the outbreak of the Latin American Debt crisis in 1982. After banks had increased their lending to developing countries for many years, the crisis led to a reassessment of sovereign risk and, with that, questioned the solvency of both international banks and regional banks that had engaged in syndicated loans.[26] One impulse seemed to be of particular relevance for the later evolution of the Basel Accord. The US Congress debated the increase of the US quota at the International Monetary Fund in 1983. In this context, the US Congress demanded a review of banking regulation and capital requirements for large domestic commercial banks. Moreover, fearing competitive

---

[22] The press communiqué published on 10 September 1974 is cited in Goodhart, *The Basel Committee on Banking Supervision*, p. 39.

[23] See notes for the preparation of the opening remarks for the first BCBS meeting by George Blunden, cited in: Goodhart, *The Basel Committee on Banking Supervision*, p. 45.

[24] The necessity of the principle of home country control was demonstrated by the failure of Banco Ambrosiano in 1982, which had a holding company in Luxembourg and subsidiaries in Italy and Panama. See, for example, Ethan B. Kapstein, 'Architects of Stability? International Cooperation among Financial Supervisors', BIS Working Papers, 2006, p. 7; Charles A. E. Goodhart, 'Financial Supervision from an Historical Perspective: Was the Development of Such Supervision Designed, or Largely Accidental?', in *The Structure of Financial Regulation*, ed. Charles A. E. Goodhart, David G. Mayes, and Geoffrey E. Wood, *Routledge International Studies in Money and Banking* (London: Routledge, 2007), pp. 43–64 (p. 58).

[25] It had already been frequently discussed by the Groupe de Contact. Goodhart, *The Basel Committee on Banking Supervision*, pp. 12–25.

[26] Kapstein, *Governing the Global Economy*, pp. 104–6; Wood, *Governing Global Banking*, p. 72.

disadvantage as compared to foreign banks, the Congress also asked to promote the international convergence of capital requirements.[27] Developing a level playing field was certainly of importance both from the US and the European perspectives. The Japanese banks were traditionally operating with much lower capital ratios than their US-American and most of their European competitors.[28] Moreover, Japanese banks were controlling about one-eighth of all US assets, and the United States and Japan were in a trade conflict.[29]

On the US side, a group of supervisors started to work on a new system to measure capital adequacy.[30] Internationally, Paul Volcker, Chairman of the Federal Reserve, took the matter to the meeting of the governors at the BIS in 1984. Volcker even suggested the introduction of a leverage ratio of 5%, which was rejected by the governors.[31]

Even though this first attempt for an internationally agreed capital requirement failed, the BCBS continued its work on a framework for capital adequacy. One of the key problems was the variety of different national standards and definitions of capital, which made the measuring of capital adequacy across countries more difficult. In 1984, the BCBS started to assess the capital level of large international banks using several definitions for capital.[32] Nevertheless, the issue of fundamental differences in the national regulatory systems remained. In January 1987, the United States and the United Kingdom announced that they had reached an agreement on regulating capital adequacy. The bilateral agreement bypassed the work of the BCBS. It consisted of a common definition of capital, the use of a risk-weighted assets approach, and the inclusion of off-balance-sheet items. Later in the year, the agreement was extended to Japan. Confronted with this fait accompli, the BCBS's negotiations were severely accelerated. In December 1987, the supervisors in the BCBS agreed to a common framework for the measurement and adequacy of capital.[33]

---

[27] Kapstein, *Governing the Global Economy*, pp. 92–95.

[28] Wood, *Governing Global Banking*, p. 77.

[29] Solomon, *Confidence Game*, p. 415.

[30] Supervisors from the Federal Reserve Board in Washington and the Federal Reserve of the Bank of New York were involved in this process. Kapstein, *Governing the Global Economy*, p. 110.

[31] Drach, *Liberté surveillée*, chap. IX.

[32] Goodhart, *The Basel Committee on Banking Supervision*, pp. 151–67; Alexis Drach, 'Liberté surveillée: Supervision bancaire et globalisation financière au Comité de Bâle, 1974–1988' (European University Institute, 2016), pp. 335–41.

[33] The existing literature discusses various reasons that led to the breakthrough in the negotiations. Kapstein established the first narrative by emphasising the leadership of the United States and the United Kingdom, together with the growing recognition for risks in banking (Kapstein, *Resolving the Regulator's Dilemma*; Kapstein, *Governing the Global Economy*). Oatley and Narbors highlight the role of competition and the interest of the United States on a level playing field (Oatley and Narbors, *Redistributive Cooperation*). Drach provides a more differentiated view, incorporating several European countries and showing that Basel I was not simply the result of pressure by the United States and the United Kingdom, but resulted also from a desire for regulatory convergence on a European level, as well as the aim of most European countries to strengthen the capital position of their banks (Drach, *Supervision bancaire et globalisation financière*).

The central bank governors at the BIS adopted the Basel Accord in 1988. The Accord defined capital, set weights for calculating risk-weighted assets, and introduced a capital requirement. The capital requirements specifically addressed credit risks and left the regulation of other risk types to national authorities.[34] The agreement differentiated between core capital (Tier 1) and supplementary capital (Tier 2). The former consisted of paid-up equity capital and disclosed reserves, whereas the latter included hidden reserves, revaluation reserves, general provisions, hybrid debt capital instruments, and subordinated debt. At least 50% of the required capital had to be Tier 1 capital.[35]

The two-tier structure of capital was a compromise between the varying national traditions. The British perceived subordinated debt as comparable to equity capital. In the United States, banking supervisory agencies had varying opinions on the use of subordinated debt for capital requirements. In Switzerland, hidden reserves had been used as part of the required capital since 1961. The Basel Accord also set five risk classes for on- and off-balance sheet items, which allowed for the calculation of risk-weighted assets. Tier 1 and Tier 2 capital would have to be at least 8% of the risk-weighted assets.

The 8% capital ratio was based on a compromise, too. Goodhart argues that the 8% 'emerged naturally', as analyses had shown that the ratios of most banks already ranged in the area of 7–10%.[36] Drach highlights that the BCBS had already been running analyses and solvency calculations since 1984. Suggestions in 1985 and 1987 targeted 10% and 9% as a total capital ratio (Tier 1 and 2 capital). According to the BCBS analyses, Banks in France and Japan were undercapitalised compared to the discussed capital requirements. For the United Kingdom and the United States, the inclusion of subordinated debt was crucial to meet the requirements. The Swiss banks were comparably well capitalised, and meeting the standards did not seem to be an issue.[37]

The BCBS was clearly not where the idea of risk-weighted assets as a tool to assess capital adequacy originated. Goodhart points out that several individuals were a member of two or even three of the committees working on capital adequacy at the same time (the unofficial Groupe de Contact, the official Advisory Committee by the EEC, and the BCBS).[38] Thus, much of the knowledge on bank capital that was further developed by the BCBS was rooted in the work at the domestic and European levels.

[34] Basel Committee on Banking Supervision, *Basel I*, p. 2.
[35] Basel Committee on Banking Supervision, *Basel I*, pp. 3–7.
[36] Goodhart, *The Basel Committee on Banking Supervision*, p. 178.
[37] Drach, *Supervision bancaire et globalisation financière*, pp. 335–42.
[38] Goodhart, *The Basel Committee on Banking Supervision*, p. 24.

5.2 FROM INFORMAL TO FORMAL: THE REGULATION AND SUPERVISION OF BANKING AND CAPITAL IN THE UNITED KINGDOM

Britain's approach towards banking regulation and supervision was different to that in Switzerland and most other continental European countries. On the regulatory side, there was no legislation regulating the financial system and its players. Instead, several Acts evolved after the 1940s that affected specific areas of the financial system. This fragmented regulatory system was, to some extent, reunified by the Banking Act of 1979.[39] On the supervisory side, banking supervision was conducted by the Bank of England without a legal mandate.[40]

In the 1960s and 1970s, the evolution of the domestic and international financial environment charged the British regulatory and supervisory system with tension. The emergence of the Eurodollar markets from the 1950s led to the rebirth of the City of London as an international financial centre.[41] On a domestic level, there were mergers again for the first time in four decades, a wholesale market for the borrowing and lending of large deposits between financial institutions developed, and, with that, the secondary banks emerged. Moreover, politically there was a desire for more competition within the financial system.

It was a crisis that brought the various evolutions to a halt. The secondary banking crisis in 1973/4 paved the way towards a reconsideration of both regulation and supervision. This triggered a review of the financial system (the Wilson Committee) and also a series of joint working papers by the Bank of England and the clearing banks on supervision, capital adequacy, and liquidity.

What were the consequences of these developments for the regulation of capital? The impact was small: the Banking Acts of 1979 and 1987 stated that the capital should be 'appropriate'. Determining capital adequacy was left to the Bank of England, which was already the case before and after the introduction of the Banking Acts. Nonetheless, relevant changes took place from the 1960s to the 1980s. A framework on how to measure capital emerged in the form of a risk-adjusted model. This framework was the result of discussions between the BoE and the clearing banks. The guiding ratio used to assess solvency in supervisory practice changed from the 'free resources ratio' to the 'risk assets ratio'. Another driving factor was the trend towards the harmonisation of capital and liquidity requirements on the European and the international levels. The following sections trace the evolution of capital regulation and the role of supervision in the United Kingdom.

---

[39] *Banking Act 1979*, C. 37, 1979.
[40] On the Bank of England and banking supervision, see Harold James, *Making a Modern Central Bank: The Bank of England 1979–2003*, Studies in Macroeconomic History (Cambridge: Cambridge University Press, 2020), chap.
[41] Cassis, *Capitals of Capital*, pp. 223–5.

5.2.1 The Irrelevance of Capital: 1945 to 1973

From the 1920s to the 1970s, capital in banking was an issue of only secondary importance in the United Kingdom. In 1918, the topic received significant public exposure for the last time. Discussions surrounding the amalgamation movement increased public attention and created political pressure. The banks raised fresh capital after the First World War. During the inter-war period, the question of capital adequacy was of little importance, most likely because the British banking system went through this period without entering a crisis. The stability of the banking sector was never publicly questioned.[42] Moreover, it was often believed that this stability was rooted in high liquidity requirements.

The irrelevance of capital was emphasised by the reports of several parliamentary committees. In 1929, the Committee on Finance and Industry, known as the Macmillan Committee, investigated the reasons for the depressed British economy.[43] The committee also analysed joint-stock banks. Even though the liability side of the banks' balance sheets was discussed, equity capital as a source of funding that influences the structure of the asset side was disregarded.[44] The final recommendations concerning joint-stock banks focused entirely on liquidity ratios and the control of credit supply by the BoE's policy on reserve ratios.[45]

Another committee was appointed in 1957 to investigate Britain's monetary policy during the 1950s.[46] The Radcliffe Committee discussed the background of the monetary policy, the work and organisation of the BoE, as well as the role of the banks in the economy. In the context of banking, the committee analysed the macroeconomic importance of deposits, advances, and overdrafts. The topic of capital in banking was – once again – neglected. Discussing liquidity, the committee concluded that the 30% liquidity ratio that was followed by the banks in the 1950s was probably too high.[47]

---

[42] Malcolm George Wilcox, 'Capital in Banking: An Historical Survey', in *UK Banking Supervision*, ed. Edward P. M. Gardener, Reprint of an Article in the Journal of the Institute of Bankers, June 1979 (London: Allen & Unwin, 1986), pp. 205–17 (p. 210).

[43] Committee on Finance and Industry (Macmillan Committee), 'Committee on Finance and Industry (Macmillan Committee): Report of Committee', 1931, The National Archives, T 200/7.

[44] Committee on Finance and Industry (Macmillan Committee), *Committee on Finance and Industry, BNA, T200/7*, p. 37.

[45] Committee on Finance and Industry (Macmillan Committee), *Committee on Finance and Industry, BNA, T200/7*, pp. 33ff, 152ff.

[46] Committee on the Working of the Monetary System (Radcliffe Committee), *Committee on the Working of the Monetary System: Report of Committee* (London: Her Majesty's Stationary Office, 1960).

[47] The liquid assets consisted of cash, call money, and bills and were measured as a percentage of the deposits; 8% of customers' deposits were held as deposits at the Bank of England. Cash in tills and vaults was also considered as 'cash'. Another 6.5–9% was usually at call at the discount market. The rest was usually held as bills, a small portion in commercial bills. and a larger amount in government bills. Committee on the Working of the Monetary System (Radcliffe Committee), *Committee on the Working of the Monetary System: Report of Committee*, para. 147.

Capital in banking did not even become a pressing topic once British banks' capital/assets ratio hit a historical low point of 2.4% in 1953. The background for this drop in the capital levels was the interest rate hikes of the 1950s. From 1932 to 1950, the Bank Rate had been at 2%. The interest rate was raised to 7% in 1957, putting pressure on market prices for government securities. Government papers still contributed about half of the total assets on the banks' balance sheets at the time, so the falling market prices translated into heavy losses for banks. Moreover, the ability of the banks to build up reserves through retained profits was severely restricted. The earnings of the banks on advances were low due to the BoE's credit control.[48] As previously shown, the banks wanted to increase their capital at the time. The BoE – prioritising monetary policy – declined these requests until 1958.[49]

Figure 5.2 shows British banks' capital/assets ratio from 1940 to 1990. The impact of the capital issuances after 1958 was substantial. The capital assets/ratios almost doubled between 1957 and 1965, to 5%. Figure 5.3 displays the capital structure of the Big Five banks from 1940 to 1973, illustrating the build-up of the nominal capital over time. The jump in the capital/assets ratio in 1969 was due to the legal disclosure of hidden reserves. A closer look at the balance

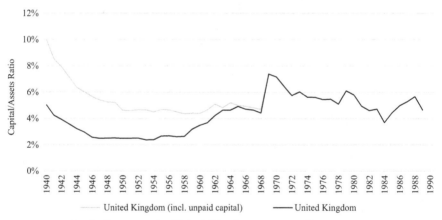

FIGURE 5.2 Capital/assets ratio, United Kingdom, 1940–90[50]

---

[48] Wilcox, *Capital in Banking: An Historical Survey*, p. 211. For an overview on profitability in banking, see also Capie and Billings, *Profitability in English Banking*.

[49] On monetary policy and more narrowly exchange rate policy, see Alain Naef, *An Exchange Rate History of the United Kingdom: 1945–1992*, Studies in Macroeconomic History (Cambridge: Cambridge University Press, 2022).

[50] Data United Kingdom: 1880–1966, Sheppard, *The Growth and Role of UK Financial Institutions.*; 1967–78: Data obtained from individual annual reports of Big Four/Big Five due to lack of data availability in official statistics; 1979–83, clearing banks: Revell, *Costs and Margins in Banking: Statistical Supplement*; 1984–2008, all banks: OECD, *Income Statement and Balance Sheet Statistics*.

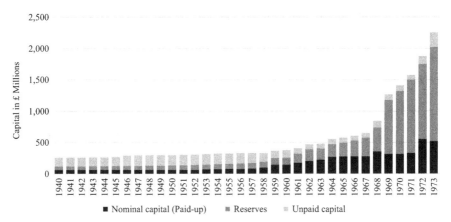

FIGURE 5.3 Paid-up capital, reserves and unpaid capital in £ millions, Big Five banks, 1940–73[51]

sheets of the Big Five reveals that the total reserves grew by £480m in 1969, which was equivalent to almost 3% of the banks' total balance sheets. The increase in public reserves can be attributed almost exclusively to hidden reserves, as shown by the archival research of Billings and Capie.[52]

Until 1979, the BoE maintained its traditional role as an informal banking supervisor. Technically, the Bank of England Act of 1946, which nationalised the BoE, gave it the power to issue directives to banks.[53] This measure, however, was never used.[54] The regulation of financial institutions was based on a mixture of statutory and non-statutory regulations. The BoE distinguished between two types of non-statutory regulation. Self-regulation was based on following commonly accepted guidelines set up by institutions or a group of institutions. The other form of non-statutory regulation was the exercise of authority over financial institutions – a role which was derived from its role and responsibilities as a central bank.[55]

A system often referred to as the 'ladder of recognition' emerged on the statutory side. The status of a bank depended on the level of recognition it received. The BoE viewed the various recognitions as a 'status ladder' via which banks could 'progress as their reputation and expertise developed'.[56] Climbing the ladder of recognition and becoming a fully authorised bank of the highest

---

[51] Author's calculations. Data obtained from individual balance sheets of Barclays, Lloyds, Midland, National Provincial, and Westminster.

[52] Billings and Capie, *Capital in British Banking*.

[53] *Bank of England Act 1946*, 9 & 10 Geo 6, para. 4 (3).

[54] Blunden, 'The Supervision of the UK Banking System'.

[55] Cooke, *Self-Regulation and Statute – the Evolution of Banking Supervision*, p. 90.

[56] Bank of England, 'Supervision of Banks and Other Deposit-Taking Institutions', *Quarterly Bulletin*, Q2 (1978), p. 383.

standing took eight to fifteen years.[57] The complex web of regulations also had implications for the capital of banks.

The recognitions were based on lists that were related to the respective acts. The Exchange Control Act of 1947 tasked the Bank of England with maintaining a list of banks that were authorised to deal with foreign exchange.[58] Thus, these banks were referred to as 'authorised banks'. The Companies Act 1948 created a list of banks that were allowed to have hidden reserves.[59] These banks were the 'Schedule 8' banks and were perceived as banks of the 'highest standing'.[60]

Other acts were also applicable to banks, such as the Prevention of Fraud (Investments) Act of 1958, which stipulated a licence requirement for banks dealing with securities for customers.[61] Another example was the Protection of Depositors Act of 1963, which restricted the use of the term 'bank' when advertising for deposits.[62] Initially, the banks allowed to use 'bank' in advertising were the same as the 'Schedule 8' banks. In 1967, however, a section was amended in the Companies Act 1967 for banks exempted from the depositor protection legislation.[63] The amendment created another list: the 'Section 127' banks.

Another recognition was based on Section 54 of the Income and Corporation Taxes Act 1970, which allowed banks to pay and receive interest gross of tax.[64] Yet another recognition was based on the Companies Act of 1967, which allowed the Department of Trade to recognise institutions that conducted banking business ('Section 123' banks). Besides these recognitions, there were also minor forms of recognition, such as membership in the British Bankers Association, having obtained a clearing code from the Committee of London Clearing Banks, or being included in the Bankers Almanac.[65]

The large number of recognitions often came with certain requirements, some of them also in connection with capital. The Section 123 list, for example, required banks to hold capital of at least £250,000 and to conduct a range of banking services, such as issuing cheque books and offering current and deposit accounts. Inclusion in the Section 127 list required capital of £1m, offering a variety of banking services, having adequate liquidity, and good quality of management and a good reputation.[66] For the Big Five banks, these

[57] Capie, *The Bank of England*, p. 597.
[58] *Exchange Control Act 1947*, 1947, c. 14.
[59] *Companies Act 1948*, 1948, c. 38.
[60] Blunden, 'The Supervision of the UK Banking System', p. 188.
[61] *Prevention of Fraud (Investments) Act 1958*, C. 45. See also Capie, *The Bank of England*, p. 591.
[62] *The Protection of Depositors (Accounts) Regulations 1963*, 1963.
[63] *Companies Act 1967*, 1967, c. 81.
[64] *Income and Corporation Taxes Act 1970*, C. 10. For a discussion, see Edward P. M. Gardener, 'Supervision in the United Kingdom', in *UK Banking Supervision*, ed. Edward P. M. Gardener (London: Allen & Unwin, 1986), pp. 70–81 (p. 72).
[65] Capie, *The Bank of England*, p. 598.
[66] Capie, *The Bank of England*, pp. 596–7.

capital requirements in absolute terms (rather than ratios) were irrelevant, given their large capitals in absolute terms (see Figure 5.3).

A government department – the Department of Trade – was responsible for granting legislative approvals for the various lists. The BoE, as an informal supervisor, however, was always consulted when banks were added to the lists. In this role, the BoE monitored liquidity and solvency ratios and conducted regular interviews with the banks. The actual supervision was usually conducted in informal meetings between representatives of the bank and the BoE's Discount Office when banks submitted their accounts.[67]

The capital ratio used by the BoE during the 1950s to measure solvency was the 'ratio of free resources'. The minimum 'ratio of free resources' ranged between 1:10 for newly established banks to 1:30 for discount houses. These ratios were not applied as target ratios in a strict manner but acted as signal that would alert the supervisors.[68] For liquidity purposes the BoE observed the 'quick assets ratio'.[69]

Given the complicated regulatory framework, it was not surprising that its complexity was about to be identified as a deficiency of the system. Moreover, as it turned out, the legislation failed to target new forms of financial institutions: the so-called secondary banks.

5.2.2 The Relevance of Capital: The Secondary Banking Crisis

The 1960s and 1970s were marked by structural change in Britain's banking sector, which had a lasting impact on competition, the market participants, and their balance sheets. After the Second World War, investments in government debt gradually lost importance. Towards the end of the 1950s, government investments were no longer the largest balance sheet item on the asset side. Advances became the most important asset item again, for the first time since 1929.

The 1960s also brought about the first mergers in four decades. The National Provincial Bank acquired the District Bank in 1962. In 1968, the Westminster Bank merged with National Provincial. In 1969, Martins Bank was acquired by Barclays. Moreover, the British clearing banks developed from domestic to international institutions within a few years, and the number of international banks in London grew rapidly. The clearing banks' balance sheets expanded by, on average, 8.9% p.a. during the 1960s and 20.0% p.a. in the 1970s.[70]

Domestically, policy changes aimed to replace the system of direct control by the BoE with market-guided mechanisms. The implementation of the 'Competition and Credit Control' (CCC) paper lifted many constraints on the

---

[67] Bank of England, *Supervision of Banks and Other Deposit-Taking Institutions.*
[68] Revell, *Solvency and Regulation of Banks*, p. 47.
[69] Definition: Assets immediately realisable as a percentage of the deposits.
[70] Author's calculations. Data: Individual annual reports.

banks in 1971, suggesting a new approach towards monetary policy.[71] Under the CCC policy, the clearing banks gave up their cartel, which had previously fixed the rates paid on deposits and set minimum rates for advances. In return, the clearing banks were allowed to enter the newly emerged wholesale market.[72] This change allowed them to place funds and raise deposits at other banks, which had previously had to be done through subsidiaries. Moreover, the paper suggested that a universal reserve ratio and adjustments in interest rates and open market operations should replace the existing quantitative control of lending through cash and liquidity ratios.[73]

In contrast to the previous system of credit control, not only clearing banks but all banks would be subject to reserve ratios. Thus, a new type of bank – the secondary (or fringe) banks – was also to be affected by CCC. The BoE already considered that the fringe banks should be invited to adhere to a 10% reserve ratio. However, these attempts were halted by the advent of the secondary banking crisis in 1973.[74]

The fringe banks emerged in the late 1950s and early 1960s. These institutions borrowed on the wholesale market and lent mostly for properties. Both the fringe banks and the wholesale market grew rapidly during the period of expansionary monetary policy between 1971 and 1973.[75] Moreover, the fringe banks competed with the traditional clearing banks in the lending and deposit markets. During 1973 and 1974, falling housing prices put many smaller financial institutions under threat of bankruptcy and the BoE, together with the London and Scottish clearing banks, launched various rescue operations to stabilise the market.[76]

Several issues became apparent as a result of the secondary banking crisis, and some of them would affect the banking legislation to come. Firstly, many financial institutions were not supervised at all. There was only informal supervision of recognised banks by the Bank of England. Fringe banks and foreign banks were out of the supervisory scope. With the secondary banking crisis, the 'old' system based on the informal control of a small number of clearing banks came to an end. Secondly, after a long period of financial stability, awareness of the importance of protecting depositors grew as a result of the crisis. Lastly, the system of the ladder of recognition was too complex and, therefore, hard to understand for the public.[77]

---

[71] Bank of England, 'Competition and Credit Control', *Quarterly Bulletin*, Q2 (1971), 189–93.

[72] The cartel emerged during the First World War. Turner argues that it 'can be viewed as a quid pro quo to the banks' in exchange for the acceptance of the Bank of England's leadership in supervision. Turner, *Banking in Crisis*, p. 175.

[73] See Capie's chapter on CCC for an overview: Capie, *The Bank of England*, pp. 483–523.

[74] Capie, *The Bank of England*, p. 599.

[75] Capie, *The Bank of England*, p. 524.

[76] Most famously the lifeboat operation. See, for example, Margaret Reid, *The Secondary Banking Crisis 1973–75: Its Causes and Course* (London: Macmillan, 1982). Capie, *The Bank of England*, pp. 524–86.

[77] Blunden, 'The Supervision of the UK Banking System', pp. 189–90.

During 1974 and 1975, it became apparent within the BoE that new legislation was both 'inevitable and desirable', as Peter W. Cooke, at the time responsible for banking supervision at the BoE, noted.[78] The bank also reorganised its system of supervision internally. Until 1974, the Discount Office had been responsible for banking supervision. As a result of the secondary banking crisis, a new supervisory office – the Banking Supervision Division (BSD) – was formed.[79]

As the protection of depositors was questioned, the topic of capital adequacy received attention as well. In 1974, the BoE created a working group to reconsider the purpose of capital, as well as to discuss methods to assess capital adequacy and liquidity. The working group consisted of representatives of the London and Scottish clearing banks and officials from the BoE.

The working group published its results in a paper titled 'The Capital and Liquidity Adequacy of Banks' in 1975.[80] This was the first time since the First World War that the topic of capital had received wider public attention. Moreover, it was also a novelty for the BoE to openly discuss methods for measuring capital adequacy. Until 1975, capital adequacy had been part of the supervisory practice but was only discussed directly between banks and the BoE. The working paper described the existing approaches towards capital adequacy and showed in which direction capital measures were to be developed.

At this time, similar discussions on capital adequacy were also underway in the EEC. The United Kingdom joined the EEC in 1973 and, as Peter Cooke pointed out, tried to influence the debates at the European level towards their interests.[81] With regards to capital adequacy, the British definitions were already quite close to those established by the EEC.

The working paper of 1975 described two methods of assessing capital adequacy. The first approach was based on the 'free resources ratio', measuring the 'free capital resources' as a percentage of the liabilities. A second approach was the 'risk assets ratio'. This new approach related the riskiness of different asset categories to the amount of capital resources. According to the working group, cash and balances with the BoE, advances to

---

[78] Cooke, *Self-Regulation and Statute – the Evolution of Banking Supervision*, p. 88.

[79] In 1974, the supervisory part of the Discount Office consisted of fifteen people. Until 1978, the number of people working for the BSD increased to about seventy. Bank of England, *Supervision of Banks and Other Deposit-Taking Institutions*, p. 384.

[80] Bank of England, 'The Capital and Liquidity Adequacy of Banks', *Quarterly Bulletin*, Q3 (1975).

[81] Cooke, *Self-Regulation and Statute – the Evolution of Banking Supervision*, p. 89: 'In the course of this process, the United Kingdom took a strong lead in redirecting the energies of the European Commission toward an approach to harmonisation in the banking field more consistent with the realities of the marketplace. An approach, we in the Bank believed, more likely in practice to lead to agreement because it was addressing major points of principle rather than detailed statutory provisions.'

(or guaranteed by) the United Kingdom's public sector, and advances to banks listed in the United Kingdom were regarded as risk free. Thus, such assets would not require banks to hold capital.[82]

The working paper also defined capital. There were two types of capital. The 'free capital resources' were defined as capital minus the book value of infrastructure, also referred to as 'fixed assets'. This definition was closely related to the idea of the purpose of capital at the time. Capital was perceived as necessary to cover fixed assets, and fixed assets were considered the most illiquid asset, especially in times of crisis. The remaining amount of capital should 'protect depositors from losses as a result of business risks' and 'engender the confidence of potential depositors and trading partners'.[83]

A second form of capital, which was used to calculate the solvency ratios, was 'capital resources'. Besides paid-up share capital and reserves, the 'capital resources' also included provisions and loan capital. This was a comprehensive definition of capital. Loan capital was medium- to long-term subordinated debt. According to the view at the time, subordinated debt (in earlier years called 'loan stock') ranked after any other debt in the case of bankruptcy constituted an 'additional line of defence' for depositors.[84]

The inclusion of provisions as a part of capital and the use of subordinated debt is debatable. One can argue that non-specific provisions are a form of capital as they are comparable to general reserves and augmented by retained profits. Specific provisions, however, usually relate to an expected loss and therefore do not serve as a general loss absorber. Yet both forms of provisions were defined by the working paper as being a part of capital resources. Thus, the working group opted for an all-encompassing definition of capital. No ratio that included 'hard' capital, consisting of share capital and reserves alone, was discussed.

The working group deliberately avoided specific minimum ratios, arguing that quantification would reduce the flexibility to consider the different circumstances of individual banks. Nevertheless, it should be possible 'to develop over time broad numerical standards for the different groups of banks which may be used as yardsticks'.[85] Being the product of a joint working group by the BoE and the clearing banks, it is not surprising that much of the paper gives the impression of being a compromise. Regarding numerical capital requirements, the paper explicitly states that 'the special position which the clearing banks occupy in the financial system is recognised'.[86] Nevertheless, it must be remembered that this approach towards capital adequacy was in keeping with the BoE's general principles

---

[82] Bank of England, *The Capital and Liquidity Adequacy of Banks*, p. 241.
[83] Bank of England, *The Capital and Liquidity Adequacy of Banks*, p. 240.
[84] Wilcox, *Capital in Banking: An Historical Survey*, p. 207.
[85] Bank of England, *The Capital and Liquidity Adequacy of Banks*, p. 240.
[86] Bank of England, *The Capital and Liquidity Adequacy of Banks*, p. 240.

and understanding of regulation and supervision at the time. It was flexible, avoiding rigid rules. It allowed each bank to be judged individually in a personal manner. Moreover, it was an outcome of the Bank's participative approach.[87]

The working paper set the course for the perception of capital in the 1970s and 1980s. Subordinated debt was accepted as an essential part of the capital. In the BoE's statistical publications on the banking market, no differentiation was made between the various types of capital. The Bank's Quarterly Bulletins (Statistical Annexes) reported total capital resources only. The same applies to the international statistics provided by the OECD at the time.[88] For a detailed assessment of a 'narrowly defined' capital base consisting of share capital and reserves only, one has to turn to the annual statements of individual banks.

Now that capital adequacy had finally emerged as a topic, was it viewed as an essential source of stability for British banks? Before the 1970s, the focus was clearly on liquidity, which was linked to the fact that credit control – or, more broadly, monetary policy – can be exercised through liquidity requirements. In 1975, George Blunden, at the time responsible for banking supervision at the BoE, still highlighted that 'liquidity is probably even more important than capital adequacy'. Blunden argued that the secondary banking crisis had been a liquidity problem and not one of inadequate capital.[89] The developments in the working groups on the European and international levels, however, seem to have shifted the focus from liquidity to solvency.

5.2.3 The Banking Acts of 1979 and 1987

By the mid-1970s, it was clear that British banking needed a new regulatory framework. The Banking Act was introduced in 1979 and represented the first legislation since the mid-nineteenth century that specifically regulated banks. The previous regulation, based on general Companies Laws and several pieces of legislation affecting different areas of banking, was mostly replaced. With regards to bank capital, however, the new Act did not introduce specific capital ratios. The Banking Act was in the tradition of British banking supervision, leaving the Bank of England as a supervisor with substantial discretionary flexibility.

The 1979 Act was primarily concerned with deposit-taking. Other areas, such as foreign exchange, securities dealing, and payment services, were left aside. All deposit-taking institutions had to be authorised by the BoE. The Act differentiated between licensed and recognised institutions. Both types of institutions were allowed to take deposits. The main difference was the type

---

[87] Blunden, *The Supervision of the UK Banking System*, p. 191.
[88] Jack Revell, *Costs and Margins in Banking: An International Survey*, ed. Organisation for Economic Co-Operation and Development OECD (Paris: OECD, 1980); Revell, *Costs and Margins in Banking: Statistical Supplement*.
[89] Blunden, 'The Supervision of the UK Banking System', p. 193.

of supervision. The Act ensured that the supervision of recognised banks could continue mostly on a non-statutory basis – as was already the case.[90]

The Banking Act set minimum capital requirements of £250,000 for licensed institutions and £5m for recognised institutions.[91] There were no prescribed capital ratios, but a general statement on capital adequacy for licensed institutions:

The institution ... will maintain net assets of such amount as, together with other financial resources available to it of such a nature and amount as are considered appropriate by the Bank, is sufficient to safeguard the interests of its depositors, having regard to the factors specified in subparagraph (2) below.[92]

Subparagraph 2 was defined as follows:

The factors referred to in subparagraph (1) (a) above are (a) the scale and nature of the liabilities of the institution and the sources and amounts of deposits accepted by it; and (b) the nature of its assets and the degree of risk attached to them.[93]

The paragraph on solvency for recognised institutions was formulated similarly, but was slightly less detailed.[94] The Banking Act defined 'net assets' as paid-up capital and reserves. The definition of capital also opened the door for the use of other forms of capital, referred to as 'other financial resources'. In practice, this meant subordinated debt and guarantees from third parties.[95]

The BoE further detailed the capital adequacy regime in another joint working paper with the British Bankers' Association (BBA), which succeeded the Committee of London Clearing Bankers as a representative body in the discussions with the bank. The paper, titled 'The Measurement of Capital', described the methods and criteria that the bank employed when assessing the capital adequacy of financial institutions and was published in 1980.[96]

The discussions between the involved parties for the working paper were also the basis for the articles on capital adequacy in the Banking Act 1979. When developing the paper, Peter W. Cooke, Head of Banking Supervision at the BoE,

---

[90] For licensed institutions, the Banking Act established a series of information obligations. The Bank of England could make inquiries about 'the nature and conduct of the institution's business and its plans for future development'. *Banking Act 1979*, para. 16.

[91] The £5m applied to banks that were providing a 'wide range of banking services'. Banks that were offering 'highly specialised banking services' had to hold a capital of £250,000. *Banking Act 1979*, sch. 2, para. 5 & 9.

[92] *Banking Act 1979*, sch. 2, para. 10.

[93] *Banking Act 1979*, sch. 2, para. 10.

[94] The net assets and other financial resources had to be 'considered appropriate by the Bank' as well, but it was not outlined any further how this was measured. In contrast to the paragraph on licensed institutions, the interests of depositors were not mentioned, nor the extent of the liabilities or the risk of the assets. Neglecting these points did not mean that they were unimportant, but probably more that they were taken for granted. *Banking Act 1979*, sch. 2, para. 6.

[95] Ian Morison, Paul Tillet, and Jane Welch, *Banking Act 1979* (London: Butterworths & Co., 1979), p. 42.

[96] Bank of England, 'The Measurement of Capital', *Quarterly Bulletin*, Q3 (1980).

stressed that the Bank aimed to develop a strict method for the measurement for capital adequacy. Referring to the attempts to harmonise capital adequacy in Europe, Cooke also stressed that other countries would not accept a system of 'excessive vagueness'. At the same time, Cooke highlighted that the BoE would judge the assessment resulting from the application of the measurement methods in a flexible way.[97] The representatives of the BBA emphasised that the BoE's proposals were generally acceptable, but they were concerned about moving towards a 'more inflexible, formalised system of supervision'.[98]

The final paper on the 'Measurement of Capital' published in 1980 took the banks' as well as the BoE's concerns into account. It once again confirmed that the regulation and supervision of capital adequacy should be flexible, considering the individual characters of the institutions. It also took a clear stance against fixed minimum ratios, which – according to the paper – could be an incentive for overtrading. The paper also argued that capital ratios should not be public knowledge as this could weaken the ability to issue new capital when a bank is in crisis.[99]

The BoE clearly preferred opaqueness over transparency, adding that 'the Bank's views on capital adequacy have been discussed with individual banks in confidence for some time past. This will continue.'[100] In the internal discussions leading to this final statement, the BBA lobbied strongly for this policy. According to the representatives of the banks, publishing a capital ratio 'could lead to banks carrying more capital than was absolutely necessary in order to avoid a run on confidence'.[101] The BBA also warned about a 'potential risk of misunderstanding' if detailed information on capital adequacy were to be published, as this could undermine 'confidence in international banking' and harm the availability of credit.[102]

The paper on 'The Measurement of Capital' endorsed the same two capital ratios as the first paper in 1975. The 'free resources ratio' ratio was slightly adapted and now termed the 'gearing ratio'. For the second ratio – the 'risk assets ratio' – the BoE stressed that this was more useful and was the concept of

---

[97] British Bankers' Association, *Note of the Meeting between the British Bankers' Association and the Bank of England on the Measurement of Capital, Held at the Bank of England*, Committee of London Clearing Bankers. Capital and Liquidity Adequacy of Banks' (73/3) (London, 12 September 1979), pp. 2, 5, London Metropolitan Archives, CLC/B/029/MS32152B/001.

[98] British Bankers' Association, *Note Meeting BBA – BoE September*, LMA, CLC/B/029/MS32152B/001, pp. 2–3.

[99] Bank of England, *The Measurement of Capital*.

[100] Bank of England, *The Measurement of Capital*, p. 325.

[101] British Bankers' Association, *Note Meeting BBA – BoE September*, LMA, CLC/B/029/MS32152B/001, p. 6.

[102] British Bankers' Association, *Note of the Meeting between the British Bankers' Association and the Bank of England on the Measurement of Capital, Held at the Bank of England*, Committee of London Clearing Bankers. Capital and Liquidity Adequacy of Banks' (73/3) (London, 13 November 1979), p. 2, London Metropolitan Archives, CLC/B/029/MS32152B/001.

reference going forward.[103] The definitions of the risk assets were much more detailed than in 1975. The paper stated exact weights for different asset classes. Balances with the BoE, for example, had zero weight; loans had a 100% weight. Interestingly, there was also a 200% weight for property owned by a bank, which was probably due to the still recent experience of collapsing property prices at the time.[104] The BoE and the BBA spent much time discussing these risk coefficients in the working group. The BBA aimed for a more comprehensive system with many different risk categories. For advances, for example, the BBA argued that several risk groups should exist, and one risk category alone would not lead to meaningful results. In addition, the BBA argued strongly for the use of the 'risk assets ratio' and questioned the validity of the 'gearing ratio'.[105]

One important area that had changed until 1980 compared to the preceding working paper on bank capital in 1975 was the definition of capital. Provisions for expected losses were excluded from the capital, which was an outcome of the EEC's Advisory Committee recommendations, formulated after the EEC Banking Directive in 1977. However, the importance of subordinated debt as a form of capital had grown substantially. While it was still clear that subordinated debt could not absorb losses, it was increasingly emphasised that it could also be used to finance fixed assets.[106] In 1975, this role was attributed only to equity capital. The working paper of 1980, therefore, manifested the rise of subordinated debt as a substitute for capital.[107]

The working papers of the BoE and the regulation of capital and liquidity in the Banking Act were mostly the results of technical discussions between BoE officials and bank representatives. However, on a broader level, questions were also raised about the regulation and supervision of British financial markets. In 1980, a report by the Committee to Review the Functioning of Financial Institutions (Wilson Committee) was published. As well as its general analysis of the financial system, the committee also discussed the capital levels of the banks. It concluded that capital ratios had been falling during the first half of the 1970s, mainly because inflation had driven the balance sheet growth. The Wilson Committee also noted that the fall in capital ratios would have been even more severe if there had not been an extensive 'raising of loan capital', which underlines the importance of subordinated debt.[108]

---

[103] Bank of England, *The Measurement of Capital*, pp. 324–27.
[104] Bank of England, *The Measurement of Capital*, p. 329, Appendix A.
[105] British Bankers' Association, *Note Meeting BBA – BoE September*, LMA, CLC/B/029/ MS32152B/001, p. 6.
[106] Bank of England, *The Measurement of Capital*, p. 326.
[107] Jack Revell, 'Capital Adequacy, Hidden Reserves and Provisions', in *UK Banking Supervision*, ed. Edward P. M. Gardener (London: Allen & Unwin, 1986), pp. 218–33 (p. 220).
[108] Committee to Review the Functioning of Financial Institutions (Wilson Committee), *Committee to Review the Functioning of Financial Institutions*, Cmnd. 7937 (London: Her Majesty's Stationary Office, 1980), para. 278–84.

Various interest groups submitted reports to the Wilson Committee, among them the Committee of the London Clearing Bankers. The clearing banks highlighted their opinion that simple capital/deposits ratios had lost importance, emphasising instead the trend towards 'measures that reflect the varying degrees of risk attached to different assets'.[109] The Committee of the London Clearing Bankers clearly favoured a 'risk assets ratio'. The clearing banks argued that treasury bills could be financed fully with deposits, as risks of price fluctuations or defaults were negligible. At the other end of the scale, properties could fluctuate and were difficult to sell in a crisis. These characteristics would have to be considered by a capital adequacy framework.[110]

The BoE's working papers on capital adequacy in 1975 and 1980, together with the Banking Act 1979 and the EEC's Banking Directive 1977, had set the stage for the assessment of capital adequacy. The initial catalyst that had brought the topic of capital adequacy back onto the domestic agenda was the secondary banking crisis. However, the development of the framework for assessing capital adequacy on a domestic level interacted with international developments.

The Banking Act of 1979 was replaced by a new Banking Act in 1987. The new Act was mostly the consequence of the rescue of Johnson Matthey Bankers by the BoE in 1984. The bank's failure was followed by another parliamentary report in 1985, which reviewed banking supervision in the United Kingdom.[111] The Act of 1987 brought many changes: it ended the two-tier system of recognised and licensed banks, among other things, and increased the power of the BoE as a supervisor. With regards to the regulation of capital, however, not much altered.

The Banking Act 1987 still required each bank to 'conduct its business in a prudent manner'. This meant that 'net assets' and 'other financial resources' would have to be considered appropriate by the BoE.[112] The amount of capital that a bank needed to maintain would depend on the nature and scale of the institution's operations and the 'risks inherent in those operations'.[113] The Banking Supervision Division of the BoE further outlined the definition of capital adequacy based on its initial working paper from 1980. In a paper on subordinated loan capital, the BSD further specified the requirements of

---

[109] *The London Clearing Banks: Evidence by the Committee of London Clearing Bankers to the Committee to Review the Functioning of Financial Institutions*, ed. Committee of London Clearing Bankers (London: Committee of London Clearing Bankers, distributed by Longman, 1978), p. 59.

[110] Committee of London Clearing Bankers, *The London Clearing Banks*, p. 69.

[111] Committee Set up to Consider the System of Banking Supervision, *Report of the Committee Set up to Consider the System of Banking Supervision*, Cmnd. 9550 (London: Her Majesty's Stationary Office, 1985).

[112] *Banking Act 1987*, C. 22, 1987, sch. 3, para. 4 (2).

[113] *Banking Act 1987*, sch. 3, para. 4 (3).

subordinated debt to be part of 'other financial resources'.[114] The risk-weighting approach for credit risks on the asset side, developed in 1980, was expanded in a paper in 1986.[115] Other types of risks, such as operational and foreign exchange risks, were also discussed and formed part of the BoE's assessment. Based on an individual analysis of each bank, the BSD defined a minimum capital ratio, termed the 'trigger ratio', and a goal for the capital requirement, referred to as the 'target ratio'.[116] However, little was known publicly about the exact process that led to setting the individual ratios.

When the BCBS issued its first common framework for the assessment of capital adequacy in 1988, the BSD issued a paper on how the international framework could be implemented in the United Kingdom.[117] The BSD noted that the international convergence would not change much for UK banks.[118]

The United Kingdom transferred to a Basel-compliant framework by the end of 1989. One of the key differences was that it also took off-balance-sheet items into account. However, the general approach towards the regulation of capital did not change. Capital requirements in the form of 'triggers' and 'target risk assets ratios' were still set based on individual evaluations of banks and continued to be confidential. The BoE noted that British banks would already meet the 8% capital requirement, and that it would not revise the individual 'triggers' or 'target ratios'.[119]

The introduction of Basel I in the United Kingdom marked the end of the process. Capital in banking had been almost irrelevant from the 1920s to the 1960s, until the secondary banking crisis at the beginning of the 1970s revived discussions about capital adequacy and initiated a series of papers by the BoE on the topic. Risk-based approaches to solvency found increasingly more attention in supervisory practice after 1975. Basel I and its application in 1988 represented only a gradual evolution that built on the already existing domestic framework for capital regulation. As such, this is not surprising. The United Kingdom took part in the discussions at the European and international levels and certainly influenced these discussions. The inclusion of subordinated debt as part of the Tier 2 capital under Basel I, for example, was clearly in the interests of the United Kingdom. At the same time, the international approach towards solvency certainly influenced domestic evolution as well (e.g. the treatment of provisions).

[114] Bank Supervision Division, Bank of England, 'Subordinated Loan Capital', 1986.
[115] Bank Supervision Division, Bank of England, 'Measurement of Capital', 1986.
[116] Graham Penn, *Banking Supervision: Regulation of the UK Banking Sector under the Banking Act 1987* (London, Edinburgh: Butterworth, 1989), p. 167.
[117] Bank Supervision Division, Bank of England, 'Implementation of the Basle Convergence Agreement in the United Kingdom', 1988.
[118] Bank of England, *Bank of England Banking Act Report 1988/89* (London: Bank of England, 1989), p. 15.
[119] Bank of England, *Bank of England Banking Act Report 1989/90* (London: Bank of England, 1990), p. 18.

Despite all the regulatory changes, approaches on the supervisory side did not change to any great extent. The BoE remained independent in setting individual minimum capital ratios for banks, and there was never a legally prescribed capital ratio.

5.3 REGULATION IN SWITZERLAND – AND HOW IT WAS INFLUENCED

The Great Depression and its severe effects, especially on Switzerland's big banks, led to a breakthrough of banking legislation in Switzerland in 1934. Swiss banks were subject to banking legislation on a national level for the first time. Among various other areas, this banking legislation also covered capital and liquidity requirements. The new legislation was comprehensive, regulating many aspects of banking, but light in terms of the strictness of rules. A former Director of the Secretariat of the Federal Banking Commission (FBC), Bernhard Müller, once stated that it was 'easier to open a bank than a restaurant' before the 1970s.[120] Müller's statement might have been an exaggeration, but it emphasises the liberal spirit with which the law was drafted, and the comparably weak position of the supervisor.

Introduced in 1934, it was not until 1961 that the first revisions of the banking legislation were undertaken. The regulatory changes coincided with the growth and internationalisation of Switzerland's banking market. The first revision of the Banking Ordinance in 1961 was significant for regulating capital. It was the basis for later changes in the capital requirements. On a broader level, the revision of the Banking Act in 1971 was even more relevant.[121] It enlarged the circle of supervised institutions to all deposit-taking banks. Moreover, the Banking Act of 1971 incorporated stricter licencing rules for domestic and foreign banks. The revised Banking Act also gave the FBC more power in supervision.[122]

The period between the 1950s and the 1980s became the 'golden age' of Swiss banking, marked by Switzerland's rise as a global financial centre. Two major developments became apparent in the process of the internationalisation of Switzerland's financial centre. Firstly, capital inflows accelerated after the war, triggering monetary problems. There were probably several drivers that contributed to these capital inflows. The Swiss franc was undervalued under the

---

[120] Müller, *Entwicklung der Bankenaufsicht*, p. 6. Müller was the Director of the Secretariat of the FBC from 1976 to 1985.

[121] *Bundesgesetz über die Banken und Sparkassen vom 11. März 1971*, 1971.

[122] An example of the increasing supervisory power of the FBC was the frequent use of the provision that required the management to have a 'good reputation and guarantee the proper conduct of their business' (Art. 3), *BankG 1971*; Tobias Straumann and Jürg Gabathuler, 'Die Entwicklung der Schweizer Bankenregulierung', in *Krisenfeste Schweizer Banken? Die Regulierung von Eigenmitteln, Liquidität und 'Too big to fail'*, ed. Armin Jans, Christoph Lengwiler, and Marco Passardi (Zurich: NZZ Libro, 2018), pp. 57–86 (pp. 76–7).

fixed exchange rate regime.[123] Switzerland was both economically and politically stable, and banking secrecy was also a key factor. The Swiss National Bank (SNB) was challenged to maintain monetary control over its currency and tried to lower inflation. In this context, various administrative measures were taken to reduce foreign capital inflows. Examples are gentlemen's agreements with the banks on non-interest payments on short-term foreign liabilities (from 1950), on negative interest rates on foreign deposits (1972/4), and the ban on investments in domestic securities and the real estate market (1972).[124]

The capital inflows were both a blessing and a curse. While they created monetary distortions, they also allowed Switzerland to gain considerable international weight. In the 1950s and 1960s, the Swiss financial centre became by far the largest foreign buyer of securities in the United States.[125] By 1970, Swiss investors held about half of the German debt which was invested by foreigners.[126] Moreover, estimates by Max Iklé, member of the SNB's governing board from 1956 to 1968, indicate that Swiss banks bought about 30–40% of the Eurobond issuances in the 1960s.[127] Swiss banks were also major players in the Eurodollar market. By 1963, Swiss banks held Eurodollar assets of USD 1.7bn and liabilities of USD 1.1bn. On par with Japan, Switzerland was the second largest lender on the Eurodollar market after the United Kingdom, and the fourth largest borrower that year.[128]

A second dimension of the internationalisation of Switzerland's financial hub was the attraction of foreign banks. These foreign banks were either established in Switzerland as independent (but foreign-controlled) banks or as subsidiaries.

---

[123] After the end of Bretton Woods, the Swiss franc tended to be overvalued often, which contributes to the argument that undervalued currency was not the sole driver of capital inflows. See Peter Bernholz, 'Die Nationalbank 1945–1982: Von der Devisenbann-Wirtschaft zur Geldmengensteuerung bei flexiblen Wechselkursen', in *Schweizerische Nationalbank, 1907– 2007*, ed. Schweizerische Nationalbank SNB (Zurich: Verlag Neue Zürcher Zeitung, 2007), pp. 119–211 (pp. 123–24).

[124] Swiss National Bank, *75 Jahre Schweizerische Nationalbank, 1907–1982* (Zurich, 1982), pp. 34, 102, 104, 127. For an overview of Switzerland's monetary policy, see also Bernholz, *Die Nationalbank 1945–1982*.

[125] Board of Governors of the Federal Reserve System (US), *Banking and Monetary Statistics, 1941–1970*, 1976, pp. 967–75, 1002: https://fraser.stlouisfed.org/title/41 (accessed 31 July 2018).

[126] Deutsche Bundesbank, 'Die Kapitalertragsbilanz Der Bundesrepublik Im Aussenwirtschafts-verkehr', 1971: www.bundesbank.de/resource/blob/690748/8e5a5e61e9bbcdafe9cfc59122c 559bb/mL/1971-03-monatsbericht-data.pdf.

[127] Max Iklé, *Die Schweiz als internationaler Bank- und Finanzplatz* (Zurich: Orell Füssli, 1970), p. 136.

[128] Schenk, *The Origins of the Eurodollar Market in London*, p. 235. For a discussion of why Switzerland did not promote a Eurodollar market in Switzerland, see Tobias Straumann, 'Finanzplatz und Pfadabhängigkeit: Die Bundesrepublik, die Schweiz und die Vertreibung der Euromärkte (1955–1980)', in *Europas Finanzzentren: Geschichte und Bedeutung im 20. Jahrhundert*, ed. Christoph Maria Merki (Frankfurt a.M.: Campus, 2005), pp. 245–68.

By 1970, 76 out of 473 banks in Switzerland were controlled by foreign owners. In 1980, there were 83 foreign-controlled banks and 16 subsidiaries of foreign banks. Therefore, the revision of the Banking Act in 1971 also addressed issues in supervising these foreign banks. For example, before 1968, establishing foreign banks or takeovers by foreign banks did not require authorisation. However, the rapid growth of foreign banks was perceived as a threat.[129] In response, the Swiss parliament introduced licencing requirements for foreign banks in 1968, which were later incorporated in the revised Banking Act.[130]

Besides the number of foreign banks in Switzerland, Swiss banks also attracted substantial foreign capital. One of the prerequisites for the rapid growth of the foreign capital flows was certainly the transition to convertibility of the major European currencies in 1958. In the years from 1960 to 1970, the share of foreign assets in Swiss banks' balance sheets grew from 13.3% to 33.7%. The share of foreign liabilities developed similarly. The numbers regarding foreign assets and liabilities are also impressive when looking at the volumes. In 1958, the volume of foreign assets was CHF 5.9bn. In 1970, foreign assets reached a volume of CHF 70.8bn, and CHF 182bn in 1980. These numbers represent balance sheet data only. Data on the share of foreign customers' securities is not available, but would likely show a significant foreign exposure too.

Most foreign activities stemmed from the three largest big banks (Credit Suisse, the Union Bank of Switzerland, the Swiss Bank Corporation). The rest of the capital flows were directed to or came from foreign banks and private banks in Switzerland. Other banks, such as the cantonal banks or savings banks, played a minor role.[131]

Table 5.1 shows the growth of the total assets of banks in Switzerland. From the 1950s to the 1980s, the average annual growth rate of total assets was between 7.4% and 13.5%. The big banks reached annualised growth rates of 18.3% in the 1960s. Because the total assets grew faster than the equity capital, the capital/assets ratios declined. However, the rapid growth among the big banks became a problem as capital requirements could not be met in certain years.

---

[129] The Federal Council wrote that some foreign institutions would make 'blatant and intrusive' use of the Swiss banking secrecy and that there are foreign banks with 'most serious grievances'. Moreover, the Federal Council feared a further increase of the monetary base that would lead to domestic credit expansion. Bundesrat, 'Botschaft des Bundesrates an die Bundesversammlung zum Entwurf eines dringlichen Bundesbeschlusses über die Bewilligungspflicht für ausländisch beherrschte Banken', *Bundesblatt*, 2.48 (1968), 756–71 (pp. 759–61).

[130] '*Bundesbeschluss über die Bewilligungspflicht für ausländisch beherrschte Banken vom 21. März 1969*'). For the regulatory history of foreign banks in Switzerland, see Thibaud Giddey, 'The Regulation of Foreign Banks in Switzerland (1956–1972)', *Foreign Financial Institutions & National Financial Systems*, The European Association for Banking and Financial History, 2013, 449–85.

[131] See Henner Kleinewefers, *Das Auslandsgeschäft der Schweizer Banken*, Schriften zum Bankenwesen (Zurich: Schuthess, 1972); Kurt Speck, *Strukturwandlungen und Entwicklungstendenzen im Auslandsgeschäft der Schweizerbanken*, Prospektivstudie über das schweizerische Bankgewerbe (Zurich: Juris Druck Verlag, 1974).

TABLE 5.1 *Decadal average growth rates (p.a.) of total assets, total capital, inflation (consumer price index) and average capital/assets ratio, 1951–90*[1]

	Total assets (growth p.a.)		Total capital (growth p.a.)		Capital/assets ratio (average)		
	All banks	Big banks	All banks	Big banks	All banks	Big banks	*Inflation*[2]
1951–1960	7.4%	8.2%	4.6%	5.0%	7.6%	7.4%	1.5%
1961–1970	13.5%	18.3%	11.3%	15.2%	6.3%	5.8%	3.3%
1971–1980	8.8%	9.8%	10.5%	12.9%	6.3%	5.7%	5.0%
1981–1990	8.3%	8.1%	8.5%	8.4%	6.2%	5.9%	3.4%

[1] Bank data: Swiss National Bank, *Historical Time Series.*; Consumer Price Index: HSSO, *Historische Statistik der Schweiz* Online, Tab. H.39, p. 39.

[2] The decadal averages of the inflation rates might be misleading since the time periods do not capture the business cycles. A more appropriate view would be a focus on the periods 1958–66 and 1967–75. The first cycle was marked by strong GDP growth (on average 5.3% p.a.) and moderate inflation (3.9% p.a.). The annual GDP growth fell by about 50% in the second cycle, and inflation rates grew to 6.2% p.a. See Swiss National Bank, *75 Jahre Schweizerische Nationalbank, 1907–1982*, pp. 57–67.

5.3.1   Banking Legislation in the 1930s

Swiss banking legislation consisted of three layers. The banking regulation introduced in 1934/5 was based on the Banking Act and the Banking Ordinance.[132] The former was passed by the government in November 1934 and became effective in March 1935.[133] The latter – the Banking Ordinance – outlined the application of the Banking Act and was introduced in 1935.[134] A third level was introduced in 1936: the Circulars issued by the FBC outlined its position on certain questions over the application of the law. The Circulars were not legally binding but gained soft law character over time. In the Circulars, the commission described how it applied banking legislation in supervisory practice.[135]

The responsibilities for each layer of the banking legislation were and still are different. New laws and amendments have to be passed by the Swiss parliament. In contrast to the Banking Act, the Ordinance requires only the approval of the Federal Council.[136] The Circulars are in the power of the FBC.

[132] *BankG 1934; BankV 1935.*

[133] *BankG 1934.*

[134] *BankV 1935.*

[135] See also Amrein, *Eigenmittel der Schweizer Banken im historischen Kontext.*

[136] The Federal Council is Switzerland's highest executive body consisting of seven ministers.

The three-layer system – Banking Act, Ordinance, and Circulars – remains the same today.[137]

The Banking Act was the first comprehensive banking regulation on the national level in Switzerland. The newly introduced legal framework also regulated capital requirements.[138] Article 4 of the Banking Act stated:

> Banks have to make sure, that there is an appropriate ratio between their own capital and their total liabilities. . . . The Ordinance defines the rules that have to be followed under normal circumstances by taking into account the business activities and types of banks.[139]

The Banking Ordinance (Art. 10) further expanded upon Article 4 of the Banking Act. Regulatory capital was defined as paid-up capital, 50% of non-paid-up capital (liability), guarantees from municipalities, disclosed reserves, and retained profits (or losses).[140]

In Article 12, the Banking Ordinance set two different minimum capital requirements, depending on the type of bank and the structure of its assets. Cantonal banks and cooperative banks with the unlimited liability of their members were required to hold a capital equivalent to at least 5% of the liabilities. All other banks had to hold a minimum of 5% of the liabilities that were invested in assets covered by domestic real securities (i.e. mortgages) and government securities.[141]

The Banking Act also stipulated liquidity requirements.[142] There were two types of liquidity ratios: one that included only cash and reserves at the SNB, and one that considered a broader range of liquid assets.[143] The liquidity ratios were measured as a percentage of short-term liabilities.

The roots of the Banking Act of 1934 reach back to a first legislative draft developed between 1914 and 1916. After a series of bank defaults from 1910 to 1914, the Federal Council commissioned Julius Landmann, Professor of

---

[137] One key difference in the regulatory structure is that the Federal Banking Commission was replaced by the Swiss Financial Market Supervisory Authority FINMA in 2009.

[138] Another important feature of the new legislation was the codification of the banking secrecy in Art. 47 of the Banking Act. For an overview on the history of the banking secrecy, see Guex, 'The Origins of the Swiss Banking Secrecy Law and Its Repercussions for Swiss Federal Policy'; Vogler, 'The Genesis of Swiss Banking Secrecy'. For a more general and contemporary overview, discussing also the developments since the last financial crisis, see Stefan Tobler, *Der Kampf um das Schweizer Bankgeheimnis: Eine 100-jährige Geschichte von Kritik und Verteidigung*, NZZ Libro (Zurich: NZZ Libro, 2019).

[139] Art. 4, *BankG 1934*.

[140] Art. 10, *BankV 1935*.

[141] Art. 12, *BankV 1935*.

[142] 'Banks must ensure that there is an appropriate ratio between tangible assets and readily realisable assets on the one hand and short-term liabilities on the other.' Art. 4, *BankG 1934*.

[143] Liquid (tangible) assets were defined as discountable securities (discountable at the SNB), sight deposits at banks (maturity <1m), treasury bills and acceptances (maturity <3m). Short-term liabilities were defined as sight deposits from customers (maturity <1m), cheques, 15% of saving deposits, bonds and short-term notes (maturity <1m). Art. 13–17, *BankV 1935*.

Economics at the University of Basel, to develop a draft for the regulation of banking.[144] Landmann suggested a discretion-based framework for Switzerland's bank regulation. Given that Swiss banks followed various activities, ad-hoc judgements would ensure that different business models were considered. Moreover, Landmann claimed that a governmental authority would usually be too late to intervene in a rule-based system, proposing flexible regulation without detailed rules. Specific capital and liquidity ratios should result from the 'practice of regulation'.[145]

Landmann's discretion-based approach and a substantial part of his first draft served as a blueprint for the Banking Act of 1934. The pressure of the Great Depression and two big banks on the brink of default finally led to the introduction of a national banking law.[146] When the Banking Act was submitted to the parliament, the Federal Council emphasised the discretion-based approach taken in the regulation of banking. For the regulation of capital, that meant that it was 'difficult or even impossible' to stipulate a universally valid ratio between capital and liabilities for all banks. The Banking Act should provide guidelines only. Nevertheless, specific minimum capital ratios were set in the Banking Ordinance, according to the Federal Council, considering the 'nature of the different institutes'.[147]

The main goals of the new banking regulation were to increase security for creditors, ensure the supply of capital for the economy, and improve the degree of information available to the SNB to enhance transparency.[148] The role of capital was seen as being an absorber of losses to safeguard depositors.[149] The liquidity requirements were viewed as being equally as important as capital adequacy for the stability of banks. Both measures were usually mentioned together and perceived as an instrument for the protection of depositors. The statement by the Federal Council in 1934 is fairly representative of the time: 'It is not sufficient for the deposits to be secured

---

[144] A study by the Federal Department of Economic Affairs on the banking crisis of 1910–14 counted seventeen defaults, twenty-one liquidations, five restructurings, and two mergers. The total losses were estimated at about CHF 110m. For a discussion of the crisis, see Julius Landmann, *Entwurf eines Bundesgesetzes: betreffend den Betrieb und die Beaufsichtigung von Bankenunternehmungen nebst Motivenbericht* (Bern: Schweizerisches Volkswirtschaftsdokument, 1916), p. 31. Wetter, *Bankkrisen und Bankkatastrophen*.

[145] Landmann, *Entwurf eines Bundesgesetzes*, p. 91.

[146] In that sense, the introduction of banking regulation was very much a story of crises and opportunities, as described by Youssef Cassis: Cassis, *Crises and Opportunities*.

[147] Bundesrat, 'Botschaft des Bundesrates an die Bundesversammlung betreffend den Entwurf eines Bundesgesetzes über die Banken und Sparkassen vom 2. Februar 1934', *Bundesblatt*, 1.6 (1934), 171–224 (p. 176).

[148] Bundesrat, *Botschaft des Bundesrates an die Bundesversammlung betreffend den Entwurf eines Bundesgesetzes über die Banken und Sparkassen vom 2. Februar 1934*, p. 175.

[149] Bundesrat, *Botschaft des Bundesrates an die Bundesversammlung betreffend den Entwurf eines Bundesgesetzes über die Banken und Sparkassen vom 2. Februar 1934*, p. 176.

in principle [by capital and reserves]; they must also be able to be withdrawn within the specified time limits.'[150]

The Federal Department for Finance and Customs was charged with developing the Banking Act and Ordinance.[151] In an internal report, the department analysed the capital structure of the Swiss banks in February 1934.[152] The authors remarked that there was a strong relationship between the level of capital and the share of mortgages: savings and Raiffeisen banks held the lowest capital and had the comparatively highest shares of mortgages on the asset side. The group of cantonal banks, also mainly focused on the mortgage business, held only slightly more capital than the other two bank groups. The authors of the report believed that banks with a predominant mortgage business have lower risks than the big banks. The Federal Department for Finance and Customs also discussed the liability of the banks' owners. Most cantonal banks at the time had government guarantees, and Raiffeisen banks were cooperative banks with unlimited joint guarantees of their members. The department therefore proposed that the mortgage share and the form of the liability should be considered if capital requirements were introduced.[153] Both recommendations found their way into the banking legislation.

The experts developing the law believed that using a bank's mortgage share and liability situation to determine adequate capital was only the second-best option. They thought that capital should depend on the risks of each bank and that the risks could be 'found in the assets'.[154] However, they concluded that 'it is impossible to find a measure for the risks on the asset side; it is not like reading the temperature on a thermometer'.[155] Nevertheless, one could argue that the

---

[150] Bundesrat, *Botschaft des Bundesrates an die Bundesversammlung betreffend den Entwurf eines Bundesgesetzes über die Banken und Sparkassen vom 2. Februar 1934*, p. 177. See also Paul Rossy and Robert Reimann, *Bundesgesetz über die Banken und Sparkassen vom 8. November 1934: Mit Vollziehungsverordnung vom 26. Februar 1935 und Verordnung des Bundesgerichts betreffend das Nachlassverfahren von Banken und Sparkassen vom 11. April 1935* (Zurich: Polygraphischer Verlag, 1935), p. 21: 'The provisions of this section are intended to safeguard creditors. On the one hand, they oblige banks to ensure a sound financial basis so that depositors do not risk losses in the event of any shock. On the other hand, they require adequate liquidity to be maintained so that a bank does not have to resort immediately to the National Bank when withdrawing funds.'

[151] 'Eidgenössisches Finanz- und Zolldepartement'/'Département fédéral des finances et des douanes'.

[152] Eidgenössisches Finanz- und Zolldepartement, *Bericht über die statistischen Grundlagen für die Aufstellung von Ausführungsbestimmungen zu Art. 10 des Entwurfes zu einem Bundesgesetz über die Banken und Sparkassen vom 2. Februar 1934* (Bern, 2 February 1934), Swiss Federal Archives, E6520A#1000/1059#5*.

[153] Eidgenössisches Finanz- und Zolldepartement, *Bericht statistische Grundlagen*, SFA, E6520A#1000/1059#5*, pp. 4–5.

[154] Eidgenössisches Finanz- und Zolldepartement, *Bericht statistische Grundlagen*, SFA, E6520A#1000/1059#5*, p. 4.

[155] Eidgenössisches Finanz- und Zolldepartement, *Bericht statistische Grundlagen*, SFA, E6520A#1000/1059#5*, p. 4.

final legislation already provided a simple risk-weighted approach; it was just that there were only two risk categories: mortgages and government securities on the one hand, and all other assets on the other hand. Instead of a risk-weighting of assets, two different minimum capital ratios were applied to the two classes.

When discussing various possible capital ratios, the group of experts of the Federal Department for Finance and Customs debated the idea that capital requirements should balance the interests of creditors and shareholders. For creditors, the experts emphasised the role of capital as a buffer against losses. Regarding shareholders and banks, it was argued that excessive capital ratios could lead to more risk-taking by banks since they would be pressured to provide sufficiently high returns to their shareholders.[156]

The considerations for an appropriate liquidity requirement were almost identical to those on capital adequacy. The group of experts argued that banks with a high share of mortgages bore a lower risk. Thus, they should be allowed to have lower liquidity ratios. Furthermore, the experts noted that bigger banks, measured by total assets, should hold more liquid assets as they were systemically more relevant 'to maintain the ability to pay'.[157]

Apart from this argument on the systemic stability of the financial market, another issue became apparent in the context of liquidity: in contrast to capital adequacy, liquidity was perceived as relevant for monetary policy. Liquidity ratios were not actively used to influence the individual business policies of banks, such as domestic lending policies, accepting foreign capital, or investing abroad.[158] The relevance of liquidity ratios for monetary policies, however, was recognised. One of the central concerns of the Banking Act was to increase the transparency of the banking market for the SNB. The commercial banks had to submit monthly or quarterly balance sheets (depending on their size) that allowed the SNB to assess their liquidity.

The final introduction of a minimum capital ratio in the Banking Ordinance is somewhat surprising, given the liberal character of the legislation that was meant to be restricted to a 'few general principles'.[159] The banks themselves did not resist these capital requirements. During the consultation process, various interest groups submitted their suggestions for changes in the draft of the law. Credit Suisse's general manager, Adolf Jöhr, was primarily concerned that private banks should not be excluded from capital

---

[156] Eidgenössisches Finanz- und Zolldepartement, *Bericht statistische Grundlagen*, SFA, E6520A#1000/1059#5*, pp. 6–11.

[157] Eidgenössisches Finanz- und Zolldepartement, *Bericht statistische Grundlagen*, SFA, E6520A#1000/1059#5*, p. 20.

[158] Another important feature with regards to the foreign capital flows, however, was that the Swiss National Bank could veto certain foreign transactions. Art. 8, *BankG 1934*.

[159] Bundesrat, *Botschaft des Bundesrates an die Bundesversammlung betreffend den Entwurf eines Bundesgesetzes über die Banken und Sparkassen vom 2. Februar 1934*, p. 174.

requirements.[160] The cantonal banks wanted to be excluded from being subjected to banking legislation altogether, claiming that the regulation of cantonal banks would undermine cantonal sovereignty.[161] And the Berne Audit Association, a self-regulatory body auditing its member banks, suggested a capital/deposits ratio of 10%, as its member banks already voluntarily adhered to this ratio.[162]

The use of capital ratios was already well accepted as a vital factor for the soundness of a bank before the introduction of banking legislation in the 1930s. There were already conventions among the banks with regard to capital adequacy for different groups of banks (e.g. that of the Berne Audit Association). Also, the bank group (e.g. cantonal banks, big banks) served as a proxy for the riskiness of a business model. To some extent, the capital requirements formalised conventions that already existed before. The introduction of a capital threshold was further facilitated by most banks fulfilling the requirements. Based on the year-end figures of 1932, the Federal Department of Finance and Customs had discussed potential capital/liability ratios of between 5% and 15%. The department's analysis showed that most banks would have fulfilled these requirements.[163] On a broader level, the big banks had little negotiating power once they accumulated significant losses in the 1930s.

5.3.2 The Evolution of Capital Regulation: 1934–91

Figure 5.4 visualises the evolution of capital regulation in Switzerland from 1934 to 1991. There are two key components of the regulation: capital requirements (required capital), and the definition of capital from a regulatory point of view (regulatory capital). In 1961, the Banking Ordinance and its capital requirements were revised for the first time. Changes were made on two levels. First, a lowered ratio for investments made in liquid assets was introduced, which reduced the required capital. For banks that were not cantonal or cooperative banks, that meant that were three risk classes on the asset side: liquid assets, assets invested in government securities or covered by mortgages, and all other assets. Second, the definition of the regulatory capital was broadened. The revised Banking Ordinance allowed any kind of 'free

---

[160] Adolf Jöhr, *Letter from Credit Suisse's General Manager Dr. Adolf Jöhr to the Director of the Department of Finance* (Zurich, 26 December 1933), Swiss Federal Archives, E6520A#1000/1059#5*.

[161] *Letter from the President of the Association of Swiss Cantonal Banks to Minister of Finance* (Basel, 14 October 1933), Swiss Federal Archives, E6520A#1000/1059#23*.

[162] President and Secretary of the Auditing Association, *Letter from the Association for the Auditing of Banks and Savings Banks in Berne to the Minister of Finance ('Revisionsverband der bernischen Banken und Sparkassen')* (Bern, 2 December 1933), Swiss Federal Archives, E6520A#1000/1059#27*.

[163] Schweizerisches Bundesarchiv, E6520A#1983/50#62*.

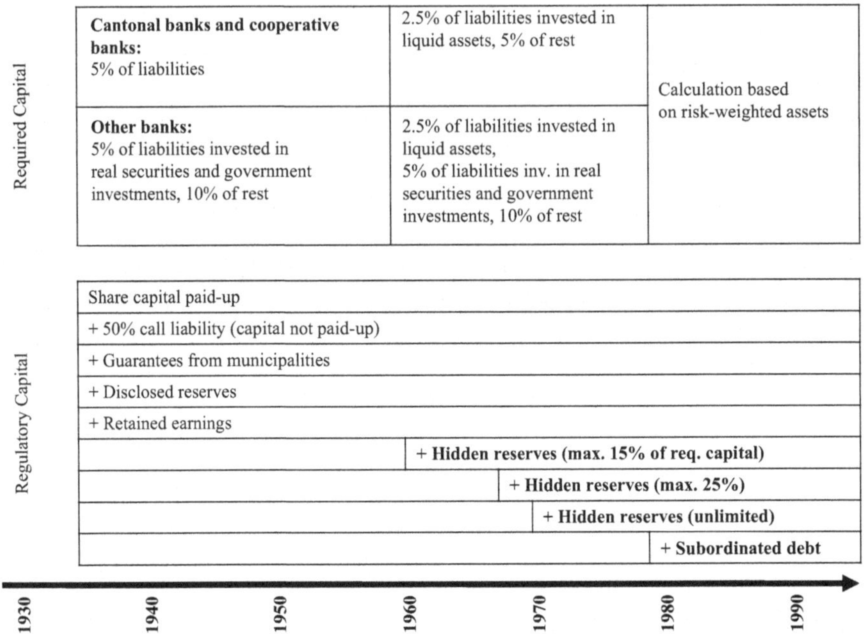

Required Capital

Cantonal banks and cooperative banks: 5% of liabilities	2.5% of liabilities invested in liquid assets, 5% of rest	Calculation based on risk-weighted assets
Other banks: 5% of liabilities invested in real securities and government investments, 10% of rest	2.5% of liabilities invested in liquid assets, 5% of liabilities inv. in real securities and government investments, 10% of rest	

Regulatory Capital

Share capital paid-up			
+ 50% call liability (capital not paid-up)			
+ Guarantees from municipalities			
+ Disclosed reserves			
+ Retained earnings			
	+ Hidden reserves (max. 15% of req. capital)		
		+ Hidden reserves (max. 25%)	
			+ Hidden reserves (unlimited)
			+ Subordinated debt

1930   1940   1950   1960   1970   1980   1990

FIGURE 5.4 Capital regulation in Switzerland, 1934–95

reserves' to be used as part of the capital. That included hidden reserves. The extent of this use could be set by the FBC.[164]

The FBC allowed that up to 15% of the required capital could consist of hidden reserves. The ratio was increased to 25% in 1967. After 1972, hidden reserves could be used as part of the required capital without any restrictions at all. After 1981, banks could also use subordinated debt as part of their required capital (up to 10%; the ratio was further increased in 1988). Thus, the definition moved closer towards what came to be Tier 2 capital in Basel I in 1988. By 1981, the definition of regulatory capital in Swiss legislation was almost identical to that in the Basel Accord.

The revision of the Banking Ordinance of 1981 also brought the introduction of a risk-weighted approach. For the first time, capital was not measured against liabilities, but against assets. According to the FBC, the new approach allowed a better consideration of banks' different business activities.[165]

Having presented capital regulation as introduced in 1934/5, and the changes it subsequently underwent up to 1991, the question remains as to

---

[164] *Vollziehungsverordnung zum Bundesgesetz über die Banken und Sparkassen vom 30. August 1961, 1961* Art. 9f.
[165] Eidgenössische Bankenkommission, *Jahresbericht 1980 der Eidgenössischen Bankenkommission* (Bern, April 1981), p. 5.

whether or not banks actually met the statutory capital requirements. In order to assess this, one can divide the regulatory capital by the required capital. The percentage is the so-called capital coverage ratio.[166] If the ratio is above 100%, a bank holds more capital than legally required. Until the revision of the Banking Ordinance in 1961, most balance sheet items relevant for calculating the capital coverage ratio were public. After 1961, the opacity of the banking market was significantly increased as hidden reserves could be used as well. In 1953, however, the SNB started to publish the capital coverage ratio for all bank groups in Switzerland.[167] Based on a few assumptions, one can estimate the capital coverage ratio for the period 1935–53 (see footnote 168).

Figure 5.5 shows the capital coverage ratio from 1935 to 1991. The average of all Swiss banks together was above the minimum capital requirement of 100% for the entire period. However, the capital coverage of the group of big

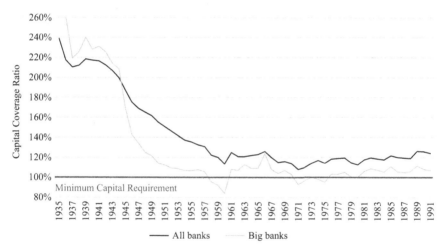

FIGURE 5.5 Capital coverage ratio (regulatory capital vs. required capital), all banks and big banks in Switzerland, 1935–91[168]

---

[166] In German, the ratio was called 'Eigenmitteldeckungsgrad'.

[167] Swiss National Bank, 'Das Schweizerische Bankwesen 1952' (Zurich: Orell Füssli, 1953).

[168] Calculations and data: 1935–49: Author's calculations and estimates based on balance sheet data of bank groups, taking into account collateralised loans and government securities. It was assumed that 80% of the loans to customers were collateralised. For the calculation of the regulatory capital, the Banking Ordinance of 1935 also allowed the use of municipal guarantees and 50% of unpaid capital. It was assumed that these two forms of capital contributed 1% to the regulatory capital (assumption based on data from the 1960s, for which the detailed disaggregated capital is available). 1950–89: Author's calculation. Data on investments in (respectively loans to) the Federal government, the Federal Railway, cantons, and municipalities were used to adjust for a lower capital requirement for these assets. Data: Swiss National Bank, *Die Banken in der Schweiz (annual issues 1906–2015)*.

banks deteriorated rapidly after the end of the Second World War, and in the mid-1950s the big banks increasingly struggled to meet capital requirements. The capital coverage still reached 105.7% in 1957, but in 1958 it fell below the 100% capital requirement, to 95.5%, for the first time. The low point was reached with a capital coverage ratio of 84% in 1960, meaning that the banks lacked 16% of the required capital. The ratio recovered in the 1960s, only to drop below the minimum capital requirement in 1971 (93.0%). It was only in the 1980s that the big banks managed to improve their capital coverage to above the minimum threshold.

5.3.3   The Influence of Banks on the Evolution of Banking Regulation

The number of non-compliant banks did not change significantly over time. What changed, however, was the relevance of the banks concerned. In 1959, the FBC granted eleven approvals to Raiffeisen banks, savings banks, and one cantonal bank. Besides these banks, the Union Bank of Switzerland and the Swiss Bank Corporation (SBC) also failed to meet capital requirements.[169] At the beginning of the 1960s, Credit Suisse also failed to meet capital requirements.[170] This gap in the capital requirements meant that the three most significant financial institutions in Switzerland lacked capital from a regulatory point of view. The three banks represented about a fourth of Switzerland's banking market (measured by total assets).[171]

Such a situation triggers a reaction from a banking supervisor. Theoretically, a non-compliant bank may be forced to terminate its business and be liquidated or sold. Alternatively, the bank may continue its business by (1) issuing new shares, (2) restructuring (e.g. reducing the total of assets), (3) being granted an exceptional approval for not complying with the regulatory standards, or (4) the regulation is changed altogether and the capital requirements are lowered. In the Swiss case, apart from divesting and reducing the balance sheet sizes, all these alternative options were used.

The Swiss banks frequently sold new shares to their shareholders. The Union Bank of Switzerland increased its paid-up capital in 1959, 1961, 1962, and 1965. Within seven years, the paid-up capital had doubled. Credit Suisse issued fresh capital in 1961, 1963, and 1965. The SBC raised its nominal capital in 1961, 1963, and 1966. The FBC also frequently granted exceptional approvals

---

[169] Eidgenössische Bankenkommission, *Geschäftsbericht der Eidgenössischen Bankenkommission an den Bundesrat für das Jahr 1959* (Bern, 1960), Swiss Federal Archives, E6520A#1983/50#62*.

[170] Eidgenössische Bankenkommission, *Eigene Mittel der Grossbanken. Notiz an Mitglieder der Eidg. Bankenkommission* (Bern, 21 March 1963), Swiss Federal Archives, E6520A#1983/50#48*.

[171] In 1960, the three banks had a cumulated balance sheet total of around CHF 5bn. For detailed figures, see Swiss National Bank, 'Das Schweizerische Bankwesen 1960' (Zurich: Orell Füssli, 1961), p. 240ff.

for non-compliant banks based on the Banking Act (Art. 23, 3d). In the long run, however, the capital requirements were further eased through lower capital requirements and broader definitions of capital, as shown in Section 5.3.2. Naturally, non-compliant banks have a distinct interest in their regulatory framework. What was the role of the banks in the regulatory changes which took place from the 1960s to the 1980s?

The regulatory changes outlined herein were made upon requests from banks. Besides the big banks, the Swiss Bankers Association (SBA), as a representative body for banking interests, lobbied for the continuous development of banking legislation. The SBA had been established in 1912. One of its goals was to coordinate and promote banking interests domestically and abroad. Since then, it had become one of Switzerland's most influential business interests associations. The SBA also had well-established connections at the political and administrative levels. Members of the SBA were frequently present in extra-parliamentary commissions.[172] There were also links between the SBA and the SNB: several board members of the SBA were also members of the SNB's 'bank council', while some were even members of the SNB's 'governing board'.[173]

The first requests to lower the capital requirements were brought to the FBC by the Swiss Bank Corporation in 1955 and 1956. A second attempt was made in 1957 by the group of the big banks together with the SBA. The banks and the SBA suggested that hidden reserves should be counted as part of the regulatory capital and that the required ratio for liquid assets should be lowered.[174]

The banks used a range of arguments to convince the FBC to broaden the definition of capital. The general directors of the big banks argued that their business activities had changed strongly in the last couple of years: large-scale

---

[172] Thomas David and others, 'Networks of Coordination: Swiss Business Associations as an Intermediary between Business, Politics and Administration during the 20th Century', *Business and Politics*, 11.4 (2009), 1–38.

[173] The following persons were members of the SBA and SNB bank council (in chronological order): Mauderli Fridolin, Frey Julius, Waldkirch von-Bock Oskar, Sarasin-Iselin Alfred, Bersier Henri, Kurz Hermann, Curchod Gustave, Barbey-Gampert Edmond, Gautier-Fatio Victor, Speich-Jenny Rudolf (Thomas), Gisling Alfred, Leemann Eduard, Schaefer-Hunziker Alfred, Givel Roger, Generali Claudio, Studer Fritz, Gysi Alfredo. The following persons were members of the SBA and the SNB Governing Board: Hirs Alfred, Lusser Markus, Blattner Niklaus. Jöhr Adolf was even a member of the SNB Governing Board (1915–18), the SBA (1920–39), and the SNB bank council (1939–51). For an analysis of links between the SBA and SNB, see also Sancey, *Quand les banquiers font la loi*. Data: Université de Lausanne, Faculté des sciences sociales et politiques, 'Observatoire des élites suisses (OBELIS)', *Données*: www.unil .ch/obelis/home.html.

[174] Eidgenössische Bankenkommission, *Anrechnung stiller Reserven als eigene Mittel. Notiz betr. die Anrechnung stiller Reserven als eigene Mittel vom 11.12.1963*. (Bern, 11 December 1963), Swiss Federal Archives, E6520A#1983/50#49*. Eidgenössische Bankenkommission, *Vorschriften über eigene Mittel. Protokoll der Sitzung vom 20. Januar 1958 zwischen Bankenkommission und Vertretern der Banken* (Bern, 20 January 1958), Swiss Federal Archives, E6520A#1983/50#48*.

industrial investments had become less relevant, their foreign exposure had become more diversified, and, overall, they were developing more towards deposit banks. Furthermore, they argued that liquid assets especially were mostly risk free, and regulation should take this into account. Overall, the proposed changes would, according to the bank managers, not affect the protection of creditors, and the lower risk would justify lower capital requirements.[175] The general director of Credit Suisse argued that 'the solid tradition, with which the banks are run, leads to safety buffers that would allow a more liberal regulation'.[176]

The banks also argued that the high growth rates of the balance sheet totals caused by foreign capital inflows in the previous years might not be sustainable. Thus, balance sheets might contract again, leaving banks overcapitalised.[177] Finally, comparisons to foreign competitors were also often used. The general director of the Union Bank of Switzerland, for example, highlighted that 'the high share capitals of the Swiss banks have proven their worth but are also their most expensive source of capital. Besides, the Swiss dividend rates for bank shares are far below the foreign dividend.'[178]

During the 1930s and 1940s, the position of the FBC had been that the capital requirements were generally too low. The FBC even proposed to the Federal Council that the Banking Ordinance should be revised, and minimum capital, as well as liquidity requirements, increased.[179] The tightening of the requirements failed because 'no agreement with the interested banking groups could be reached', according to the FBC's former Head of the Secretariat.[180]

The view of the FBC changed in the 1950s. Considering the proposals made by the Swiss Bankers Association and the big banks, the FBC drafted a revised Ordinance and submitted it for consultation to the SNB in 1958 and the SBA in 1959.[181] The proposed legislation was then discussed in a conference between the FBC, the SNB, the SBA, and representatives of the big banks in December 1959.

---

[175] Eidgenössische Bankenkommission, *Protokoll 1958*, SFA, *E6520A#1983/50#48**, pp. 11–18.

[176] Eberhard Reinhardt, General Director of Credit Suisse. Eidgenössische Bankenkommission, *Protokoll 1958*, SFA, *E6520A#1983/50#48**, p. 16.

[177] Samuel Schweizer, General Director of Swiss Bank Corporation. Eidgenössische Bankenkommission, *Protokoll 1958*, SFA, *E6520A#1983/50#48**, p. 14.

[178] Alfred Schäfer, General Director Union Bank of Switzerland. Eidgenössische Bankenkommission, *Protokoll 1958*, SFA, *E6520A#1983/50#48**, p. 11.

[179] Eidgenössische Bankenkommission, *Geschäftsbericht der Eidgenössischen Bankenkommission an den Bundesrat für das Jahr 1939* (Bern, 25 April 1940), pp. 3–4, Swiss Federal Archives, *E6520A#1983/50#62**.

[180] Robert Reimann, *Kommentar zum Bundesgesetz über die Banken und Sparkassen*, 3. Auflage (Zurich: Poly. Verlag, 1963), pp. 12–13. Robert Reimann was the Secretary of the Federal Banking Commission.

[181] Eidgenössische Bankenkommission, *Notiz Anrechnung stiller Reserven*, SFA, *E6520A#1983/50#49**.

The most crucial change in the draft of the Banking Ordinance was that the FBC would be responsible for setting the percentage of hidden reserves that could be used as regulatory capital. The question discussed in the meeting of the interest groups was where to set the limit on the use of hidden reserves. The SNB had opposed the extensive use of hidden reserves for regulatory purposes. The big banks wanted to use as many hidden reserves as possible. Interestingly, although hesitant at first, the FBC sided with the big banks. The representatives of the Commission argued that the big banks had struggled to fulfil capital requirements for some time and that if there was no change in regulation, the commission would have to continue granting exceptional approvals for non-compliance with the capital requirements. The meeting between the various interest groups in 1959 led to the compromise that 15% of the required capital could be composed of hidden reserves.[182]

According to the FBC, the 15% rule was meant to be a temporary exception to support some undercapitalised big banks. In the view of the FBC, this temporary solution would prevent even bigger capital issuances. The commission was aware that the need for further capital was mainly driven by the large inflows of foreign capital to the big banks.[183] The effect of the regulatory change in 1961 on the capital coverage ratio was striking. Down at 84% in 1960, the ratio of the big banks grew to 108% in 1961 (see Figure 5.5). About half of this increase came from the use of hidden reserves. Archival material indicates that the big banks used at least CHF 104m of hidden reserves for regulatory purposes in 1961.[184] The rest of the change in the capital coverage ratio can be attributed to capital issuances by the big banks (CHF 95m) in the same year. From a regulatory point of view, the banks were suddenly substantially better capitalised.

The cycle of proposals from the banks to the supervisor leading to a compromise that eased capital regulation was repeated several times in later years. A first request to use more hidden reserves by the Union Bank of Switzerland in 1963 was declined.[185] In 1967, however, the SBA asked for an increase of the hidden reserves allowed for regulatory purposes to 30%. The FBC confirmed a 'benevolent' consideration of the Bankers Association's proposal and decided – as a compromise – on 25%.[186]

---

[182] Reimann, *Kommentar zum Bundesgesetz über die Banken und Sparkassen*, p. 13.

[183] Reimann, *Kommentar zum Bundesgesetz über die Banken und Sparkassen*, p. 13.

[184] Eidgenössische Bankenkommission, *Anrechnung stiller Reserven*, SFA, E6520A#1983/50#49*.

[185] Eidgenössische Bankenkommission, *Verhandlungen der Eidgenössichen Bankenkommission vom 29. April, 1963* (Bern, 29 April 1963), Swiss Federal Archives, E6520A#1983/50#49*.

[186] Sekretariat der Eidgenössische Bankenkommission, *Brief des Sekretariats an die Mitglieder der Eidgenössischen Bankenkommission, Bankenkammer. Betrifft Anrechnung stiller Reserven als eigene Mittel / Abänderung der Verfügung vom 30.08.1961.* (Bern, 8 December 1967), Swiss Federal Archives, E6520B#2007_62#239.

In 1971 and 1972, the Banking Act and the Banking Ordinance were revised.[187] During the preparation of the Ordinance, a delegation of the SBA bypassed the FBC and talked directly to Switzerland's Minister of Finance, Nello Celio. The FBC was disappointed to have been excluded from these discussions, even more so as the Minister of Finance made various concessions. At this point, the FBC was clearly against a further weakening of the capital requirements. The experts' group of the FBC tasked with preparing a new Banking Ordinance suggested that a maximum of 80% of the regulatory capital could be hidden reserves. The Minister of Finance, however, decided to allow the unlimited use of hidden reserves.[188]

Publicly, the government argued that the revisions of the Banking Act and the Banking Ordinance in 1971 increased the liquidity and solvency requirements.[189] Both changes were undertaken against the background of the internationalisation of the Swiss financial centre. The revised Banking Ordinance required a minimum capital of CHF 2m for the foundation of a bank (this was what was meant by the 'stricter' capital requirements). The requirement targeted mainly new market entrants – many of them foreign institutions. Established banks in Switzerland, however, were not affected by this change.

The stricter liquidity requirements were the result of growing criticism of the large-scale foreign investments of the big banks. In the consultation process for the new Banking Act, the Social Democrat Party as well as the Workers Union had voiced their concerns that foreign investments – specifically referring to the Euromarkets – had increased the risks of the banks. The Federal Council shared this opinion, commenting that 'the increasing shift of liquidity from the domestic to the foreign market cannot be denied and poses a number of risks' and suggested that the liquidity requirements should be increased.[190]

In 1981, capital regulation in the Banking Ordinance was revised again.[191] For the first time, subordinated debt was allowed to be counted as part of the regulatory capital. The banks had been attempting to introduce such a change

---

[187] *BankG 1971. Vollziehungsverordnung zum Bundesgesetz über die Banken und Sparkassen vom 17. Mai 1972*, 1972.

[188] Sekretariat der Eidgenössischen Bankenkommission, *Bericht an die Mitglieder der Eidgenössischen Bankenkommission betr. Revision der Vollziehungsverordnung* (Bern, 16 February 1972), Swiss Federal Archives, E6520A#1983/50#49*.

[189] See, for example, the statement of the Federal Council on the revision of the Banking Act: Bundesrat, 'Botschaft des Bundesrates an die Bundesversammlung über die Revision des Bankgesetzes', *Bundesblatt*, 10570, 1.24 (1970), 1144–203.

[190] Bundesrat, *Botschaft des Bundesrates an die Bundesversammlung über die Revision des Bankgesetzes*, p. 1169.

[191] Another relevant change due to the Banking Ordinance was the use of consolidated balance sheets. *Vollziehungsverordnung zum Bundesgesetz über die Banken und Sparkassen vom 1. Dezember 1980*, 1981.

for several years.[192] It was also the first time that Switzerland moved to a capital adequacy model that exclusively focused on the asset risk.[193] The assets were differentiated according to fifteen different categories, and each category was matched with a capital requirement ratio. The underlying idea was the same as in the Basel I framework that was introduced in Switzerland in 1991 and 1994.[194] The application, however, was different. Basel I used risk-weights for each asset category and multiplied the risk-weighted assets with 8%. The Swiss approach in 1981 assigned a capital requirement ratio to each asset category (instead of a risk weight). Despite this, when the Basel I requirements were introduced into Swiss banking legislation ten years later, it did not bring fundamental changes. Subordinated debt, hidden reserves, and hybrid capital instruments could already be partially credited as Tier 2 capital. In addition, taking into account off-balance-sheet items was not an innovation, but rather a development of the existing framework.

Were all these regulatory changes relevant to the big banks? Figure 5.6 shows the structure of the regulatory capital used by the big banks from 1970 to 1995. There is no data available for the period before 1970. In the first half of the 1970s, the hidden reserves were even bigger than the paid-up capital. By 1974, for example, the hidden reserves held by the big banks were CHF 2.2bn, while the paid-up capital was CHF 1.9bn. Thus, the inclusion of hidden reserves as part of the regulatory capital was fundamental. Similarly, the relevance of subordinated debt grew over time. By 1994, the paid-up share capital of the big banks was CHF 9.4bn; the subordinated debt was CHF 11.1bn. Finally, it is also important to note that the largest part of the regulatory capital was disclosed reserves, and not paid-up share capital.

The broadening of the capital definition was absolutely crucial for the growth of the big banks. Estimates show that the total assets of the big banks would have had to be about 15–35% smaller if the capital regulation was not changed. Thus, changing capital requirements was an important factor that allowed banks to grow at such a rapid pace.

Despite the lobbying of the big banks, the change in capital requirements in the 1960s and 1970s is rather surprising, given Switzerland's macroeconomic context at the time. The SNB was constantly fighting foreign capital inflows

---

[192] Eidgenössische Bankenkommission, *Jahresbericht 1978 der Eidgenössischen Bankenkommission* (Bern, April 1979), p. 13.

[193] Eidgenössische Bankenkommission, *Jahresbericht 1980 der Eidgenössischen Bankenkommission*, p. 5.

[194] The revision of the Banking Ordinance in 1990 harmonised the risk classifications of Swiss legislation and the Basel Accord. In 1994, the capital requirements were changed from a direct to an indirect model. Until then, different requirements ratios were used for the risk classes. After 1994, the risk classes were weighted according to the Basel Accord and then multiplied with the requirement ratio of 8%. *Vollziehungsverordnung zum Bundesgesetz über die Banken und Sparkassen*, 1990; *Vollziehungsverordnung zum Bundesgesetz über die Banken und Sparkassen*, 1994; *Bundesgesetz über die Banken und Sparkassen*, 1994.

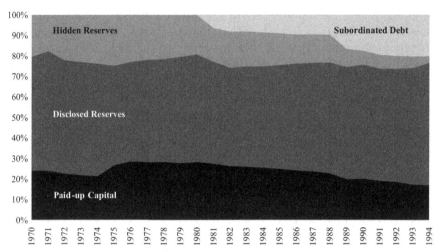

FIGURE 5.6 Structure of the regulatory capital, big banks, 1970–94[195]

during these decades. It took defensive measures to limit the inflow of capital from abroad – for example, by prohibiting investments and negative interest rates on the deposits of non-residents, as well as restricting borrowing abroad.[196] The Swiss economist Edgar Salin termed the state of the economy a 'Devisenbann-Wirtschaft' ('currency ban economy').[197] The assessment made of this period, which lasted until 1979, both by economists and officially by the SNB itself, is clear: the defensive measures by the SNB were largely ineffective.[198]

One measure that might have been effective, however, was stricter capital requirements for the big banks. It is likely that stricter capital requirements would have acted as a brake for the balance sheet growth of undercapitalised banks, which was driven substantially by foreign capital flows. In retrospect, there might be two reasons why stricter capital rules were not considered as a tool for monetary policy.

Firstly, the FBC and various political actors (the Federal Council, parliament) could change the regulatory environment for banks (Banking Act,

[195] Author's calculations. The data was collected from: Eidgenössische Bankenkommission, *Anrechnung stiller Reserven, SFA, E6520A#1983/50#49**; and various editions of Swiss National Bank, *Die Banken in der Schweiz (annual issues 1906–2015)*.
[196] Bernholz, *Die Nationalbank 1945–1982*, pp. 127–43.
[197] Edgar Salin, 'Devisen-Bann-Wirtschaft: über die beginnende Anarchie im westlichen Währungssystem', *Kyklos*, 1964, 149–64.
[198] Kurt Schiltknecht, 'Beurteilung der Gentlemen's Agreements und Konjunkturbeschlüsse der Jahre 1954–1966: Unter besonderer Berücksichtigung der Auslandgelder' (ETH Zurich, 1970), p. 127ff; Swiss National Bank, *75 Jahre Schweizerische Nationalbank, 1907–1982*, p. 102; Bernholz, *Die Nationalbank 1945–1982*, p. 123.

Ordinance, Circulars). The SNB attended conferences that discussed regulatory revisions but could only make recommendations. The archival material suggests that the SBA and the big banks were much more closely involved in the regulatory process than the SNB. The FBC acted more as a mediator between the interests of the banks and the SNB than as an independent supervisory voice. Furthermore, the FBC was a weak supervisor until the revision of the Banking Act in 1971. Its enforcement mechanisms were – even in its own view – 'not sufficient'.[199] In cases of non-compliance with the Banking Act, the commission could make either a criminal complaint to the cantonal prosecution authorities or fine the bank. The handling of such complaints, however, would often take years and reach the statutes of limitations. The FBC also had little success with regulatory fines, as the maximum amount was too low (CHF 20,000).[200] The ultimate threat for a bank – withdrawal of its banking licence – was only possible after 1971.

Second, the SNB had to strike its own bargain with the big banks and the SBA. Many measures to reduce foreign capital inflows were based on gentlemen's agreements – for example in 1950, 1955, 1960, 1962, 1975, and 1976 – negotiated through the SBA.[201] The SNB depended on the cooperation of the banks for these measures. Overall, the regulatory changes in the 1960s and 1970s were clearly in the interest of the banks, and the banks took part in shaping their regulatory environment.

Publicly, the regulatory changes and the non-compliance of the major big banks with the capital requirements were noted, but did not trigger a public debate on the topic. The revision of the Banking Ordinance in 1961, which was a crucial technical change with a significant impact on the growth of the big banks, received little public attention. The *Neue Zürcher Zeitung*, for example, simply described the regulatory changes or the capital ratios of the banks, without further comments.[202] The banks themselves were also silent about their struggle to meet capital requirements at their annual meetings.[203]

The interest of banks in developing the regulatory environment certainly persisted in the 1980s. However, the changes mainly followed trends that were already apparent on an international level. Risk-weighted approaches to

[199] Eidgenössische Bankenkommission, *Jahresbericht 1984 der Eidgenössischen Bankenkommission* (Bern, April 1985), p. 12.
[200] Eidgenössische Bankenkommission, *Jahresbericht 1984 der Eidgenössischen Bankenkommission*, p. 12. See Art. 46, *BankG 1934*.
[201] See the chronicle of monetary and exchange rate policies by the SNB in Swiss National Bank, *75 Jahre Schweizerische Nationalbank, 1907–1982*.
[202] Neue Zürcher Zeitung, 'Keine Revision des Bankengesetzes: Eine neue Vollziehungsverordnung', *Abendausgabe Nr. 3162* (Zurich, 30 August 1961), p. 13; Neue Zürcher Zeitung, 'Das schweizerische Bankwesen im Jahre 1961' (Zurich, 15 January 1963), p. 14.
[203] Neue Zürcher Zeitung, 'Schweizerischer Bankverein' (Zurich, 24 February 1959); Neue Zürcher Zeitung, 'Generalversammlung der Schweizerischen Bankgesellschaft' (Zurich, 9 March 1963).

measuring capital adequacy were being discussed at the beginning of the 1970s at the European level and later in the BCBS. Switzerland took part in the negotiations in the BCBS. In this context, the introduction of the Swiss framework in 1981 is not surprising. Moreover, the use of subordinated debt for regulatory purposes came into fashion too.

5.4 THE UNITED STATES: FINDING THE RIGHT WEIGHT

The Great Depression of the 1930s started a new era for banks in the United States. Only four days after the bank holiday on 5 March 1933, the United States Congress passed the Banking Act (Glass–Steagall), giving the Federal Reserve and the Office of the Comptroller of the Currency (OCC) the authority to reopen or close banks. The Banking Acts of 1933 and then 1935 and the following supervisory changes created a new regulatory regime in US banking. This new regime meant less competition for existing banks, as market entry was controlled. The legislature separated commercial banking from investment banking. Regulation Q introduced a maximum interest rate on savings and prohibited interest rates on demand deposits. Deposit insurance was established, and a new federal bank supervisor, the Federal Deposit Insurance Corporation, was created.[204] Moreover, banking supervision practice changed from a rule-based approach to one where bank examiners received more discretion.[205]

The years from the Second World War into the 1960s were a period with few bank failures, creating a perception of a stable banking system. The environment changed in the 1970s. Domestically, a part of the banking industry collapsed, and the Savings and Loans sector failed entirely.[206] Among the failing banks were also larger institutions, such as the United States National Bank (USNB) of San Diego in 1973 and the Franklin National Bank of New York in 1974, ranking 86th and 20th by size.[207] With growing instability in the banking market, criticism of banking supervision grew.

---

[204] Milton Friedman and Anna J. Schwartz, *A Monetary History of the United States 1867–1960*, Studies in Business Cycles; No. 12 (Princeton: Princeton University Press, 1963), chap. 8.

[205] Eugene N. White, '"To Establish a More Effective Supervision of Banking": How the Birth of the Fed Altered Bank Supervision', in *The Origins, History, and Future of the Federal Reserve: A Return to Jekyll Island*, ed. Michael D. Bordo and William Roberds, Studies in Macroeconomic History (Cambridge: Cambridge University Press, 2013), pp. 7–54.

[206] Eugene White, 'Banking and Finance in the Twentieth Century', in *The Cambridge Economic History of the United States: Volume 3: The Twentieth Century*, ed. Robert E. Gallman and Stanley L. Engerman, Cambridge Economic History of the United States (Cambridge: Cambridge University Press, 2000), Vol. III, 743–802

[207] Roger Tufts and Paul Moloney, 'The History of Supervisory Expectations for Capital Adequacy: Part I (1863–1983)', *Moments in History – Office of the Comptroller of the Currency*, 2022, p. 10.

The 1970s were also marked by increased competition domestically and internationally. The banking market in the United States was internationalised internally, with the group of foreign banks being the fastest-growing segment of banks in the United States. And, at the international level, the large international US banks – often referred to as money centre banks – gradually lost importance. By 1970, six out of the ten largest banks in the world were from the United States. Ten years later, only two US banks ranked among the ten largest banks. Japanese banks in particular were expanding quickly.[208]

Nevertheless, measured by total assets, the banks in the United States grew rapidly. Their balance sheet total increased by an annual average of 15% during the first half of the 1970s. The growth rates of the total equity capital averaged about 9% per year.[209] The fact that the expansion of total assets outpaced that of capital resulted in decreasing capital/assets ratios. The capital ratios of US banks fell sharply during the Second World War, recovered to 8.6% in 1962, and entered a period of steady decline to 5.3% in 1980. Much of the decline – about 2.0 percentage points – occurred between 1971 and 1974. A significant change in terms of the structure on the liabilities side of the US banks was the shift towards long-term borrowing. Until the 1960s, savings of consumers and demand deposits were essential funding sources. From the 1970s, the issuance of long-term debt gained importance, a factor which should eventually also alter the definition of capital in banking.[210]

Figure 5.7 shows US banks' capital/assets ratios from 1969 to 1984 for different size groups of banks (measured by total assets). A crucial feature of the declining capital ratios in the 1970s was that large banks were the main driver of this trend. Between 1970 and 1980, for example, the capital/assets ratio of small banks grew, while that of banks with assets between $1bn and $5bn and above $5bn dropped by 0.5 percentage points and 1.2 percentage points, respectively.

The federal bank supervisory agencies had emerged from the Second World War with a new view on capital adequacy. The classic 10% capital/deposit ratio was gone in supervisory practice, and the new perception was that the quality of assets– among other factors – should determine the required amount of capital in a bank. After the Second World War, using a capital/risk-assets ratio was common in supervisory practice. However, the methods to assess capital adequacy soon started to diverge again.

The OCC, the Federal Reserve Board, and the Federal Deposit Insurance Company determined capital adequacy on the level of bank-specific

---

[208] Wolfgang H. Reinicke, *Banking, Politics and Global Finance: American Commercial Banks and Regulatory Change, 1980–1990*, Studies in International Political Economy (Aldershot: Edward Elgar Publishing, 1995), p. 92.

[209] Refers to FDIC-insured commercial banks. Federal Deposit Insurance Corporation, *Historical Bank Data*, tbl. CB14.

[210] James G. Ehlen, 'A Review of Bank Capital and Its Adequacy', *Economic Review*, Federal Reserve Bank of Atlanta, 54.11 (1983), 54–60 (p. 56).

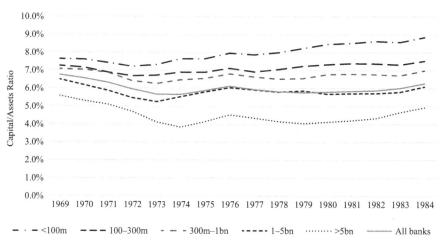

FIGURE 5.7 Capital/assets ratio by bank size (total assets), 1969–84[211]

assessments, providing bank examiners with a certain degree of discretion. Legally, the agencies had limited authority to enforce capital requirements.

The methods for assessing capital adequacy among three federal agencies and the importance of the topic varied between the 1950s and the 1970s. In the 1950s, the three federal bank supervisory agencies publicly discussed their supervisory frameworks for capital. The discourse was rooted in the legacy of the Second World War, leaving banks with high shares of government debt in their balance sheets and challenging traditional measures for capital adequacy.

The Federal Reserve was the leading voice in measuring capital adequacy from the 1940s to the 1980s. Its Analyzing Bank Capital (ABC) formula for capital requirements, developed in the 1950s, was the most advanced measurement method, and the OCC and the FDIC adopted many of the FED's principles.[212] The FED's approach already consisted of a risk-weighting of assets. The capital was then compared to the 'risk assets'.

However, in the 1960s, the question of capitalisation in banking lost some of its importance. The OCC was the federal agency that most emphasised determinants beyond capital when assessing banks. In 1962, the OCC shifted its focus from the risk-assets approach to a total of eight potential factors relevant for analysing a bank's financial stability, such as management quality, earnings and earnings retention, quality and character of ownership,

[211] Data obtained from 'Letter by Paul Volcker to Timothy Wirth, Chairman Subcommittee on Telecommunications, Consumer Protection, and Finance, House of Representatives', in *Hearing Before the Subcommittee on Telecommunications, Consumer Protection, and Finance, 99th Congress, First Session on H.R. 2032*, 99–38 (Washington, DC: US Government Printing Office, 1985), pp. 461–68 (p. 467).

[212] Reinicke, *Banking, Politics and Global Finance*, p. 34.

and deposit volatility.[213] By 1971, the relevance of capital ratios in the OCC's supervisory practice had deteriorated even further.[214]

The FDIC has worked with several capital ratios after the Second World War. The FDIC deducted expected losses both from capital and assets, leading to a net-sound capital and adjusted assets. The Federal Reserve Board used its ABC formula, which it revised in 1972. Among the three government agencies, it was the only one using a risk-weighted assets approach until the 1970s.[215]

Besides the measuring approaches of capital adequacy, the definition of capital itself was also the subject of intensive debate. Banks had aimed to use subordinated or long-term debt as a substitute for equity capital since the 1960s.[216] The Federal agencies answered such requests with different guidelines, leading to varying definitions of capital. The FED was the most hesitant to accept subordinated debt as a part of the capital and considered paid-up capital and reserves as capital from 1970.[217] The OCC and the FDIC followed more liberal approaches than the FED. Under certain conditions, the OCC allowed that up to one-third of banks' capital could consist of subordinated debt after 1962.[218] The OCC analysed aspects such as the ratio of 'earnings to interest on long-term debt' and 'retained earnings to repayments of long-term debt'.[219]

The opinion of the FDIC on subordinated debt seemed to be evolving. It acknowledged the use of subordinated debt with a maturity of more than seven years as a part of bank capital, serving as a protection for depositors against losses.[220] In 1980, the FDIC took a stronger stance and argued that subordinated debt should not have the same quality as equity capital as it cannot absorb unanticipated losses – one of the critical functions of equity capital.[221] In the official statistical appendix of the FDIC's annual report, 'notes and debentures' was listed as an individual item under the banks'

---

[213] Orgler and Wolkowitz, *Bank Capital*, p. 70.

[214] In the revised version of the 'Comptroller's Manual for National Banks' in 1971, the topic of capital adequacy was no longer discussed in detail. Tufts and Moloney, *The History of Supervisory Expectations for Capital Adequacy: Part I (1863–1983)*, p. 10.

[215] Putnam, *Early Warning Systems and Financial Analysis in Bank Monitoring*, p. 9.

[216] Ehlen, *A Review of Bank Capital and Its Adequacy*, p. 54.

[217] See Amendments to Regulation D (Reserves of Member Banks) and Regulation Q (Interest on Deposits), 12th June 1970 and 4th June 1976. Federal Reserve, 'Annual Report of the Board of Governors of the Federal Reserve System 1970', 1971, p. 73; Federal Reserve, 'Annual Report of the Board of Governors of the Federal Reserve System 1976', 1977, p. 139.

[218] Office of the Comptroller of the Currency, 'Annual Report of the Comptroller of the Currency 1963', 1964, pp. 18–19.

[219] Orgler and Wolkowitz, *Bank Capital*, pp. 67, 76.

[220] FDIC, 'Annual Report of the Federal Deposit Insurance Corporation 1970', 1971, p. 168.

[221] Lee Davison, 'Banking Legislation and Regulation', in *An Examination of the Banking Crises of the 1980s and Early 1990s*, ed. Federal Deposit Insurance Corporation (Federal Deposit Insurance Corporation, 1997), pp. 87–136 (p. 111). Federal Deposit Insurance Corporation, 'Statement on Policy of Capital Adequacy', Federal Register, 46.248 (1981), 62693–4 (p. 62694).

capital from 1966 to 1975. From 1975, it was neither assigned to capital nor liabilities. Proportionally, 'notes and debentures' represented about 5–7% of the banks' total capital (if one views it as capital) between 1966 and 1979.[222]

In the 1970s, the three federal bank supervision agencies arrived at a point where all had acknowledged the importance of the 'quality of assets' to assess capital adequacy. However, the approaches to measuring capital adequacy and the definition of capital varied.

5.4.1   Changes in Capital Adequacy Standards in the 1970s

The increased banking instability in the United States in the 1970s put pressure on the regulators and supervisors. In particular, the criticism towards the supervisors grew, and one of the key arguments was that banking supervisors had not been able to detect 'problem banks' early enough. Moreover, many policymakers identified a second deficiency in the varying measurement approaches and definitions of capital. The Federal bank supervisors concluded that more uniformity in banking supervision and also in the issue of bank adequacy was needed.[223] Aiming to reform bank supervision in the United States, the FDIC, the OCC, and the FED (together with the Federal Home Loan Bank Board and the National Credit Union Administration) established an interagency body, the Federal Financial Institutions Examination Council (FFIEC) in 1979. The purpose of the FFIEC was to promote uniform principles and standards in bank supervision, which also encompassed the measurement and definition of capital.[224]

The OCC made the first attempts to strengthen capital requirements in 1980, suggesting stricter rules for the definition of capital.[225] The banking sector strongly opposed these suggestions, and the OCC eventually refrained from introducing narrower definitions for capital.[226] The work of the FFIEC was more successful than the OCC's first attempt. It published a first draft proposal for a uniform definition of capital and capital requirements in June 1981.[227] By the end of 1981, responding to the call for uniformity, the Federal Reserve and

---

[222] Author's calculations. Data: FDIC, 'Annual Reports of the Federal Deposit Insurance Corporation 1966–1979', 1980. (all banks)

[223] Reinicke, *Banking, Politics and Global Finance*, p. 136.

[224] Federal Financial Institutions Examination Council, *Annual Report 1979* (Washington, DC, 1980).

[225] Statement of the Comptroller of the Currency, John G. Heimann, before the Senate Committee on Banking, Housing and Urban Affairs, Washington, DC, 21 May 1980. See Office of the Comptroller of the Currency, 'Annual Report of the Comptroller of the Currency 1980', 1981, p. 199.

[226] Reinicke, *Banking, Politics and Global Finance*, p. 137.

[227] Federal Financial Institutions Examination Council, *Annual Report 1980* (Washington, DC, 1981); Federal Financial Institutions Examination Council, 'Proposed Definition of Bank Capital to Be Used in Determining Capital Adequacy', Federal Register, 46.120 (1981), 32498–500.

the OCC issued common guidelines for defining capital and capital requirements. The FDIC adopted slightly different criteria, as the agencies disagreed on the definition of capital.[228]

The FFIEC chose a middle-way between the two positions on using subordinated debt or not-for-capital requirements by defining two types of capital: primary capital consisted of common and preferred stock, surplus, undivided profits, mandatory convertible debt instruments, reserves for loan losses, and other capital reserves. The FFIEC defined other forms of capital, such as limited-life preferred stock and subordinated debt, as secondary capital.[229]

The guidelines of the FED and the OCC largely followed the suggestions of the FFIEC and categorised banks according to three different groups: multinational, regional, and community banks. The guidelines also included numerical minimum capital ratios for the very first time. Regional banks (total assets $1bn to $15bn) had to reach a primary capital/assets ratio of 5% and a capital/assets ratio of 5.5%. Community banks (total assets <$1bn) were required to meet a 6% primary capital/ratio and a 6.5% capital/assets ratio. The FED and the OCC excluded multinational banks from minimum capital requirements, arguing that the complexity of their businesses would require individual analyses. Contemporaries contended that the exclusion was because these banks failed to meet the capital requirements.[230] This argument is underlined by the large banks' capital/assets ratio (total assets above $5bn) in Figure 5.7, which was below the 5% threshold from 1972 to 1984. Both the FED and the OCC were well aware of the difficulties that large banks faced if they had to meet a 5% capital requirement in 1981 and might have opted for informal pressure on these banks instead.[231] Multinational banks reacted and issued substantial amounts of primary capital after 1981.[232]

The FDIC set a 5% minimum capital/assets ratio for all banks and a 6% minimum requirement for all state non-member banks. Several deviations from the concepts of the OCC and the FED emerged. The FDIC guidelines did not differentiate between bank sizes. Moreover, the FDIC adjusted both the capital and the assets by deducting losses and one-half of the doubtful assets. For capital, the FDIC used primary capital, disregarding secondary capital.[233]

Thus, by 1981, the Federal bank supervisory agencies had introduced leverage ratios, and the capital requirements and definitions became – despite some remaining differences – more harmonised between 1979 and 1981. However, three issues remained unresolved.

---

[228] Reinicke, *Banking, Politics and Global Finance*, pp. 140–1.
[229] Reinicke, *Banking, Politics and Global Finance*, p. 139.
[230] Ehlen, *A Review of Bank Capital and Its Adequacy*, p. 57.
[231] Reinicke, *Banking, Politics and Global Finance*, p. 139.
[232] Ehlen, *A Review of Bank Capital and Its Adequacy*, p. 57.
[233] Federal Deposit Insurance Corporation, *Statement on Policy of Capital Adequacy*.

Firstly, bank supervisors' enforcement of capital requirements – and, respectively, their authority – was still limited. The guiding principles issued by the three federal agencies in 1981 formalised capital requirements, but they were based on guidelines and not on law. Before 1981, there was no direct legal authority to enforce capital requirements, and the OCC, the FED, and the FDIC had to rely on persuasion. Beyond moral suasion, this could mean declining branch or acquisition applications or invoking cease-and-desist orders.[234] However, even with the new guidelines in 1981, the legal reach of the agencies was limited. The FDIC, for example, communicated in its official policy statement that it would use its authority by withholding the 'approval of applications of various types' to impose capital requirements.[235] A case in point for the limited legal authority of the federal agencies was the case of the OCC v. the First National Bank of Bellaire (Texas), which became a catalyst for an extension of the legal authority of the three Federal agencies.[236]

The OCC had issued a cease-and-desist order against Bellaire in May 1981, arguing that the bank was operating without adequate capital. Through the order, the OCC requested that the bank issued additional capital to reach a capital/assets ratio of 7% or higher. Bellaire challenged the ruling. In May 1983, the United States Court of Appeals, Fifth Circuit, decided in favour of Bellaire, stating a lack of substantial evidence by the OCC proving that the bank was 'unsafe and unsound'.[237] The court decision undermined the mandate of the OCC, the FED, and the FDIC to set and enforce capital requirements for banks.

Secondly, the new capital ratios introduced in 1981 did not quantitively consider the riskiness of assets, even though all three federal agencies had declared already in the 1930s that asset quality was the most relevant determinant for the required amount of capital and developed capital ratios that to some degree considered asset risk. The FED had even applied its ABC formula for capital adequacy in banking supervision since the 1950s.

5.4.2 The Latin American Debt Crisis as a Driver of Capital Standards

Between 1982 and 1986, the regulation and supervision of bank adequacy was completely transformed. The driver for the change was no longer internal financial instability but increasing international financial instability, leading to further harmonisation of capital requirements in the United States.

The debt of Latin American countries has been growing steadily since the 1970s. External borrowing by Argentina, Brazil, Mexico, and Venezuela grew

---

[234] Reinicke, Banking, Politics and Global Finance, p. 35.

[235] Federal Deposit Insurance Corporation, Statement on Policy of Capital Adequacy, p. 62694.

[236] Reinicke, Banking, Politics and Global Finance, p. 148; Tufts and Moloney, The History of Supervisory Expectations for Capital Adequacy: Part I (1863–1983), p. 12.

[237] First Nat. Bank, Bellaire v. Comp. of Currency, 697 F.2d 674, 1983.

by multiples of 7 to 32 from 1970 to 1981.[238] Large US multinational banks were among the major lenders to what was referred to as the less developed countries (LDC). Data from the eight largest US banks indicates that their loan exposure to LDC countries grew from $32.5bn in 1977 to $53.7bn and peaked in 1985 at $58.5bn. Such volumes represented more than 10% of their total assets, or more than three times their capital and reserves (1981).[239]

In 1982, the largest borrowers among the LDC countries – Mexico, Argentina, and Brazil – announced their inability to pay interest and repay their debt. Given the involvement of large US banks in LDC lending, these defaults had potentially severe effects on solvency. Moreover, it triggered the involvement of the US Congress.

The International Monetary Fund (IMF) aimed to substantially increase its resources, including the share of the United States. Such an increase, in turn, required the approval of the US Congress. The new situation changed the balance of power between the legislature, supervisors, and banks. Banks depended on the IMF's support for the LDC countries to avoid severe losses, threatening their own survival. The IMF required additional resources from the United States, which was subject to approval by the US Congress. Moreover, the perception in the hearings of the respective committees on banking in the Senate and the House of Representatives was that banks' capital resources should be strengthened. To a lesser degree, US banks' competitive position in capitalisation was a topic too.[240]

The FED and the OCC reacted to the debate on capital requirements by amending their 1981 guidelines. The multinational banks, previously excluded from capital requirements, had to meet a 5% primary capital/assets ratio.[241] Reinicke emphasises that twelve of the seventeen multinational banks had reached the 5% threshold by then.[242]

In November 1983, Congress passed the International Lending Supervision Act (ILSA). Section 908 of ILSA dealt specifically with capital adequacy and had implications on two levels. Domestically, ILSA gave the Federal banking agencies – for the first time – the legal authority to impose statutory capital requirements. On an international level, the chairman of the Federal Reserve, Paul Volcker, received a mandate to 'encourage

---

[238] Data: The World Bank, *International Debt Statistics, Data Bank*: https://databank.worldbank .org/source/international-debt-statistics (accessed 20 January 2022).

[239] Timothy Curry, 'The LDC Debt Crisis', in *An Examination of the Banking Crises of the 1980s and Early 1990s*, ed. Federal Deposit Insurance Corporation, 1997, pp. 191–210 (pp. 196–7). Data refers to loans from at the time called less developed countries (LDC). Sixteen out of the LDC countries were from Latin America. About three-quarters of the outstanding LDC debt was from contributed from Argentina, Brazil, Mexico, and Venezuela.

[240] Reinicke, *Banking, Politics and Global Finance*, p. 145ff. Tarullo, *Banking on Basel*, p. 46.

[241] Federal Reserve, 'Annual Report of the Board of Governors of the Federal Reserve System 1983', 1984, p. 74.

[242] Reinicke, *Banking, Politics and Global Finance*, p. 148.

governments, central banks, and regulatory authorities of other major banking countries to work toward maintaining and, where appropriate, strengthening the capital bases of banking institutions involved in international lending'.[243]

During 1984 and 1985, the three federal bank supervisory agencies worked on new, uniform capital requirements. They agreed on a minimum primary capital/assets ratio of 5.5% and a 6% total capital (primary and secondary)/ assets ratio for all federally supervised banks.[244] Another outcome of interagency cooperation was the increased emphasis on certain aspects that should determine capital adequacy: The agencies expressed their concern that capital/assets ratios exclude considerations on risk in the balance sheet and risk exposure resulting from off-balance-sheet items. The FED noted that the multinational banks had substantial off-balance sheet risks in the range of 5–15% of total assets.[245] Moreover, the FED noted a shift from low-risk, highly liquid assets to assets with higher risk exposure. Altogether, this meant that the overall risk exposure of large banks likely increased. Capital/assets ratios could not capture such changes and incentivised additional risk-taking by banks. Furthermore, the increasing capital/assets ratios of large banks during the first half of the 1980s even provided an impression of improved financial stability, which was not the case. The solution to these problems was a risk-based capital requirement.[246]

The FED, the OCC, and the FDIC published a series of proposals for risk-based capital ratios between 1986 and 1988. The proposals largely followed the Federal Reserve's ABC formula, placing assets into different risk categories, leading to the 'weighted risk asset and off-balance sheet total' as the denominator.[247] Dividing the primary capital by the risk-weighted assets resulted in the 'risk-based capital ratio'. From 1986 onwards, the proposals for capital adequacy rules also started to integrate elements from discussions on the international level. As a first step, the agencies started integrating the agreement between the federal agencies of the United States and the BoE into

---

[243] United States. Congress, *International Lending Supervision Act of 1983*, 1983, p. 1281, (3)(C).

[244] Board of Governors of the Federal Reserve System, 'Membership of State Banking Institutions; Bank Holding Companies and Change in Bank Control; Capital Maintenance; Rules of Procedure', Federal Register, 50.79 (1985), 16057–71 (pp. 16058–59); Federal Deposit Insurance Corporation, 'Capital Maintenance', Federal Register, 50.53 (1985), 11128–43.

[245] Often in the form of standby letters of credit, binding loan commitments, or interest rate swaps.

[246] Board of Governors of the Federal Reserve System, 'Bank Holding Companies and Change in Bank Control; Capital Maintenance; Supplemental Adjusted Capital Measure', Federal Register, 51.21 (1986), 3976–84 (pp. 3976–7).

[247] Board of Governors of the Federal Reserve System, *Bank Holding Companies and Change in Bank Control; Capital Maintenance; Supplemental Adjusted Capital Measure*; Federal Deposit Insurance Corporation, 'Capital Maintenance', Federal Register, 51.34 (1986), 6126–32; Office of the Comptroller of the Currency, 'Minimum Capital Ratios; Risk-Based Capital Standard for National Banks', Federal Register, 51.59 (1986), 10602–7.

their proposals for capital adequacy guidelines in 1987.[248] Once the Basel Committee on Banking Regulations and Supervisory Practices reached an agreement in the summer of 1988, the agencies published the final rules incorporating the Basel agreement in January and March 1989, with transition periods until the end of 1992.[249]

Methodologically, the risk-weighted assets approach followed the ABC formula developed by the FED in the 1950s. However, there were differences in the classification of assets and the weights assigned to these risk classes, as well as the treatment of off-balance sheet assets. Beyond that, the Basel I approach multiplied the risk-weighted assets by 8% (respectively, lower percentages in the transition period), which led to the required capital. The definition of capital under Basel I also consisted of two capital tiers, as it was already the approach taken by the United States Federal Agencies. A key difference was the treatment of loan-loss reserves. The federal agencies had previously counted loan-loss reserves as primary capital. Basel I defined such reserves as Tier 2 capital.

The new capital requirements introduced in 1989 supplemented but did not replace risk-unweighted capital thresholds in the United States. The FDIC and the FED did not replace the requirement of 6% total capital/assets. The OCC, however, aimed to introduce a substantially lower total capital/assets requirement of 3%. The three agencies agreed on a compromise of 3% for banks in the best rating category. All other banks had to maintain additional capital between 1% and 2%, resulting in a capital/assets ratio of at least 4–5% for most banks.[250]

The use of unweighted-capital requirements was further strengthened by the Federal Deposit Insurance Improvement Act (FDICIA) in 1991. After more than a decade of increased banking instability in the United States, the FDICIA introduced 'prompt corrective action' (PCA), which aimed to detect undercapitalised banks early and to force such banks to strengthen their capital. Numerical capital requirements were used as triggers that initiated severe supervisory actions. The 5% total capital/assets ratio thus became a de facto threshold.

[248] Federal Deposit Insurance Corporation, 'Capital Maintenance; Risk-Based Capital Proposal', Federal Register, 52.68 (1987), 11476–92; Board of Governors of the Federal Reserve System, 'Capital Maintenance; Revision to Capital Adequacy Guidelines', Federal Register, 52.56 (1987), 9304–12; Office of the Comptroller of the Currency, 'Minimum Capital Ratios; Issuance of Directives', Federal Register, 52.116 (1987), 23045–55.

[249] Office of the Comptroller of the Currency, 'Risk-Based Capital Guidelines', Federal Register, 54.17 (1989), 4168–84; Board of Governors of the Federal Reserve System, 'Capital; Risk-Based Capital Guidelines', Federal Register, 54.17 (1989), 4186–221; Federal Deposit Insurance Corporation, 'Capital Maintenance; Final Statement of Policy on Risk-Based Capital', Federal Register, 54.53 (1989), 11500.

[250] Davison, *Banking Legislation and Regulation*, p. 116.

5.5 CONCLUDING REMARKS

Crises in the United Kingdom, the United States, and Switzerland triggered the introduction of statutory capital requirements. The United States has the longest and richest tradition of banking regulation and supervision among the three countries. The three federal banking supervision agencies had already informally applied a capital/deposits ratio of 10% until the 1930s. However, minimum capital ratios were formalised and harmonised only in the 1970s and 1980s due to increasing domestic financial instability. In 1981, the FDIC, the OCC, and the FED introduced minimum capital/assets ratios of at least 5%. The OCC and the FED, however exempted the large multinational banks from capital requirements in 1981, which many would have failed to meet.

Switzerland introduced banking legislation and capital requirements in 1934/5. The group of the big banks had been profoundly affected by the Great Depression, and losses on foreign loans and securities led to solvency problems. Most of the Swiss banks did not even reject a statutory capital requirement. There were several reasons for this. Firstly, capital has always played an essential role in the Swiss system. It was perceived as a source of stability and trust. Banks often considered the risk of their business activities when considering further capital issuances. Unwritten conventions developed on what amount of capital was deemed adequate for which banking group. The new minimum requirements replaced these informal conventions. Secondly, most banks had already fulfilled the capital requirements and were thus unaffected by the implementation of the new law. Moreover, the banks most affected by higher capital requirements lacked bargaining power on the topic of solvency in the middle of the Great Depression.

The introduction of statutory banking regulation in the United Kingdom came comparatively late. The Banking Act of 1979 was the first comprehensive banking legislation. Before that, banking legislation consisted of several individual pieces of legislation, affecting different areas of banking. Supervision was conducted informally and flexibly by the BoE. The role of capital in British banking was also unimportant until the 1970s. Until then, solvency was rarely discussed publicly, and the BoE attached its primary attention to liquidity. Change was ultimately initiated by the secondary banking crisis, as well as growing competition from foreign banks.

The United Kingdom did not go through a crisis that would have required government rescues of insolvent banks in the 1930s. The absence of solvency problems probably even reinforced British belief in liquidity as the critical determinant of banking stability. Moreover, the 1930s and the Second World War gave rise to a strict monetary policy. This subjected financial policy to monetary goals, enforced by the strict but informal control of the BoE. It took another crisis, decades later, for banking legislation to be reconsidered. The secondary banking crisis in 1973 revealed many of the problems of the existing regulatory framework. It also triggered a reassessment of liquidity and solvency in banking between 1975 and 1980 through working groups of the BoE and representatives of the clearing banks.

All three countries had already developed risk-weighted capital adequacy frameworks before the Basel Accord of 1988. The BoE's working paper on the 'Measurement of Capital' (1980) set out a system of assessing solvency similar to the Basel I framework. Similarly, Switzerland introduced a risk-weighted approach in 1981. The roots of the Federal Reserve's ABC formula reach back to the 1950s. Academic publications by authors in the United States had already proposed risk-adjusted capital requirements in the 1940s. And Switzerland's initial capital regulations of 1934/1935 were also adjusting for risk. It was just a different methodology with two categories of assets (mortgages and government securities versus all other assets) requiring a different percentage of capital. The development towards the risk-based capital adequacy guidelines of Basel I was an evolution, not a revolution.

Beyond the domestic discourses, financial globalisation and international instability initiated discussions on capital adequacy on the international level. Key venues for these discussions were the committees in the European Economic Community and the Basel Committee on Banking Supervision. The discourses at the BCBS and the EEC interacted with the evolution of the national capital requirements framework. In the United Kingdom, the discussions between the BoE and the clearing banks coincided with attempts by the EEC to harmonise financial legislation in the 1970s. While not the catalyst for the reassessment of capital adequacy in the United Kingdom, the discussions on the European level certainly provided impulses for British policy change. This development can also be traced in the supervisory practice of the BoE. Up until the 1970s, the BoE still used the 'free resources ratio'. From the late 1970s, the 'risk assets ratio' became more fashionable, categorising the assets into different risk categories and attaching a certain risk weight to each category. Similarly, the US federal bank supervision agencies had already started the process of integrating 'international' elements from the BCBS negotiations into domestic guidelines in 1986.

While financial crises triggered the implementation of capital requirements, financial globalisation and the rapid growth of large banks were the driver of change for the definition of capital and capital requirements. During the 1960s and 1970s, average annual growth rates of British, Swiss, and US banks' total assets in the range of 10% were common, and large banks grew even faster. Given this rapid growth, it was increasingly challenging for large banks to meet capital requirements. Subordinated debt was a vital funding source in all three countries, allowing banks to grow despite thin equity cushions. In the United Kingdom, subordinated debt was perceived as equal to equity capital from the 1970s. For US banks, the FDIC and the OCC allowed banks to use subordinated capital from 1962. Swiss banks could use subordinated debt as regulatory capital from 1981 (the use of hidden reserves for that purpose had already been allowed since 1961).

A commonality of the banking regulation in the three countries lies in the involvement of banks in shaping the regulatory environment. In Switzerland, the changes in capital regulation were initiated by the big banks and the Swiss Bankers Association. In the United Kingdom, the system of supervision was, by definition, participative and personal. The Committee of London Clearing Bankers and later the British Bankers' Association were part of joint working groups led by the BoE from the 1970s. These working groups developed the relevant policy papers for assessing capital adequacy. In the United States, first attempts by the OCC to introduce a minimum capital ratio in 1980 failed due to banks' lobbying. Once capital ratios were introduced in 1981, the large international US banks were exempted from these requirements until 1983.

However, it has to be mentioned too that banking and government interests might have been congruent many times – and the outcomes regarding capital requirements were more than the simple result of lobbying. Regulatory development occurred in the context of financial globalisation and growing international competition. In particular, the topic of foreign competition seemed to be the standard argument in discussions between banks and supervisors, whether in Switzerland, the United Kingdom, or the United States. Nevertheless, there was a clear imbalance in the involvement of interest groups other than banks in the regulatory development process.

The banking crises of the twentieth century, resulting in capital regulation and changes in capital requirements, seemed to be a missed chance. In particular, three common features across the twentieth century and in all three countries stand out. First of all, new capital requirements were never strict. Average ratios of existing banks were often taken as the benchmark for what was considered adequate. There were usually a few banks below the new requirements, but these were exempted in some cases (money centre banks in the United States) or not penalised if they failed to meet requirements (big banks in Switzerland).

Secondly, capital requirements were seldom (United States: once) or never (Switzerland, United Kingdom) increased – not even in the aftermath of crises, which would have been the opportunity for new measures. Basel I, specifically, was a missed opportunity. The threat of financial instability as a result of financial globalisation was recognised. This triggered international financial cooperation. Many countries already had risk-weighted capital adequacy frameworks in place. With regards to stricter capital requirements, however, the threat of financial instability was not acted upon. Instead, requirements oriented themselves on already existing capital ratios, and the definition of capital was a compromise incorporating the capital definitions of various countries. In retrospect, the goal for a level playing field for international banks – and, thus, national interests – seemed to win over financial stability concerns.

Third, and related to that, financial stability seemed to receive little attention when it came to drafting new rules. The history of capital regulation presents itself as highly path dependent. New regulations always addressed problems of the past by further developing existing regulatory frameworks. The framework that should provide financial and banking stability was never fundamentally questioned.

6

Epilogue

The Basel I framework of 1988 led to a new set of capital regulations in Switzerland, the United States, the United Kingdom, and many other countries. One of the critical aspects was the risk-adjusted view on capital requirements. The capital/assets ratio, as a simple measure of a bank's leverage, disappeared from the public discourse. Only during the financial crisis from 2008 did non-risk-adjusted capital ratios gain importance again. The subsequent reforms of the Basel framework – the revised version of Basel II and then Basel III – led to a revival of risk-unweighted capital requirements in the form of a leverage ratio. Moreover, risk-weighted capital measures were revised, and requirements were increased. Does that leave us with a more stable banking system?

6.1 BASEL CAPITAL REQUIREMENTS AND THE CHARACTERISTICS OF LEVERAGE BEFORE THE 2007/2008 FINANCIAL CRISIS

The 2007/8 financial crisis led to increased concern over a highly leveraged banking system.[1] Figure 6.1 shows banks' capital/assets ratios in the United Kingdom, Switzerland, and the United States from 1990 to 2020. Several distinct features must be considered when analysing bank capital in the period leading up to the 2007/8 financial crisis. Firstly, capital ratios from 2000 to 2006/7 indicate increasing leverage in the British and Swiss banking systems. The trend in the United States was different, indicating continuously growing capital/assets ratios among commercial banks from 1990 to 2006. However, the data is somewhat misleading and conceals that a significant part of the banking system was highly leveraged. The data excludes investment

---

[1] Erkki Liikanen and others, 'High-Level Expert Group on Reforming the Structure of the EU Banking Sector – Final Report', 2012, p. 90. Basel Committee on Banking Supervision, *Basel III*.

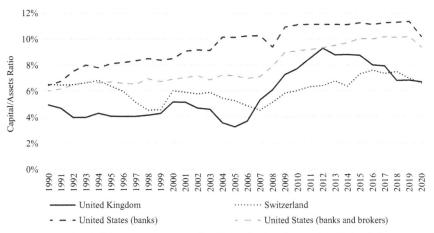

FIGURE 6.1 Capital/assets ratios in the United Kingdom, the United States, and Switzerland, 1990–2020[2]

banks, which increased their leverage substantially from the early 2000s.[3] Therefore, a second line combines banks and brokers in the United States. Overall, the leverage in the United States banking system was relatively stable from 2000 to 2007, ranging around the 7% mark, but one specific segment of the US banking market became particularly vulnerable to losses. After 2007, the banking markets of all three countries deleveraged substantially. Banks' capital/assets ratios in all three countries peaked between 2012 and 2019 at levels unseen for several decades.

A second peculiarity during the period before the 2007/8 crisis was that large global banks operated with higher leverage than the rest of the banking market. In Switzerland, the capital/assets ratio of UBS and Credit Suisse by the end of 2007 was 1.5 percentage points lower than that of the Swiss banking market. In the United Kingdom, the six largest banks had average capital/ assets ratios 0.7 percentage points lower than the market average.[4] In the United States, the deviation in the capital/assets ratio of the five largest banks

---

[2] Data: United Kingdom: 1990–2008, all banks (OECD, *Income Statement and Balance Sheet Statistics*), 2009–2020, 'ECB Statistical Data Warehouse (Series T00/L60)'. Switzerland: 1990–2020, all banks (Swiss National Bank, 'Datenportal Der Schweizerischen Nationalbank', online: https://data.snb.ch/de (accessed 20 December 2021). United States: 1990–2009, all banks (OECD, *Income Statement and Balance Sheet Statistics*); 2010–2020: Federal Deposit Insurance Corporation, *Historical Bank Data*.

[3] Bordo, Redish, and Rockoff, *Why Didn't Canada Have a Banking Crisis in 2008 (or in 1930, or 1907, or ...)?*, fig. 7.

[4] Sample consists of Barclays, Lloyds, HBOS, HSBC, NatWest, and StandardChartered. Data: Banks' annual reports. Bloomberg LP, 'Bloomberg', 2023; FitchSolutions, 'FitchConnect', 2023.

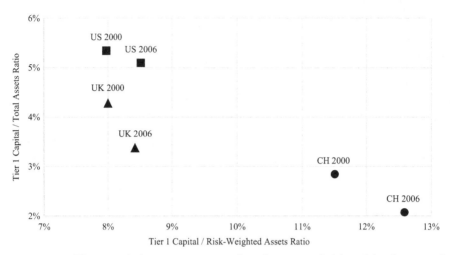

FIGURE 6.2 Tier 1 capital as a percentage of total assets and risk-weighted assets of large banks in the United Kingdom, the United States, and Switzerland (CH) in 2000 and 2006[5]

from the rest of the banking market was even more pronounced (3.9 percentage points lower).[6]

A third feature of the pre-crisis period was that many large banks' risk-weighted and risk-unweighted capital ratios diverged from the early 2000s. The most important risk-weighted capital measure was the Tier 1 capital ratio. This measured a bank's capital and reserves against the risk-weighted assets (RWA). If the two Tier 1 ratios and the capital/assets diverge, it means that the difference between the total assets and the RWA grows, as both ratios use capital as the numerator.

Figure 6.2 shows the average risk-weighted capital ratios and risk-unweighted capital ratios of the thirteen largest commercial banks in the United Kingdom, the United States, and Switzerland in 2000 and 2006, the year before the 2007/8 financial crisis. Both ratios use Tier 1 capital as a numerator for a uniform definition of capital. The evolution of capital ratios among these thirteen global banks from 2000 to 2006 was similar: the risk-unweighted capital ratio fell, meaning the banks reduced the equity capital and

[5] The following banks are included: US: Bank of America, Citigroup, JP Morgan Chase, Wachovia, Wells Fargo. UK: Barclays, Lloyds, HBOS, HSBC, RBS/NatWest, StandardChartered. Switzerland: Credit Suisse, UBS. Data: Annual reports of respective banks. Bloomberg LP, *Bloomberg*; FitchSolutions, *FitchConnect*. Consolidated statements/bank holding companies were used. The ratios are weighted with the total assets of the banks. Note that tier 1 capital ratio can be lower than the simple capital/assets ratio due to deductions such as goodwill.

[6] Sample consists of Bank of America, Citigroup, JP Morgan Chase, Wachovia, and Wells Fargo. Data: Banks' annual reports. Bloomberg LP, *Bloomberg*; FitchSolutions, *FitchConnect*.

increased debt capital in relative terms. At the same time, however, the risk-weighted Tier 1 capital ratio increased.

The reasons for the two diverging ratios can be twofold: the riskiness of the assets as classified by the Basel framework could have been reduced, or the measurement approach to calculate RWA changed. Both adjustments result in lower RWA.[7]

A critical aspect was that the Tier 1/RWA ratio provided a perception of increased banking stability until the 2007/8 crisis, and banks actively cultivated that view. Interestingly, the two banks most keen to boast their strong capital position were the most leveraged ones. By 2006, UBS referred to itself as 'one of the best capitalised financial institutions in the world', and Credit Suisse highlighted that it had the strongest capital base in its history.[8] These statements were true when analysing the risk-weighted Tier 1 ratio for the brief period that the ratio existed (since 1988). However, the simple and risk-unweighted capital/assets ratio reveals that these banks were never more leveraged in their history than in 2006. The large US and British banks were slightly more reserved than their Swiss counterparts, underlining that they are strongly capitalised and met the statutory capital requirements.[9]

The Basel Accord in 1988 and its later versions (Basel II and Basel III) provide the framework for risk-weighted capital measurements. Many limits and weaknesses of the framework were understood and evident to policymakers and experts from the beginning of Basel I.[10] One crucial aspect was that Basel I did not cover market or operational risk. The focus on credit risk was a deliberate choice, leaving the treatment of other risk types to national regulators and supervisors. In 1996, the BCBS amended Basel I and included market risk.[11] A key characteristic was that the revision allowed banks to apply their internal risk models to derive capital requirements for their trading book. The use of proprietary risk models was subject to approval from the supervisor. This was the first time banks were allowed to use their risk models. In retrospect, it was a critical moment, as was the start of the so-called internal ratings-based (IRB) models to follow in subsequent years.

---

[7] The risk-weighted assets as a percentage to total assets is known as RWA density. From 2000 to 2006, the ratio decreased from 51% to 46% in the United Kingdom, from 74% to 68% in the United States, and from 25% to 16% in Switzerland (data: thirteen largest banks in the three countries; RWA density was weighted with total assets of respective banks).

[8] UBS, *Annual Report 2006* (Zurich, 2007), p. 3; Credit Suisse, *Annual Report 2006* (Zurich, 2007), p. 5.

[9] HSBC Holdings PLC, *Annual Report 2006* (London, 2007), p. 10; Lloyds TSB Group, *Annual Report 2006* (London, 2007), p. 10; RBS Group, *Annual Report 2006* (Edinburgh, 2007), p. 46.

[10] Giorgio P. Szegö, 'A Critique of the Basel Regulations, or How to Enhance (Im) Moral Hazards', in *Risk Management and Regulation in Banking* (Boston: Springer, 1999), pp. 147–58.

[11] Basel Committee on Banking Supervision, *Amendment to the Capital Accord to Incorporate Market Risks*, 1996.

Other issues – such as off-balance sheet activities, the securitisation and buy-back of assets (leading to lower capital requirements), and the complexity of business models among international banks – had to be addressed by a more fundamental revision of the Basel framework. The BCBS published a new framework, Basel II, in 2004.[12] The new approach also covered operational risk, previously covered implicitly by credit risk. Moreover, it allowed banks to choose different levels of sophistication in calculating the required capital. The rationale was that large banks could use more sophisticated measurement methods for risk, which would lead to more accurate risk assessments. Accuracy was rewarded with less required capital, whereas a simple approach with less accuracy would yield a higher capital requirement. The simple approach was termed the 'standard' approach. The more sophisticated versions were the banks' proprietary internal-ratings-based approaches. In retrospect, the Basel II framework is a testament to the faith in financial models to capture risk accurately. The critique that followed regarding financial modelling in general, and Basel II specifically, was widespread.[13]

In many countries, the 2007/8 financial crisis fell into the Basel II transition period. The US banking supervisory agencies published the final implementation of Basel II (for large banks only) in December 2007, with a three-year transition period.[14] In Switzerland and the United Kingdom, Basel II was introduced in 2007.[15] The BCBS addressed many crisis-related and evident problems by revising Basel II (Basel II.5) in 2009.[16] By 2010, the BCBS issued the new Basel III framework. Critical features of Basel III were a new definition of capital (CET1 capital), higher capital requirements, a leverage ratio, and liquidity requirements.[17] Finally, the BCBS published the latest revision of Basel III in December 2017.[18] The focus of the 2017 revision is on the risk models to calculate the RWA. Especially the use of internal models are more constrained again, which somewhat reverses the evolution towards such models initiated in 1996.

---

[12] Basel Committee on Banking Supervision, *Basel II*.

[13] See, for example Tarullo, *Banking on Basel*; Admati and Hellwig, *The Bankers' New Clothes*.

[14] Roger Tufts and Paul Moloney, 'The History of Supervisory Expectations for Capital Adequacy: Part II (1984–2021)', *Moments in History – Office of the Comptroller of the Currency*, 2022, p. 7.

[15] Eidgenössische Bankenkommission, 'Basel II Umsetzung in der Schweiz. Erläuterungsbericht der Eidg. Bankenkommission', 2005.

[16] Basel Committee on Banking Supervision, *Revisions to the Basel II Market Risk Framework*, 2009.

[17] Basel Committee on Banking Supervision, 'International Regulatory Framework for Banks (Basel III)', 2010.

[18] Basel Committee on Banking Supervision, *Basel III: Finalising Post-Crisis Reforms*, 2017.

6.2   THE LIMITS OF CAPITAL

The perception of an adequate level of bank capital and how it is measured has changed fundamentally since the nineteenth century. Simple rules of thumb developed into complex models. Regulatory texts and supervisory guidelines on capital grew from a few sentences to hundreds of pages. This book has presented financial crises and wars as two crucial catalysts for change in the perception of capital. Another – neglected – dimension is the role of knowledge. Before the 1950s, finance was mainly a 'literary' subject. The introduction of mathematics, modelling, and statistics as techniques for analysis triggered innovation in risk management that also found its way into the Basel framework.

If the authors of banking textbooks of the nineteenth century were presented with the capital adequacy frameworks of today, they might be positively surprised. First, the functions of capital in banking did not change since the first commercial banks emerged. The loss absorbency and the guarantee function of capital are still crucial for ensuring trust. Second, it was already apparent in the nineteenth century that the size of a bank's capital should relate to its risk. The various measurement approaches for capital adequacy developed in the twentieth century aimed to do precisely that: measuring risk more accurately to allocate the capital needed for a stable bank. However, the nineteenth century banking literature authors might be less impressed with the outcome. Never before were methods to derive capital requirements more sophisticated than now – but banks remain unstable.

In a historical perspective, the United Kingdom, the United States, and Switzerland provide various attempts to create more stable banking systems. The United Kingdom opted for a system of informal supervision with a strong focus on liquidity. Not even the Banking Acts of 1979 and 1987 introduced statutory minimum capital ratios. Switzerland introduced nationwide banking legislation with minimum solvency and liquidity ratios in 1934/5. And the United States had a long tradition of minimum capital ratios applied by bank supervising agencies but harmonised and formalised minimum capital ratios only by the 1980s. Eventually, all three countries arrived at a system that regulated capital based on a risk-weighted approach during the 1980s, before the introduction of Basel I.

Looking at the evolution of capital requirements, it is somewhat surprising that the premise of financial market stability was often not the starting point when capital requirements were discussed. Existing regulatory frameworks or conventions served as a blueprint, resulting in the ever-growing complexity of banking regulation. Instead of fundamentally reconsidering banking stability, time after time regulators focused their attention on ameliorating the weaknesses of the existing framework. This approach was often backwards looking and neglected the fact that lessons of the past are not necessarily the solution to tomorrow's problems.

At the same time, one must bear in mind that banking instability is not surprising. If banks accept deposits and lend, then by their very nature they are prone to bank runs from creditors. Capital plays an integral part in inducing trust for creditors, but it is not the only possible source of trust. Governments, shareholders, and banks can also provide guarantees that provide trust for creditors. Historically, there was a clear risk-shifting from shareholders and bank managers to the state, which took over more guarantor roles. Unlimited liability or double liability for shareholders is long gone. At the same time, states implemented capital regulation, created bank supervising agencies and deposit insurance schemes, formalised the lender-of-last-resort function, and accepted implicit and explicit government guarantees for banks. On the side of banks' management, history also provides numerous cases of speculative behaviour and mismanagement with little or limited consequences for decision-makers.

Once we accept that modern banks are unstable by their very nature, the attention falls on the impact of bank failures. Losses of failed banks must be covered by those who own a bank, and no bank should be too big to fail.

Bibliography

Acheson, Graeme G., and John D. Turner, 'The Death Blow to Unlimited Liability in Victorian Britain: The City of Glasgow Failure', *Explorations in Economic History*, 45 (2008), 235–53.

'The Impact of Limited Liability on Ownership and Control: Irish Banking, 1877–1914', *The Economic History Review*, 59 (2006), 320–46.

'Investor Behaviour in a Nascent Capital Market: Scottish Bank Shareholders in the Nineteenth Century', *The Economic History Review*, 64 (2011), 188–213.

Admati, Anat R., and Martin Hellwig, *The Bankers' New Clothes: What's Wrong with Banking and What to Do about It* (Princeton: Princeton University Press, 2014).

Allen, Arthur Meredith, S. R. Cope, Leslie J. H. Dark, and Henry J. Witheridge, *Commercial Banking Legislation and Control* (London: Macmillan, 1938).

Allen, Franklin, and Douglas Gale, *Comparing Financial Systems* (Cambridge, MA: MIT Press, 2000).

American National Biography, 'Carey, Henry Charles (1793–1879), Economist, Publisher, and Social Scientist', https://doi.org/10.1093/anb/9780198606697 .article.1400098 (accessed 4 May 2022).

'Lord, Eleazar (1788–1871), Financier, Railway President, and Theologian', https://doi.org/10.1093/anb/9780198606697.article.1001015 (accessed 4 May 2022).

Amrein, Simon, 'Eigenmittel der Schweizer Banken im historischen Kontext', in *Krisenfeste Schweizer Banken? Die Regulierung von Eigenmitteln, Liquidität und "Too Big to Fail"*, ed. Armin Jans, Christoph Lengwiler, and Marco Passardi (Zurich: NZZ Libro, 2018), pp. 87–116.

Bagehot, Walter, *Lombard Street: A Description of the Money Market* (London: Henry S. King & Co., 1873).

Balaban, Ioan, 'International and Multinational Banking under Bretton Woods (1945–1971): The Experience of Italian Banks' (unpublished thesis, European University Institute, 2021), https://cadmus.eui.eu/handle/1814/69996 (accessed 22 April 2023).

'Banking and Eurodollars in Italy in the 1950s', *Enterprise & Society*, 2022, 1–25.

Baltensperger, Ernst, and Peter Kugler, *Swiss Monetary History Since the Early 19th Century*, Studies in Macroeconomic History (Cambridge: Cambridge University Press, 2017).

Bank of England, *Bank of England Banking Act Report 1988/89* (London: Bank of England, 1989).

Bank of England Banking Act Report 1989/90 (London: Bank of England, 1990).

'The Capital and Liquidity Adequacy of Banks', *Quarterly Bulletin*, Q3 (1975), 240–243.

'Competition and Credit Control', *Quarterly Bulletin*, Q2 (1971), 189–93.

'The Measurement of Capital', *Quarterly Bulletin*, Q3 (1980), 324–330.

'A Millennium of Macroeconomic Data. A29. The National Debt', 2016 www .bankofengland.co.uk/statistics/research-datasets (accessed 6 June 2018).

'A Millennium of Macroeconomic Data. A30a. Government Debt 1727–2016', 2016 www.bankofengland.co.uk/statistics/research-datasets (accessed 6 June 2018).

'A Millennium of Macroeconomic Data. A47. Wages and Prices 1209–2016', 2016 www.bankofengland.co.uk/statistics/research-datasets (accessed 6 June 2018).

'Supervision of Banks and Other Deposit-Taking Institutions', *Quarterly Bulletin*, Q2 (1978), 383–386.

Bank of England Act 1946, 9 & 10 Geo 6.

Bank Supervision Division, Bank of England, 'Implementation of the Basle Convergence Agreement in the United Kingdom', 1988.

'Measurement of Capital', 1986.

'Subordinated Loan Capital', 1986.

Banking Act 1979, C. 37, 1979.

Banking Act 1987, C. 22, 1987.

'Banking Supplement 1916', *The Economist* (London, 21 October 1916).

'Banking Supplement 1921', *The Economist* (London, 21 May 1921).

'Banking Supplement 1923', *The Economist* (London, 19 May 1923).

'Banking Supplement 1940', *The Economist* (London, 18 May 1940).

'Banking Supplement 1941', *The Economist* (London, 20 November 1941).

'Banking Supplement 1945', *The Economist* (London, 29 December 1945).

'Banking Supplement, Various, 1861–1946', *The Economist* (London, 1946).

Barclays Bank Capital, Banking and Banking Practice: Clearing Bank Capital (London, 10 April 1958), Bank of England Archive, C40/102.

Basel Committee on Banking Supervision, Amendment to the Capital Accord to Incorporate Market Risks, 1996.

Basel II: International Convergence of Capital Measurement and Capital Standards: A Revised Framework, 2004.

Basel III: Finalising Post-Crisis Reforms, 2017.

Basel III: A Global Regulatory Framework for More Resilient Banks and Banking Systems, 2010.

Basel III Leverage Ratio Framework and Disclosure Requirements, 2014.

International Convergence of Capital Measurement and Capital Standards (Basel I), 1988.

International Regulatory Framework for Banks (Basel III), 2010.

Revisions to the Basel II Market Risk Framework, 2009.

Battilossi, Stefano, 'Introduction: International Banking and the American Challenge in Historical Perspective', in *European Banks and the American Challenge: Competition and Cooperation in International Banking Under Bretton Woods*, ed. Youssef Cassis and Stefano Battilossi (Oxford: Oxford University Press, 2002), pp. 1–36.

Bauer, Hans, *Schweizerischer Bankverein 1872–1972*, ed. Schweizerischer Bankverein (Basel, 1972).

Baumann, Jan, 'Bundesinterventionen in der Bankenkrise 1931–1937: Eine vergleichende Studie am Beispiel der Schweizerischen Volksbank und der Schweizerischen Diskontbank' (unpublished doctoral dissertation; University of Zurich, 2007).

Becker, Wolf-Dieter, Reinhold Falk, Ottokar W. Breycha, and Godehard Puckler, *Stille Reserven in den Jahresabschlüssen von Kreditinstituten: eine Studie über die Handhabung in den Ländern der Europäischen Gemeinschaft sowie in der Schweiz, in den USA und in Japan*, ed. Peat, Marwick, Mitchell and Co., and Schriften des Verbandes öffentlicher Banken (Göttingen: O. Schwartz, 1979).

Berger, Allen N., Richard J. Herring, and Giorgio P. Szegö, 'The Role of Capital in Financial Institutions', *Journal of Banking & Finance*, 19 (1995), 393–430.

Bernholz, Peter, 'Die Nationalbank 1945–1982: Von der Devisenbann-Wirtschaft zur Geldmengensteuerung bei flexiblen Wechselkursen', in *Schweizerische Nationalbank, 1907–2007*, ed. Schweizerische Nationalbank SNB (Zurich: Verlag Neue Zürcher Zeitung, 2007), pp. 119–211.

Billings, Mark, and Forrest Capie, 'Capital in British Banking, 1920–1970', *Business History*, 49 (2007), 139–62.

'Transparency and Financial Reporting in Mid-20th Century British Banking', *Accounting Forum*, Financial Accounting: Past, Present and Future, 33 (2009), 38–53.

Bloomberg LP, 'Bloomberg', 2023. Data retrieved from Bloomberg database.

Blunden, George, 'The Supervision of the UK Banking System', ed. Bank of England, *Quarterly Bulletin*, Q2 (1975).

Board of Governors of the Federal Reserve System, 'Bank Holding Companies and Change in Bank Control; Capital Maintenance; Supplemental Adjusted Capital Measure', *Federal Register*, 51 (1986), 3976–84.

'Capital Maintenance; Revision to Capital Adequacy Guidelines', *Federal Register*, 52 (1987), 9304–12.

'Capital; Risk-Based Capital Guidelines', *Federal Register*, 54 (1989), 4186–221.

'Membership of State Banking Institutions; Bank Holding Companies and Change in Bank Control; Capital Maintenance; Rules of Procedure', *Federal Register*, 50 (1985), 16057–71.

Board of Governors of the Federal Reserve System (US), *Banking and Monetary Statistics*, 1941–1970, 1976. https://fraser.stlouisfed.org/title/41 (accessed 31 July 2018).

Bodenhorn, Howard, 'Commercial Banks – Number and Assets: 1834–1980, Table Cj251-264', in *Historical Statistics of the United States, Earliest Times to the Present*, ed. Susan B. Carter, Scott Sigmund Gartner, Michael R. Haines, et al. (New York: Cambridge University Press, 2006). http://dx.doi.org/10.1017/ISBN-9780511132971.

'State Banks – Number, Assets, and Liabilities: 1834–1896, Table Cj149-157', in *Historical Statistics of the United States, Earliest Times to the Present*, ed. Susan B. Carter, Scott Sigmund Gartner, Michael R. Haines, et al. (New York: Cambridge University Press, 2006). http://dx.doi.org/10.1017/ISBN-9780511132971.

Bollmann, Erick, *Paragraphs on Banks* (Philadelphia: C. & A. Conrad & co., 1811).

Bonhage, Barbara, Marc Perrenoud, and Hanspeter Lussy, *Nachrichtenlose Vermögen bei Schweizer Banken: Depots, Konten und Safes von Opfern des nationalsozialistischen*

Regimes und Restitutionsprobleme in der Nachkriegszeit, ed. Unabhängige
    Expertenkommission Schweiz – Zweiter Weltkrieg (UEK) (Zurich: Chronos, 2001).
Bordo, Michael D., 'The Bretton Woods International Monetary System: A Historical
    Overview', in *A Retrospective on the Bretton Woods System*, ed. Michael D. Bordo
    and Barry Eichengreen (Chicago: University of Chicago Press, 1993), pp. 3–108.
Bordo, Michael D., Angela Redish, and Hugh Rockoff, 'Why Didn't Canada Have
    a Banking Crisis in 2008 (or in 1930, or 1907, or …)?', *The Economic History
    Review*, 68 (2015), 218–43.
Bordo, Michael, and Harold James, 'Die Nationalbank 1907–1946: Glückliche Kindheit
    oder schwierige Jugend?', in *Schweizerische Nationalbank, 1907–2007*, ed.
    Schweizerische Nationalbank SNB (Zurich: Verlag Neue Zürcher Zeitung, 2007),
    pp. 29–118.
British Bankers' Association, Note of the Meeting between the British Bankers'
    Association and the Bank of England on the Measurement of Capital, Held at the
    Bank of England, Committee of London Clearing Bankers. Capital and Liquidity
    Adequacy of Banks' (73/3) (London, 12 September 1979), London Metropolitan
    Archives, CLC/B/029/MS32152B/001.
Note of the Meeting between the British Bankers' Association and the Bank of
    England on the Measurement of Capital, Held at the Bank of England,
    Committee of London Clearing Bankers. Capital and Liquidity Adequacy of
    Banks' (73/3) (London, 13 November 1979), London Metropolitan Archives,
    CLC/B/029/MS32152B/001.
· *Bundesgesetz betreffend die Ergänzung des Schweizerischen Zivilgesetzbuches (Fünfter
    Teil: Obligationenrecht), (Stand am 1. April 2017)*, 1911.
Bundesgesetz über das eidgenössische Schuldbuch vom 21. September 1939, 1939.
Bundesgesetz über das Obligationenrecht vom 14. Juni 1881, 1883.
Bundesgesetz über die Ausgabe und die Einlösung von Banknoten vom 8. März 1881,
    1883.
Bundesgesetz über die Banken und Sparkassen, 1994.
Bundesgesetz über die Banken und Sparkassen vom 8. November 1934, 1934.
Bundesgesetz über die Banken und Sparkassen vom 11. März 1971, 1971.
Bundesrat, 'Botschaft des Bundesrates an die Bundesversammlung betreffend den
    Entwurf eines Bundesgesetzes über die Banken und Sparkassen vom 2. Februar
    1934', *Bundesblatt*, 1 (1934), 171–224.
'Botschaft des Bundesrates an die Bundesversammlung über die Revision des
    Bankgesetzes', *Bundesblatt*, 10570, 1 (1970), 1144–203.
'Botschaft des Bundesrates an die Bundesversammlung zum Entwurf eines dringlichen
    Bundesbeschlusses über die Bewilligungspflicht für ausländisch beherrschte
    Banken', *Bundesblatt*, 2 (1968), 756–71.
Capie, Forrest, *The Bank of England: 1950s to 1979*, Studies in Macroeconomic History
    (Cambridge: Cambridge University Press, 2010).
Capie, Forrest, and Mark Billings, 'Profitability in English Banking in the Twentieth
    Century', *European Review of Economic History*, 5 (2001), 367–401.
Capie, Forrest, and Geoffrey Edward Wood, *Banking Theory, 1870–1930*, History of
    Banking and Finance (New York: Routledge, 1999).
Carey, Henry Charles, *Principles of Social Science, Volume 2* (Philadelphia:
    J. B. Lippincott & Co., 1860).

Carey, Mathew, *Essays on Banking (Reprint)*, ed. Herman E Krooss (Clifton: Kelley, 1972).

Cassis, Youssef, *Capitals of Capital: A History of International Financial Centres 1780–2005* (Cambridge: Cambridge University Press, 2006).

'Commercial Banks in the 20th-Century Switzerland', in *The Evolution of Financial Institutions and Markets in Twentieth-Century Europe*, ed. Youssef Cassis, Gerald D. Feldman, and Ulf Olsson (Aldershot: Scolar Press, 1995), pp. 64–77.

Crises and Opportunities (Oxford: Oxford University Press, 2011).

'International Financial Centres', in *The Oxford Handbook of Banking and Financial History*, ed. Youssef Cassis, Richard S. Grossman, and Catherine R. Schenk, Oxford Handbooks (Oxford: Oxford University Press, 2016), pp. 293–318.

'Introduction: The Weight of Finance in European Societies', in *Finance and Financiers in European History, 1880–1960*, ed. Youssef Cassis (Cambridge: Cambridge University Press, 1992), pp. 1–13.

Catterall, Ralph Charles Henry, *The Second Bank of the United States* (Chicago: The University of Chicago Press, 1903).

Checkland, Sydney George, *Scottish Banking: A History, 1695–1973* (Glasgow: Collins, 1975).

Clearing Banks – Capital Increases, Internal Note, Banking and Banking Practice: Clearing Bank Capital (London, 5 November 1959), Bank of England Archive, C40/102.

Clearing Banks' Capital, Banking and Banking Practice: Clearing Bank Capital (London, 6 February 1959), Bank of England Archive, C40/102.

Clement, Piet, 'The Missing Link: International Banking Supervision in the Archives of the BIS', in *State and Financial Systems in Europe and the USA: Historical Perspectives on Regulation and Supervision in the Nineteenth and Twentieth Centuries*, ed. Stefano Battilossi and Jaime Reis (Farnham/Burlington: EABH/Ashgate, 2010), pp. 167–75.

Cleveland, Harold Van B., and Thomas F. Huertas, *Citibank 1812–1970* (Cambridge: Harvard University Press, 1985).

Cochrane, John H., 'The Grumpy Economist: Equity-Financed Banking', *The Grumpy Economist*, 2016 http://johnhcochrane.blogspot.com/2016/05/equity-financed-banking.html (accessed 22 February 2017).

Commission of the European Communities, Advisory Committee on Banking Coordination, *Notice on the Calculation of Observation Ratios for Assessing Bank Solvency*, Committee of London Clearing Bankers. Capital and Liquidity Adequacy of Banks' (London, 1 May 1980), London Metropolitan Archives, CLC/B/029/MS32152B/004.

Committee of London Clearing Bankers, ed., *The London Clearing Banks: Evidence by the Committee of London Clearing Bankers to the Committee to Review the Functioning of Financial Institutions* (London: Committee of London Clearing Bankers, distributed by Longman, 1978).

Committee of the London Clearing Bankers Minute Book 1946–1954, British Bankers' Association (London, 7 November 1946), London Metropolitan Archives, CLC/B/029/MS32006/009.

Committee on Bank Amalgamations, 'Report of the Treasury Committee on Bank Amalgamations. Treasury Minute Dated 11th March 1918', 1918, The National Archives, T 1/12325/20697.

Committee on Finance and Industry (Macmillan Committee), 'Committee on Finance and Industry (Macmillan Committee): Report of Committee', 1931, The National Archives, T 200/7.

Committee on the Working of the Monetary System (Radcliffe Committee), *Committee on the Working of the Monetary System: Report of Committee* (London: Her Majesty's Stationary Office, 1960).

Committee Set up to Consider the System of Banking Supervision, Report of the Committee Set up to Consider the System of Banking Supervision, Cmnd. 9550 (London: Her Majesty's Stationary Office, 1985).

Committee to Review the Functioning of Financial Institutions (Wilson Committee), Committee to Review the Functioning of Financial Institutions, Cmnd. 7937 (London: Her Majesty's Stationary Office, 1980).

Companies Act 1948, 1948, c. 38.

Companies Act 1967, 1967, c. 81.

Cooke, Helen J. Mellon, 'Significance of Bank Capital Ratios', *Journal of Political Economy*, 57 (1949), 75–7.

Cooke, Peter W., 'Self-Regulation and Statute – the Evolution of Banking Supervision', in *UK Banking Supervision*, ed. Edward P.M. Gardener (London: Allen & Unwin, 1986), pp. 85–98.

Council of the European Communities, *Council Directive 89/299/EEC of 17 April 1989 on the Own Funds of Credit Institutions*, 89/299/EEC, 1989.

Council Directive 89/647/EEC of 18 December 1989 on a Solvency Ratio for Credit Institutions, 89/647/EEC, 1989.

First Council Directive on the Coordination of Laws, Regulations and Administrative Provisions Relating to the Taking up and Pursuit of the Business of Credit Institutions, 1977.

Second Council Directive 89/646/EEC of 15 December 1989 on the Coordination of Laws, Regulations and Administrative Provisions Relating to the Taking up and Pursuit of the Business of Credit Institutions, 89/646/EE, 1989.

Country Bankers Act, 1826, c. 46.

Credit Suisse, *Annual Report 2006* (Zurich, 2007).

Crosse, Howard D., *Management Policies for Commercial Banks* (Englewood Cliffs, NJ: Prentice-Hall, 1962).

Curry, Timothy, 'The LDC Debt Crisis', in *An Examination of the Banking Crises of the 1980s and Early 1990s*, ed. Federal Deposit Insurance Corporation, 1997, pp. 191–210.

Daily Express, 'Money Trusts and Public Policy' (4 February 1918), London: The National Archives, T 1/12431/52485.

David, Thomas, Stéphanie Ginalski, André Mach, and Frédéric Rebmann, 'Networks of Coordination: Swiss Business Associations as an Intermediary between Business, Politics and Administration during the 20th Century', *Business and Politics*, 11 (2009), 1–38.

Davison, Lee, 'Banking Legislation and Regulation', in *An Examination of the Banking Crises of the 1980s and Early 1990s*, ed. Federal Deposit Insurance Corporation (Federal Deposit Insurance Corporation, 1997), pp. 87–136.

Deutsche Bundesbank, 'Deutsche Bundesbank – Statistics (Table BBK01.OU0322; BBK01. OU0308)', 2022 www.bundesbank.de/de/statistiken (accessed 21 February 2022).

Deutsches Geld- und Bankwesen in Zahlen, 1876–1975 (Frankfurt am Main: Knapp, 1976).

'Die Kapitalertragsbilanz Der Bundesrepublik Im Aussenwirtschaftsverkehr', 1971 www.bundesbank.de/resource/blob/690748/8e5a5e61e9bbcdafe9cfc59122c559bb/mL/1971-03-monatsbericht-data.pdf.

Dewey, Davis R., *State Banking Before the Civil War*, Congressional Documents (Government Printing Office, 1910).

Diamond, Douglas W., and Philip H. Dybvig, 'Bank Runs, Deposit Insurance, and Liquidity', *Journal of Political Economy*, 91 (1983), 401–19.

Domett, Henry Williams, *A History of the Bank of New York, 1784–1884 : Compiled from Official Records and Other Sources at the Request of the Directors*, 4th ed. (Cambridge, MA: The Riverside Press, 1922).

Drach, Alexis, *Liberté surveillée: supervision bancaire et globalisation financière au Comité de Bâle, 1974–1988*, Histoire (Rennes: Presses universitaires de Rennes, 2022).

Liberté surveillée: Supervision bancaire et globalisation financière au Comité de Bâle, 1974–1988 (Florence: European University Institute, 2016).

Dun, John, *British Banking Statistics: With Remarks on the Bullion Reserve and Non-Legal-Tender Note Circulation of the United Kingdom* (London: E. Stanford, 1876).

Dunbar, Charles F., *Chapters on Banking* (Cambridge, 1885).

Theory and History of Banking (New York: G.P. Putnam's Sons, 1891).

ECB Statistical Data Warehouse (Series T00/L60)' https://sdw.ecb.europa.eu/home.do (accessed 28 February 2022).

Ehlen, James G., 'A Review of Bank Capital and Its Adequacy', *Economic Review*, Federal Reserve Bank of Atlanta, 54 (1983), 54–60.

Eichengreen, Barry, *Globalizing Capital: A History of the International Monetary System* (Princeton: Princeton University Press, 1998).

Eidgenössische Bankenkommission, *Anrechnung stiller Reserven als eigene Mittel* (Bern, 1966), Swiss Federal Archives, E6520A#1983/50#49*.

Anrechnung stiller Reserven als eigene Mittel. Notiz betr. die Anrechnung stiller Reserven als eigene Mittel vom 11.12.1963 (Bern, 11 December 1963), Swiss Federal Archives, E6520A#1983/50#49*.

'Basel II Umsetzung in der Schweiz. Erläuterungsbericht der Eidg. Bankenkommission', 2005.

Circular, 1961.

Circular, 1968.

Circular, 1990.

Eigene Mittel der Grossbanken. Notiz an Mitglieder der Eidg. Bankenkommission (Bern, 21 March 1963), Swiss Federal Archives, E6520A#1983/50#48*.

Geschäftsbericht der Eidgenössischen Bankenkommission an den Bundesrat für das Jahr 1939 (Bern, 25 April 1940), Swiss Federal Archives, E6520A#1983/50#62*.

Geschäftsbericht der Eidgenössischen Bankenkommission an den Bundesrat für das Jahr 1943 (Bern, 14 February 1944), Swiss Federal Archives, E6520A#1983/50#62*.

Geschäftsbericht der Eidgenössischen Bankenkommission an den Bundesrat für das Jahr 1946 (Bern, 30 April 1947), Swiss Federal Archives, E6520A#1983/50#62*.

Geschäftsbericht der Eidgenössischen Bankenkommission an den Bundesrat für das Jahr 1959 (Bern, 1960), Swiss Federal Archives, E6520A#1983/50#62*.

Jahresbericht 1978 der Eidgenössischen Bankenkommission (Bern, April 1979).

Jahresbericht 1980 der Eidgenössischen Bankenkommission (Bern, April 1981).

Jahresbericht 1984 der Eidgenössischen Bankenkommission (Bern, April 1985).

Jahresbericht 1997 der Eidgenössischen Bankenkommission (Bern, April 1998).

Verhandlungen der Eidgenössichen Bankenkommission vom 29. April, 1963 (Bern, 29 April 1963), Swiss Federal Archives, E6520A#1983/50#49*.

Vorschriften über eigene Mittel. Protokoll der Sitzung vom 20. Januar 1958 zwischen Bankenkommission und Vertretern der Banken (Bern, 20 January 1958), Swiss Federal Archives, E6520A#1983/50#48*.

Eidgenössische Finanzmarktaufsicht FINMA, *Jahresbericht 2009* (2010).

Eidgenössisches Finanz- und Zolldepartement, *Bericht über die statistischen Grundlagen für die Aufstellung von Ausführungsbestimmungen zu Art. 10 des Entwurfes zu einem Bundesgesetz über die Banken und Sparkassen vom 2. Februar 1934* (Bern, 2 February 1934), Swiss Federal Archives, E6520A#1000/1059#5*.

Erb, Rudolf, *Die Stellungnahme der schweizerischen Grossbanken zu den bank- und währungspolitischen Problemen der Kriegs- und Nachkriegszeit* (Zurich: A.-G. Gebr. Leemann & Co, 1931).

Esslinger, Martin, *Geschichte der Schweizerischen Kreditanstalt während der ersten 50 Jahre ihres Bestehens* (Zurich: Orell Füssli, 1907).

Esty, Benjamin C., 'The Impact of Contingent Liability on Commercial Bank Risk Taking', *Journal of Financial Economics*, 1998, 189.

Exchange Control Act 1947, 1947, c. 14.

Farquet, Christophe, *Histoire du paradis fiscal suisse* (Paris: SciencesPo les presses, 2018).

'Quantification and Revolution: An Investigation of German Capital Flight after the First World War', *EHES Working Paper*, 2019.

FDIC, 'Annual Report of the Federal Deposit Insurance Corporation 1934', 1935.

'Annual Report of the Federal Deposit Insurance Corporation 1935', 1936.

'Annual Report of the Federal Deposit Insurance Corporation 1936', 1937.

'Annual Report of the Federal Deposit Insurance Corporation 1937', 1938.

'Annual Report of the Federal Deposit Insurance Corporation 1938', 1939.

'Annual Report of the Federal Deposit Insurance Corporation 1942', 1943.

'Annual Report of the Federal Deposit Insurance Corporation 1945', 1946.

'Annual Report of the Federal Deposit Insurance Corporation 1951', 1951.

'Annual Report of the Federal Deposit Insurance Corporation 1970', 1971.

'Annual Reports of the Federal Deposit Insurance Corporation 1966–1979', 1980.

Federal Deposit Insurance Corporation, 'BankFind Suite: Find Institution Financial & Regulatory Data'. https://banks.data.fdic.gov/bankfind-suite/financialreporting (accessed 11 April 2022).

'Capital Maintenance', *Federal Register*, 50 (1985), 11128–43.

'Capital Maintenance', *Federal Register*, 51 (1986), 6126–32.

'Capital Maintenance; Final Statement of Policy on Risk-Based Capital', *Federal Register*, 54 (1989), 11500.

'Capital Maintenance; Risk-Based Capital Proposal', *Federal Register*, 52 (1987), 11476–92.

'Historical Bank Data', 2017. www2.fdic.gov/hsob/index.asp (accessed 21 February 2017).

'Statement on Policy of Capital Adequacy', *Federal Register*, 46 (1981), 62693–4.

Federal Financial Institutions Examination Council, *Annual Report 1979* (Washington, DC, 1980).

Annual Report 1980 (Washington, DC, 1981).

'Proposed Definition of Bank Capital To Be Used in Determining Capital Adequacy', Federal Register, 46 (1981), 32498–500.

Federal Reserve, 'Annual Report of the Board of Governors of the Federal Reserve System 1943', 1943.

Annual Report of the Board of Governors of the Federal Reserve System 1946', 1946.

'Annual Report of the Board of Governors of the Federal Reserve System 1970', 1971.

'Annual Report of the Board of Governors of the Federal Reserve System 1976', 1977.

'Annual Report of the Board of Governors of the Federal Reserve System 1983', 1984.

First Nat. Bank, Bellaire v. *Comp. of Currency*, 697 F 2.d 674, 1983.

Fisher, Irving, *The Theory of Interest: As Determined by Impatience to Spend Income and Opportunity to Invest It* (New York: Macmillan, 1930).

FitchSolutions, 'FitchConnect', 2023 https://app.fitchconnect.com.

Friedman, Milton, and Anna J. Schwartz, *A Monetary History of the United States 1867–1960*, Studies in Business Cycles; No. 12 (Princeton: Princeton University Press, 1963).

Gallatin, Albert, *Considerations on the Currency and Banking* (Philadelphia: Carey and Lea, 1831).

Gardener, Edward P.M., 'Supervision in the United Kingdom', in *UK Banking Supervision*, ed. Edward P.M. Gardener (London: Allen & Unwin, 1986), pp. 70–81.

Giddey, Thibaud, 'The Regulation of Foreign Banks in Switzerland (1956–1972)', *Foreign Financial Institutions & National Financial Systems*, The European Association for Banking and Financial History, 2013, 449–85.

Gilbart, James William, *A Practical Treatise on Banking* (London: Effingham Wilson, 1827).

A Record of the Proceedings of the London and Westminster Bank, during the First Thirteen Years of Its Existence with Portraits of Its Principal Officers (London: R. Clay, Bread Street Hill, 1847).

The History and Principles of Banking (London: Longman, Rees, Orme, Brown, Green, and Longman, 1834).

The History of Banking in America (London: Longman, Rees, Orme, Brown, Green, and Longman, 1837).

The Principles and Practice of Banking (London: George Bell & Sons, 1873).

Goodhart, Charles A. E., 'Financial Supervision from an Historical Perspctive: Was the Development of Such Supervision Designed, or Largely Accidental?', in *The Structure of Financial Regulation*, ed. Charles A. E. Goodhart, David G. Mayes, and Geoffrey E. Wood, Routledge International Studies in Money and Banking (London: Routledge, 2007), pp. 43–64.

'Lessons for Monetary Policy from the Euro-Area Crisis', *Journal of Macroeconomics*, 39 (2014), 378–82.

The Basel Committee on Banking Supervision: A History of the Early Years, 1974–1997 (Cambridge: Cambridge University Press, 2011).

Gouge, William M, *A Short History of Paper Money and Banking in the United States* (Philadelphia: Ustick, 1833).

Grady, Henry Francis, *British War Finance: 1914–1919* (New York: Columbia University Press, 1927).

Gregory, Theodor Emanuel, *The Westminster Bank Through a Century*, Volume 1 (London: Oxford University Press, H. Milford, 1936).

The Westminster Bank Through a Century, Volume 2 (London: Oxford University Press, H. Milford, 1936).

Grossman, Richard S., 'Double Liability and Bank Risk Taking', *Journal of Money, Credit and Banking*, 33 (2001), 143.

'Fear and Greed: The Evolution of Double Liability in American Banking, 1865–1930', *Explorations in Economic History*, 44 (2007), 59–80.

'Other People's Money: The Evolution of Bank Capital in the Industrialized World', in *The New Comparative Economic History: Essays in Honor of Jeffrey G. Williamson*, ed. Jeffrey G. Williamson, T. J. Hatton, Kevin H. O'Rourke, and Alan M. Taylor (Cambridge, MA: MIT Press, 2007).

Unsettled Account: The Evolution of Banking in the Industrialized World since 1800, Princeton Economic History of the Western World (Princeton: Princeton University Press, 2010), pp. 141–164.

Grossman, Richard S., and Masami Imai, 'Contingent Capital and Bank Risk-Taking among British Banks before the First World War', *Economic History Review*, 66 (2013), 132–55.

Guex, Sébastien, *La politique monétaire et financière de la Confédération suisse: 1900–1920* (Lausanne: Payot, 1993).

'The Origins of the Swiss Banking Secrecy Law and Its Repercussions for Swiss Federal Policy', *Business History Review*, 2000, 237.

Halbeisen, Patrick, and Tobias Straumann, 'Die Wirtschaftspolitik im internationalen Kontext', in *Wirtschaftsgeschichte der Schweiz im 20. Jahrhundert*, ed. Patrick Halbeisen, Margrit Müller, and Béatrice Veyrassat (Basel: Schwabe Verlag, 2012), pp. 983–1075.

Haldane, Andrew G., and Vasileios Madouros, 'The Dog and the Frisbee'. Speech Presented at the Federal Reserve Bank of Kansas City's Jackson Hole Economic Policy Symposium, 2012.

Handels- und Gewerbe-Zeitung, 'Die grossen Unternehmungen der Westschweiz', *Handels- und Gewerbe-Zeitung* (Zurich, 26 April 1856), pp. 189–90.

Harris, George Taylor, *The Capital Structure in American Banking*, Dissertation (The University of Iowa, 1953).

Howson, Susan, *British Monetary Policy 1945–51* (Oxford: Clarendon Press, 1993).

Domestic Monetary Management in Britain: 1919–38, Occasional Paper. University of Cambridge, Department of Applied Economics (Cambridge: Cambridge University Press, 1975).

HSBC Holdings PLC, *Annual Report 2006* (London, 2007).

HSSO, 'Historische Statistik der Schweiz Online, Tab. H.39.', 2012. www.hsso.ch/2012/h/39.

'Historische Statistik der Schweiz Online, Tab. Q.6a.', 2012. www.hsso.ch/2012/q/6a.

'Historische Statistik der Schweiz Online, Tab. Q.16a.', 2012. www.hsso.ch/2012/q/16a.

'Historische Statistik der Schweiz Online, Tab. U.45.', 2012. www.hsso.ch/2012/u/45.

Hübner, Otto, *Die Banken* (Leipzig: Verlag von Heinrich Hübner, 1854).

Hügi, Werner, *Ökonomische Eigenarten im schweizerischen Bankgewerbe* (Bern: P. Haupt, 1927).

Hürlimann, Katja, 'Jöhr, Adolf', *Historisches Lexikon der Schweiz – Dictionnaire historique de la Suisse – Dizionario storico della Svizzera* (Bern). www.hls-dhs-dss.ch/textes/d/D46271.php (accessed 30 April 2019).

Husy, Thomas, *Die eigenen Mittel der schweizerischen Banken*, Betriebswirtschaftliche Studien (St. Gallen: Fehr, 1946).

Iklé, Max, *Die Schweiz als internationaler Bank- und Finanzplatz* (Zurich: Orell Füssli, 1970).

Income and Corporation Taxes Act 1970, C. 10.

Institute of Bankers, *Journal of the Institute of Bankers*, XXXIII (London: Blades, East & Blades, 1912).

Institute of International Finance, New York University, 'Problems of Capital-Deposit Ratio', *The Bankers Magazine*, 1940, 537–38

Internal Note by the Chief Cashier – Secret, Banking and Banking Practice: Clearing Bank Capital (London, 21 March 1961), Bank of England Archive, C40/102

James, Harold, *Making a Modern Central Bank: The Bank of England 1979–2003*, Studies in Macroeconomic History (Cambridge: Cambridge University Press, 2020) .

Jöhr, Adolf, *Die schweizerischen Grossbanken und Privatbankiers* (Zurich: Polygraphischer Verlag, 1940).

Die Schweizerischen Notenbanken: 1826–1913 (Zurich: Orell Füssli, 1915).

Letter from Credit Suisse's General Manager Dr. Adolf Jöhr to the Director of the Department of Finance (Zurich, 26 December 1933), Swiss Federal Archives, E6520A#1000/1059#5*.

Jöhr, Walter Adolf, *Schweizerische Kreditanstalt: 1856–1956* (Zurich: Schweizerische Kreditanstalt, 1956).

Joplin, Thomas, *An Essay on the General Principles and Present Practice of Banking in England and Scotland*, 2nd ed. (Newcastle upon Tyne: E. Walker, 1822).

Jordà, Òscar, Björn Richter, Moritz H. P. Schularick, and Alan M. Taylor, 'Bank Capital before and after Financial Crises', in *Leveraged the New Economics of Debt and Financial Fragility*, ed. Moritz Schularick (Chicago: The University of Chicago Press, 2022), pp. 116–33.

Jordà, Òscar, Björn Richter, Moritz Schularick, and Alan M. Taylor, *Bank Capital Redux: Solvency, Liquidity, and Crisis* (National Bureau of Economic Research, March 2017) www.nber.org/papers/w23287.

Jost, Hans Ulrich, *Politik und Wirtschaft im Krieg: die Schweiz 1938–1948* (Zurich: Chronos, 2016).

Jung, Joseph, *Von der Schweizerischen Kreditanstalt zur Credit Suisse Group: eine Bankengeschichte* (Zurich: NZZ Verlag, 2000).

Kapstein, Ethan B., 'Architects of Stability? International Cooperation among Financial Supervisors', BIS Working Papers, 2006.

Governing the Global Economy: International Finance and the State (Cambridge, MA: Harvard University Press, 1994).

'Resolving the Regulator's Dilemma: International Coordination of Banking Regulations', *International Organization*, 43 (1989), 323.

Kleinewefers, Henner, *Das Auslandsgeschäft der Schweizer Banken*, Schriften zum Bankenwesen (Zurich: Schuthess, 1972).

Knies, Karl, *Geld und Credit* (Berlin: Weidmann, 1879).

Kobrak, Christopher, and Michael Troege, 'From Basel to Bailouts: Forty Years of International Attempts to Bolster Bank Safety', *Financial History Review*, 22 (2015), 133–56.

König, Peter, 'Der Anteil der Lebensversicherungsgesellschaften an der Finanzierung des Geldbedarfes des Bundes 1939–1945', *Schweizerische Zeitschrift für Volkswirtschaft und Statistik*, 1947, 560–9.

Korajczyk, Robert A., Deborah J. Lucas, and Robert L. McDonald, 'Equity Issues with Time-Varying Asymmetric Information', *The Journal of Financial and Quantitative Analysis*, 27 (1992), 397–417.

Körnert, Jan, 'Liquiditäts- oder Solvabilitätsnormen für Banken? Zu den Anfängen eines Paradigmenwechsels und zur Einführung von Solvabilitätsnormen zwischen 1850 und 1934', *VSWG: Vierteljahrschrift für Sozial- und Wirtschaftsgeschichte*, 99 (2012), 171–88.

Kraus, Alan, and Robert H. Litzenberger, 'A State-Preference Model of Optimal Financial Leverage', *The Journal of Finance*, 28 (1973), 911–22.

Kunze, Walzer, Hans Schippel, and Otto Schoele, *Die deutsche Bankwirtschaft: Ein Schulungs- und Nachschlagewerk für das deutsche Geld- und Kreditwesen* (Berlin: Verlag der Betriebswirt, 1935).

Kurz, Hermann, *Die schweizerischen Grossbanken: Ihre Geschäftstätigkeit und wirtschaftliche Bedeutung* (Zurich: Orell Füssli, 1928).

Landmann, Julius, *Entwurf eines Bundesgesetzes: betreffend den Betrieb und die Beaufsichtigung von Bankenunternehmungen nebst Motivenbericht* (Bern: Schweizerisches Volkswirtschaftsdokument, 1916).

Langer, Marie-Astrid, and Michael Rasch, 'Interview with Eugene Fama – Banken brauchen mindestens 25 Prozent Eigenkapital', *Neue Zürcher Zeitung*, 9 November 2013.

Law, John, *Money and Trade Considered* (Edinburgh, 1705).

Leaf, Walter, *Banking* (London: Williams & Norgate Ltd., 1927).

'Letter by Paul Volcker to Timothy Wirth, Chairman Subcommittee on Telecommunications, Consumer Protection, and Finance, House of Representatives', in *Hearing Before the Subcommittee on Telecommunications, Consumer Protection, and Finance, 99th Congress, First Session on H.R. 2032, 99–38* (Washington, DC: US Government Printing Office, 1985), pp. 461–68.

Letter from Barclays Chairman to Governor of the Bank of England, Banking and Banking Practice: Clearing Bank Capital (London, 12 February 1959), Bank of England Archive, C40/102.

Letter from the President of the Association of Swiss Cantonal Banks to Minister of Finance (Basel, 14 October 1933), Swiss Federal Archives, E6520A#1000/1059#23*.

Lidbury, Charles, 'Internal Note', 1934, Archive of the Royal Bank of Scotland, Edinburgh, WES/1174/206.

Liikanen, Erkki, Hugo Bänziger, José Manuel Campa, et al., 'High-Level Expert Group on Reforming the Structure of the EU Banking Sector – Final Report', 2012.

Linder, Albert, *Die schweizerischen Grossbanken*, Beiträge zur schweizerischen Wirtschaftskunde (Bern: Stämpfli & Cie, 1927).

Lindert, Peter H, and Richard Sutch, 'Consumer Price Indexes, for All Items: 1774–2003, Table Cc1-2', in *Historical Statistics of the United States, Earliest Times to the Present*, ed. Susan B. Carter, Scott Sigmund Gartner, Michael R. Haines, et al. (New York: Cambridge University Press, 2006) http://dx.doi.org/10.1017/ISBN-9780511132971.

Lloyds Bank Limited, *Banking and Banking Practice: Clearing Bank Capital* (London, 18 April 1962), Bank of England Archive, C40/102.

Lloyds TSB Group, *Annual Report 2006* (London, 2007).

London Clearing Banks' Capital, Internal Note, Banking and Banking Practice: Clearing Bank Capital (London, 8 October 1958), Bank of England Archive, C40/102.

London Clearing Banks' Capital, Internal Note by the Chief Cashier, Banking and Banking Practice: Clearing Bank Capital (London, 13 October 1958), Bank of England Archive, C40/102.

Lord, Eleazar, *Principles of Currency and Banking* (New York: G. & C. & H. Carvill, 1829).

Lucas, Deborah J., and Robert L. McDonald, 'Equity Issues and Stock Price Dynamics', *The Journal of Finance*, 45 (1990), 1019–43.

Macey, Johnathan R. and Geoffrey P. Miller, 'Double Liability of Bank Shareholders: History and Implications', *Wake Forest Law Review*, 27 (1992).

Marquis, Ralph W., and Frank P. Smith, 'Double Liability for Bank Stock', *The American Economic Review*, 27 (1937), 490–502.

Martins Bank, Banking and Banking Practice: Clearing Bank Capital (London, 5 December 1958), Bank of England Archive, C40/102.

Mazbouri, Malik, 'A Retrospective Illusion? Reflections on the "Longevity" of Swiss Big Banks 1850-2000', in *Immortal Banks: Strategies, Structures and Performances of Major Banks*, ed. Michel Lescure (Genève: Librairie Droz, 2016), pp. 231–51.

Mazbouri, Malik, Sébastien Guex, and Rodrigo Lopez, 'Finanzplatz Schweiz', in *Wirtschaftsgeschichte der Schweiz im 20. Jahrhundert*, ed. Patrick Halbeisen, Margrit Müller, and Béatrice Veyrassat (Basel: Schwabe Verlag, 2012), pp. 468–518.

Mazbouri, Malik, and Marc Perrenoud, 'Banques suisses et guerres mondiales', in *Kriegswirtschaft und Wirtschaftskriege*, ed. Valentin Groebner and Sébastien Guex (Zurich: Chronos, 2008), pp. 233–53.

McVickar, William A., *The Life of the Reverend John McVickar* (New York/Cambridge, MA: Hurd and Houghton/Riverside Press, 1872).

Michie, Ranald Cattanach, *British Banking: Continuity and Change from 1694 to the Present* (Oxford: Oxford University Press, 2016).

Miller, Harry E., *Banking Theories in the United States before 1860* (A. M. Kelley; Cambridge, MA: Harvard University Press, 1927).

Miller, Merton H., 'Debt and Taxes', *The Journal of Finance*, 1977, 261–75.

Modigliani, Franco, and Merton H. Miller, 'Corporate Income Taxes and the Cost of Capital: A Correction', *The American Economic Review*, 1963, 433–43.

'The Cost of Capital, Corporation Finance and the Theory of Investment', *The American Economic Review*, 1958, 261–97.

Morgan, E. Victor, *Studies in British Financial Policy, 1914–25* (London: Macmillan, 1952).

Morison, Ian, Paul Tillet, and Jane Welch, *Banking Act 1979* (London: Butterworths & Co., 1979).

Mottram, Ralph Hale, *The Westminster Bank, 1836–1936* (London: Westminster Bank, 1936).

Moulton, Harold G., 'Commercial Banking and Capital Formation: III', *Journal of Political Economy*, 26 (1918), 484–508.

Müller, Bernhard, 'Die Entwicklung der Bankenaufsicht in der Schweiz', *Schweizerische Aktiengesellschaft: Zeitschrift für Handels- und Wirtschaftsrecht*, 1 (1977), 1–13.

Myers, Stewart C., and Nicholas S. Majluf, 'Corporate Financing and Investment Decisions When Firms Have Information That Investors Do Not Have', *Journal of Financial Economics*, 13 (1984), 187–221.

Naef, Alain, *An Exchange Rate History of the United Kingdom: 1945–1992*, Studies in Macroeconomic History (Cambridge: Cambridge University Press, 2022).

National Banking Act, 1864.

Neue Zürcher Zeitung, 'Das schweizerische Bankwesen im Jahre 1961' (Zurich, 15 January 1963).

'Generalversammlung der Schweizerischen Bankgesellschaft' (Zurich, 9 March 1963).

'Keine Revision des Bankengesetzes: Eine neue Vollziehungsverordnung', *Abendausgabe Nr. 3162* (Zurich, 30 August 1961).

'Schweizerische Volksbank, Delegiertenversammlung' (Zurich, 24 February 1947), section Handelsteil, p. 3.

'Schweizerischer Bankverein' (Zurich, 24 February 1959).

Nevins, Allan, *History of the Bank of New York and Trust Company, 1784 to 1934* (New York: Bank of New York and Trust Company, 1934).

Oatley, Thomas, and Robert Nabors, 'Redistributive Cooperation: Market Failure, Wealth Transfers, and the Basle Accord', *International Organization*, 1998, 35.

Obst, Georg, *Banken und Bankpolitik* (Leipzig: Verlag von Carl Ernst Poeschel, 1909).

OECD, *Income Statement and Balance Sheet Statistics* (Paris: Organisation for Economic Co-operation and Development, 13 April 2010). www.oecd-ilibrary.org/content/data/data-00270-en (accessed 8 December 2015).

Office of the Comptroller of the Currency, 'Annual Report of the Comptroller of the Currency 1914', 1914.

'Annual Report of the Comptroller of the Currency 1931', 1932.

'Annual Report of the Comptroller of the Currency 1939', 1940.

'Annual Report of the Comptroller of the Currency 1944', 1945.

'Annual Report of the Comptroller of the Currency 1945', 1946.

'Annual Report of the Comptroller of the Currency 1948', 1949.

'Annual Report of the Comptroller of the Currency 1951', 1952.

'Annual Report of the Comptroller of the Currency 1963', 1964.

'Annual Report of the Comptroller of the Currency 1980', 1981.

Annual Report of the Comptroller of the Currency, Various Years'.

'Minimum Capital Ratios; Issuance of Directives', Federal Register, 52 (1987), 23045–55.

'Minimum Capital Ratios; Risk-Based Capital Standard for National Banks', Federal Register, 51 (1986), 10602–7.

'Risk-Based Capital Guidelines', Federal Register, 54 (1989), 4168–84.

Orgler, Yair E., and Benjamin Wolkowitz, *Bank Capital* (New York: Van Nostrand Reinhold, 1976).

'Passing Events', *The Investors' Review* (London, 23 January 1915), XXXV, No. 890 edition.

Penn, Graham, *Banking Supervision: Regulation of the UK Banking Sector under the Banking Act 1987* (London, Edinburgh: Butterworth, 1989).

Porter, Tony, *States, Markets and Regimes in Global Finance*, International Political Economy Series (New York, London: St. Martin's Press, Palgrave Macmillan, 1993).

President and Secretary of the Auditing Association, *Letter from the Association for the Auditing of Banks and Savings Banks in Berne to the Minister of Finance ('Revisionsverband der bernischen Banken und Sparkassen')* (Bern, 2 December 1933), Swiss Federal Archives, E6520A#1000/1059#27*.

Preston, Howard H., *History of Banking in Iowa*, The Rise of Commercial Banking (Iowa: The State of Iowa Historical Society, 1922).

Prevention of Fraud (Investments) Act 1958, C. 45.

Putnam, Barron H., 'Early Warning Systems and Financial Analysis in Bank Monitoring', *Economic Review*, Federal Reserve Bank of Atlanta, 54 (1983), 6–12.

Rae, George, *The Country Banker, His Clients, Cares, and Work. From an Experience of Forty Years* (London: John Murray, 1885).

Raff, Herbert, *Schweizerische Bankgesellschaft: 1862, 1912, 1962* (Zurich: Schweizerische Bankgesellschaft, 1962).

Raiffeisen Schweiz Genossenschaft, 'Geschäftsbericht der Raiffeisen Gruppe 2013', 2014.

Rand McNally and Company, 'Rand McNally Bankers Directory, Various Years' (Rand McNally).

RBS Group, *Annual Report 2006* (Edinburgh, 2007).

RBS Heritage Hub, 'James William Gilbart' http://heritagearchives.rbs.com/people/list/james-william-gilbart.html (accessed 26 April 2017).

Redlich, Fritz, *Eric Bollmann and Studies in Banking*, Essays in American Economic History (New York: G. E. Stechert & co., 1944).

Reid, Margaret, *The Secondary Banking Crisis 1973–75: Its Causes and Course* (London: Macmillan, 1982).

Reimann, Robert, *Kommentar zum Bundesgesetz über die Banken und Sparkassen*, 3. Auflage (Zurich: Poly. Verlag, 1963).

Reinicke, Wolfgang H., *Banking, Politics and Global Finance: American Commercial Banks and Regulatory Change, 1980–1990*, Studies in International Political Economy (Aldershot: Edward Elgar Publishing, 1995).

Revell, Jack, 'Capital Adequacy, Hidden Reserves and Provisions', in *UK Banking Supervision*, ed. Edward P. M. Gardener (London: Allen & Unwin, 1986), pp. 218–33.

 Costs and Margins in Banking: An International Survey, ed. Organisation for Economic Co-Operation and Development OECD (Paris: OECD, 1980).

 Costs and Margins in Banking: Statistical Supplement 1978–1982, ed. Organisation for Economic Co-Operation and Development OECD (Paris: OECD, 1985).

 Solvency and Regulation of Banks: Theoretical and Practical Implications, Bangor Occasional Papers in Economics (Bangor: University of Wales Press, 1975).

Ritzmann, Franz, *Die Schweizer Banken: Geschichte, Theorie, Statistik*, Bankwirtschaftliche Forschungen (Bern: Haupt, 1973).

Robinson, Roland I., 'Bank Capital and Dividend Policies', *Harvard Business Review*, 1948, 398–409.

'The Capital-Deposit Ratio in Banking Supervision', *Journal of Political Economy*, 49 (1941), 41–57.

Ross, Stephen A., 'The Determination of Financial Structure: The Incentive-Signalling Approach', *The Bell Journal of Economics*, 8 (1977), 23–40.

Rossy, Paul, and Robert Reimann, *Bundesgesetz über die Banken und Sparkassen vom 8. November 1934: mit Vollziehungsverordnung vom 26. Februar 1935 und Verordnung des Bundesgerichts betreffend das Nachlassverfahren von Banken und Sparkassen vom 11. April 1935* (Zurich: Polygraphischer Verlag, 1935).

Rowan, D. C., 'The Monetary System in the Fifties and Sixties', *The Manchester School of Economic & Social Studies*, 41 (1973), 19–42.

Ruoss, Eveline, *Die Geldpolitik der Schweizerischen Nationalbank 1907–1929: Grundlagen, Ziele und Instrumente* (Zurich, 1992).

Ryon, Sandra L., 'History of Bank Capital Adequacy Analysis', ed. FDIC Division of Economic Research, *FDIC Working Paper*, 1969.

Salin, Edgar, 'Devisen-Bann-Wirtschaft: über die beginnende Anarchie im westlichen Währungssystem', *Kyklos*, 1964, 149–64.

Sancey, Yves, *Quand les banquiers font la loi: aux sources de l'autorégulation bancaire en Suisse et en Angleterre, de 1914 aux années 1950*, Histoire et société contemporaines (Lausanne: Ed. Antipodes, 2015).

Saunders, Anthony, and Berry Wilson, 'The Impact of Consolidation and Safety-Net Support on Canadian, US and UK Banks: 1893–1992', *Journal of Banking & Finance*, 23 (1999), 537–71.

Sayers, Richard Sidney, *Financial Policy, 1939–45* (London: Her Majesty's Stationery Office, 1956).

Modern Banking First Edition (London: Oxford University Press, 1938).

Modern Banking Sixth Edition (Oxford: Clarendon Press, 1964).

The Bank of England 1891–1944 (Cambridge: Cambridge University Press, 1976).

Schenk, Catherine R., 'Summer in the City: Banking Failures of 1974 and the Development of International Banking Supervision', *The English Historical Review*, 129 (2014), 1129–56.

'The Origins of the Eurodollar Market in London: 1955–1963', *Explorations in Economic History*, 35 (1998), 221–38.

Schiltknecht, Kurt, *Beurteilung der Gentlemen's Agreements und Konjunkturbeschlüsse der Jahre 1954–1966: Unter besonderer Berücksichtigung der Auslandgelder* (Zurich: Polygraphischer Verlag, 1970).

Schneebeli, Hermann, *Die Schweizerische Nationalbank 1907–1932* (Zurich: Swiss National Bank, 1932).

Schneider, Ernst, *Die schweizerischen Grossbanken im zweiten Weltkrieg 1939–1945* (Zurich: Brunner & Bodmer, 1951).

Schweizerische Kreditanstalt, *Jahresbericht Schweizerische Kreditanstalt 1870, 1871*.

Jahresbericht Schweizerische Kreditanstalt 1889, 1890.

Jahresbericht Schweizerische Kreditanstalt 1890, 1891.

Jahresbericht Schweizerische Kreditanstalt 1904, 1905.

Jahresbericht Schweizerische Kreditanstalt 1910, 1911.

Jahresbericht Schweizerische Kreditanstalt 1926, 1927.

Jahresbericht Schweizerische Kreditanstalt 1973, 1874.

Jahresberichte Schweizerische Kreditanstalt 1857–1914, 1914.

Schweizerische Volksbank, *Denkschrift der Schweizerischen Volksbank zur Feier ihres 50jährigen Bestandes – 1869–1919* (Bern, 1919).

Schweizerischer Bankverein, *Jahresbericht Schweizerischer Bankverein 1906* (Basel, 1907).

Jahresbericht Schweizerischer Bankverein 1912 (Basel, 1913).

Jahresbericht Schweizerischer Bankverein 1918 (Basel, 1919).

Secret Committee on Joint Stock Banks, *Report from the Secret Committee on Joint Stock Banks: Together with the Minutes of Evidence, and Appendix*, 1838.

Sekretariat der Eidgenössische Bankenkommission, *Brief des Sekretariats an die Mitglieder der Eidgenössischen Bankenkommission, Bankenkammer. Betrifft Anrechnung stiller Reserven als eigene Mittel / Abänderung der Verfügung vom 30.08.1961.* (Bern, 8 December 1967), Swiss Federal Archives, E6520B#2007_62#239.

Sekretariat der Eidgenössischen Bankenkommission, *Bericht an die Mitglieder der Eidgenössischen Bankenkommission betr. Revision der Vollziehungsverordnung* (Bern, 16 February 1972), Swiss Federal Archives, E6520A#1983/50#49*.

Sheppard, David K., *The Growth and Role of UK Financial Institutions, 1880–1962* (London: Methuen, 1971).

Shultz, William John, and M. R. Cain, *Financial Development of the United States* (New York: Prentice-Hall, 1937).

Smith, Adam, *An Inquiry into the Nature and Causes of the Wealth of Nations* (London, 1776).

Smith, Frank P., and Ralph W. Marquis, 'Capital and Surplus as Protection for Bank Deposits', *The Bankers Magazine*, 1937, 215–26.

Smith, Tynan, and Raymond E. Hengren, 'Bank Capital: The Problem Restated', *Journal of Political Economy*, 55 (1947), 553–66.

Solomon, Steven, *The Confidence Game: How Unelected Central Bankers Are Governing the Changed Global Economy* (New York: Simon & Schuster, 1995).

Somary, Felix, *Bankpolitik* (Tübingen: J. C. B. Mohr, 1915).

Erinnerungen aus meinem Leben, NZZ Libro (Zurich: Verlag Neue Zürcher Zeitung, 2013).

Speck, Kurt, *Strukturwandlungen und Entwicklungstendenzen im Auslandsgeschäft der Schweizerbanken*, Prospektivstudie über das schweizerische Bankgewerbe (Zurich: Juris Druck Verlag, 1974).

Speich, Rudolf, *75 Jahre Schweizerischer Bankverein: 1872–1947. Vergangenheit und Gegenwart: Ansprache* (Basel: Schweizerischer Bankverein, 1947).

Spyri, Johannes Ludwig, *Die Ersparnisskassen der Schweiz (1852–1862)*, Schweizerische Statistik (Zurich: Druck von Gebrüder Gull, 1864).

Steuart, James, *An Inquiry Into The Principles Of Political Economy, Volume 2* (London: A. Millar and T. Cadell, 1767).

Straumann, Tobias, 'Finanzplatz und Pfadabhängigkeit: Die Bundesrepublik, die Schweiz und die Vertreibung der Euromärkte (1955–1980)', in *Europas Finanzzentren: Geschichte und Bedeutung im 20. Jahrhundert*, ed. Christoph Maria Merki (Frankfurt a.M.: Campus, 2005), pp. 245–68.

Fixed Ideas of Money: Small States and Exchange Rate Regimes in Twentieth Century Europe, Studies in Macroeconomic History (Cambridge: Cambridge University Press, 2010).

Straumann, Tobias, and Jürg Gabathuler, 'Die Entwicklung der Schweizer Bankenregulierung', in *Krisenfeste Schweizer Banken? Die Regulierung von*

Eigenmitteln, Liquidität und 'Too big to fail', ed. Armin Jans, Christoph Lengwiler, and Marco Passardi (Zurich: NZZ Libro, 2018), pp. 57–86.

Strictures on the Report of the Secret Committee on the Joint Stock Banks with an Appendix Containing Some Valuable Tables, Compiled from the Evidence (London: Joseph Thomas, 1836).

Sutch, Richard, 'Gross Domestic Product: 1790–2002, Table Ca10', in *Historical Statistics of the United States, Earliest Times to the Present*, ed. Susan B. Carter, Scott Sigmund Gartner, Michael R. Haines, et al. (New York: Cambridge University Press, 2006) http://dx.doi.org/10.1017/ISBN-9780511132971.

Swiss National Bank, *75 Jahre Schweizerische Nationalbank, 1907–1982* (Zurich, 1982).

'Das Schweizerische Bankwesen / Die Banken in der Schweiz (annual issues 1906–2015)', various, 1906–2015 (2015).

'Das Schweizerische Bankwesen 1909–1913' (Bern: Buchdruckerei Stämpfli & Cie, 1915).

'Das Schweizerische Bankwesen 1916' (Bern: Buchdruckerei Stämpfli & Cie, 1918).

'Das Schweizerische Bankwesen 1917' (Bern: Buchdruckerei Stämpfli & Cie, 1919).

'Das Schweizerische Bankwesen 1918' (Bern: Buchdruckerei Stämpfli & Cie, 1920).

'Das Schweizerische Bankwesen 1919' (Bern: Buchdruckerei Stämpfli & Cie, 1921).

'Das Schweizerische Bankwesen 1920' (Zurich: Art. Institut Orell Füssli, 1921).

'Das Schweizerische Bankwesen 1921' (Zurich: Art. Institut Orell Füssli, 1923).

'Das Schweizerische Bankwesen 1922' (Zurich: Art. Institut Orell Füssli, 1924).

'Das Schweizerische Bankwesen 1940' (Zurich: Orell Füssli, 1941).

'Das Schweizerische Bankwesen 1942' (Zurich: Orell Füssli, 1943).

'Das Schweizerische Bankwesen 1945' (Zurich: Orell Füssli, 1946).

'Das Schweizerische Bankwesen 1946' (Zurich: Orell Füssli, 1947).

'Das Schweizerische Bankwesen 1951' (Zurich: Orell Füssli, 1952).

'Das Schweizerische Bankwesen 1952' (Zurich: Orell Füssli, 1953).

'Das Schweizerische Bankwesen 1960' (Zurich: Orell Füssli, 1961).

'Datenportal Der Schweizerischen Nationalbank', online https://data.snb.ch/de (accessed 20 December 2021).

'Historical Time Series', 2009.

Sykes, Joseph, *The Amalgamation Movement in English Banking, 1825–1924* (London: P.S. King & Son, Ltd., 1926).

Szegö, Giorgio P., 'A Critique of the Basel Regulations, or How to Enhance (Im) Moral Hazards', in *Risk Management and Regulation in Banking* (Boston: Springer, 1999), pp. 147–58.

Tarkka, Juha, 'Investment Doctrines for Banks, from Real Bills to Post-Crisis Reforms', in *Preparing for the Next Financial Crisis: Policies, Tools and Models*, ed. Esa Jokivuolle and Radu Tunaru (Cambridge: Cambridge University Press, 2017), pp. 63–88.

Tarullo, Daniel K., *Banking on Basel: The Future of International Financial Regulation* (Washington, DC: Peterson Institute for International Economics, 2008).

The Bankers' Magazine, 'Progress of Banking in Great Britain and Ireland during 1944', 1945.

'Reports of Joint Stock Banks. London and County Bank', 1880, 230–3.

'Reports of Joint Stock Banks. London and Westminster Bank', 1880, 129–32.

'Reports of Joint Stock Banks. London and Westminster Bank', 1909, 438–9.

'Reports of Joint-Stock Banks. London and County Bank', XVII (1857), 241–7.
'Reports of Joint-Stock Banks. London and County Bank', 1864, 280–3.
'Reports of Joint-Stock Banks. London and County Bank', 1872, 788–94.
'Reports of Joint-Stock Banks. London and County Bank', 1873, 854–60.
'Reports of Joint-Stock Banks. London and Westminster Bank', 1848, 264–5.
'Reports of Joint-Stock Banks. London and Westminster Bank', 1857, 167–72.
'Reports of Joint-Stock Banks. London and Westminster Bank', 1862, 90–5.
'Reports of Joint-Stock Banks. London and Westminster Bank', 1867, 804–9.
'The Great Addition About to Be Made to the Capital Employed in Banking
    Enterprise', 1880, 28–9.
'The Important London Amalgamation', 1909, 346–50.
'The Progress of Banking in Great Britain and Ireland During 1913', 1914, 850–70.
'The Progress of Banking in Great Britain and Ireland During 1918', 1919, 381–90.
    1877, 361–9.
1903 *The Protection of Depositors (Accounts) Regulations 1963*, 1963.
The World Bank, *Bank Regulation and Supervision Survey*, November 2019.
    International Debt Statistics, Data Bank https://databank.worldbank.org/source/
    international-debt-statistics (accessed 20 January 2022).
Thomas, Samuel Evelyn, *The Rise and Growth of Joint Stock Banking* (London: Sir
    I. Pitman & Sons, 1934).
Tobler, Stefan, *Der Kampf um das Schweizer Bankgeheimnis: Eine 100-jährige
    Geschichte von Kritik und Verteidigung*, NZZ Libro (Zurich: NZZ Libro, 2019).
Toniolo, Gianni, and Eugene N. White, *The Evolution of the Financial Stability
    Mandate: From Its Origins to the Present Day* (Cambridge, MA: National Bureau
    of Economic Research, January 2015).
Tucker, George, *The Theory of Money and Banks Investigated* (Boston: C. . Little and
    J. Brown, 1839).
Tufts, Roger, and Paul Moloney, 'The History of Supervisory Expectations for Capital
    Adequacy: Part I (1863–1983)', *Moments in History – Office of the Comptroller of
    the Currency*, 2022.
    'The History of Supervisory Expectations for Capital Adequacy: Part II (1984–2021)',
    Moments in History – Office of the Comptroller of the Currency, 2022.
Turner, John D., *Banking in Crisis: The Rise and Fall of British Banking Stability, 1800
    to the Present*, Cambridge Studies in Economic History (Cambridge: Cambridge
    University Press, 2014).
    'Wider Share Ownership? Investors in English and Welsh Bank Shares in the
    Nineteenth Century', *The Economic History Review*, 62 (2009), 167–92.
UBS, *Annual Report 2006* (Zurich, 2007).
United States. Bureau of the Census, ed., *Historical Statistics of the United States.
    Colonial Times to 1970*, 1975.
United States Congress, *Banking Act of 1933*, H.R. 5661, 1933.
    Banking Act of 1935, H.R. 7617, 1935.
United States. Congress, *International Lending Supervision Act of 1983*, 1983.
Université de Lausanne, Faculté des sciences sociales et politiques, 'Observatoire des
    élites suisses (OBELIS)', *Données*. www.unil.ch/obelis/home.html.
Vogler, Robert, 'The Genesis of Swiss Banking Secrecy: Political and Economic
    Environment', *Financial History Review*, 8 (2001), 73–84.

Vollziehungsverordnung zum Bundesgesetz über die Banken und Sparkassen vom 17. Mai 1972, Änderung vom 23. August 1989, 1990.

Vollziehungsverordnung zum Bundesgesetz über die Banken und Sparkassen vom 1. Dezember 1980, 1981.

Vollziehungsverordnung zum Bundesgesetz über die Banken und Sparkassen vom 17. Mai 1972, 1972.

Vollziehungsverordnung zum Bundesgesetz über die Banken und Sparkassen vom 26. Februar 1935, 1935.

Vollziehungsverordnung zum Bundesgesetz über die Banken und Sparkassen vom 30. August 1961, 1961.

Wagner, Adolph, *Beiträge zur Lehre von den Banken* (Leipzig: Voss, 1857).

System der Zettelbankpolitik: mit besonderer Rücksicht auf das geltende Recht und auf deutsche Verhältnisse – ein Handbuch des Zettelbankwesens (Freiburg i. Br.: F. Wagner, 1873).

Wallis, John Joseph, 'Federal Government Debt, by Type: 1791–1970, Table Ea650', in *Historical Statistics of the United States, Earliest Times to the Present*, ed. Susan B. Carter, Scott Sigmund Gartner, Michael R. Haines, et al. (New York: Cambridge University Press, 2006). http://dx.doi.org/10.1017/ISBN-9780511132971.

Watson, Katherine, and Charles H. Feinstein, 'Private International Capital Flows in Europe in the Inter-War', in *Banking, Currency, and Finance in Europe Between the Wars*, ed. Charles H. Feinstein (Oxford: Oxford University Press, 1995), pp. 94–130.

Weber, Adolf, 'Depositenbanken und Spekulationsbanken: ein Vergleich deutschen und englischen Bankwesens' (Rheinische Friedrich-Wilhelms-Universität, 1902).

Geld, Banken, Börsen (Leipzig: Quelle & Meyer, 1939).

Weber, Warren E., 'Antebellum US State Bank Balance Sheets', *Federal Reserve Bank of Minneapolis, Research Division*, 2018.

Wetter, Ernst, *Bankkrisen und Bankkatastrophen der letzten Jahre in der Schweiz* (Zurich: Orell Füssli, 1918).

White, Eugene, 'Banking and Finance in the Twentieth Century', in *The Cambridge Economic History of the United States: Volume 3: The Twentieth Century*, ed. Robert E. Gallman and Stanley L. Engerman, Cambridge Economic History of the United States (Cambridge: Cambridge University Press, 2000), III, pp. 743–802 https://doi.org/10.1017/CHOL9780521553087.014.

The Regulation and Reform of the American Banking System, 1900–1929 (Princeton: Princeton University Press, 1983).

'"To Establish a More Effective Supervision of Banking": How the Birth of the Fed Altered Bank Supervision', in *The Origins, History, and Future of the Federal Reserve: A Return to Jekyll Island*, ed. Michael D. Bordo and William Roberds, *Studies in Macroeconomic History* (Cambridge: Cambridge University Press, 2013), pp. 7–54.

Wilcox, Malcolm George, 'Capital in Banking: An Historical Survey', in *UK Banking Supervision*, ed. Edward P.M. Gardener, Reprint of an Article in the Journal of the Institute of Bankers, June 1979 (London: Allen & Unwin, 1986), pp. 205–17.

Wilkinson, J. Harvie, *Investment Policies for Commercial Banks* (New York: Harper, 1938)

Wilson, John Donald, *The Chase* (Boston: Harvard Business School, 1986)

Wirth, Max, *Grundzüge der National-Ökonomie: Handbuch des Bankwesens* (Köln: DuMont-Schauberg, 1870).

Wolfgang Moritz Freiherr, von Bissing, 'Die Schrumpfung des Kapitals und seine Surrogate', in *Untersuchung des Bankwesens 1933 I. Teil*, ed. Untersuchungsausschuß für das Bankwesen 1933 (Berlin: Heymanns, 1933).

Wood, Duncan, *Governing Global Banking: The Basel Committee and the Politics of Financial Globalisation*, Global Finance Series (Aldershot: Ashgate, 2005).

Worner, Bernard, *La Suisse, centre financier européen* (Argenton: Impr. de Langlois, 1931).

Index

Tobias Straumann, *Fixed Ideas of Money: Small States and Exchange Rate Regimes in Twentieth-Century Europe* (2010)

Forrest Capie, *The Bank of England: 1950s to 1979* (2010)

Aldo Musacchio, *Experiments in Financial Democracy: Corporate Governance and Financial Development in Brazil, 1882–1950* (2009)

Claudio Borio, Gianni Toniolo, and Piet Clement, Editors, *The Past and Future of Central Bank Cooperation* (2008)

Robert L. Hetzel, *The Monetary Policy of the Federal Reserve: A History* (2008)

Caroline Fohlin, *Finance Capitalism and Germany's Rise to Industrial Power* (2007)

John H. Wood, *A History of Central Banking in Great Britain and the United States* (2005)

Gianni Toniolo (with the assistance of Piet Clement), *Central Bank Cooperation at the Bank for International Settlements, 1930–1973* (2005)

Richard Burdekin and Pierre Siklos, Editors, *Deflation: Current and Historical Perspectives* (2004)

Pierre Siklos, *The Changing Face of Central Banking: Evolutionary Trends since World War II* (2002)

Michael D. Bordo and Roberto Cortés-Conde, Editors, *Transferring Wealth and Power from the Old to the New World: Monetary and Fiscal Institutions in the 17th through the 19th Centuries* (2001)

Howard Bodenhorn, *A History of Banking in Antebellum America: Financial Markets and Economic Development in an Era of Nation-Building* (2000)

Mark Harrison, Editor, *The Economics of World War II: Six Great Powers in International Comparison* (2000)

Angela Redish, *Bimetallism: An Economic and Historical Analysis* (2000)

Elmus Wicker, *Banking Panics of the Gilded Age* (2000)

Michael D. Bordo, *The Gold Standard and Related Regimes: Collected Essays* (1999)

Michele Fratianni and Franco Spinelli, *A Monetary History of Italy* (1997)

Mark Toma, *Competition and Monopoly in the Federal Reserve System, 1914–1951* (1997)

Barry Eichengreen, Editor, *Europe's Postwar Recovery*(1996)

Lawrence H. Officer, *Between the Dollar-Sterling Gold Points: Exchange Rates, Parity and Market Behavior* (1996)

Elmus Wicker, *The Banking Panics of the Great Depression* (1996)

Norio Tamaki, *Japanese Banking: A History, 1859–1959* (1995)

Barry Eichengreen, *Elusive Stability: Essays in the History of International Finance, 1919–1939* (1993)

Michael D. Bordo and Forrest Capie, Editors, *Monetary Regimes in Transition* (1993)

Larry Neal, *The Rise of Financial Capitalism: International Capital Markets in the Age of Reason* (1993)